# The Hidden Intelligence

## Innovation through Intuition

**Sandra Weintraub**

Boston  Oxford  Johannesburg  Melbourne  New Delhi  Singapore

158.7
W42h

**Library of Congress Cataloging-in-Publication Data**
Weintraub, Sandra, 1946-
    The hidden intelligence : innovation through intuition / Sandra Weintraub.
       p.      cm.
    Includes bibliographical references and index.
    ISBN 0-7506-9937-X (pbk. : alk. paper)
    1. Creativity in business. 2. Intuition. 3. Psychology, Industrial. 4. Management—Psychological aspects. I. Title.
    HD53.W45  1998
    158.7—dc21
                              98-14881
                                     CIP

**British Library Cataloguing-in-Publication Data**
A catalogue record for this book is available from the British Library.

The publisher offers special discounts on bulk orders of this book. For information, please contact:

Manager of Special Sales
Butterworth–Heinemann
225 Wildwood Avenue
Woburn, MA 01801–2041
Tel: 781-904-2500
Fax: 781-904-2620

For information on all Butterworth–Heinemann publications available, contact our World Wide Web home page at: http://www.bh.com

10 9 8 7 6 5 4 3 2 1

Printed in the United States of America

*To my mother, Rose Brodinsky Glatky*

# Contents

# Acknowledgments

To my husband, Bob, without whose encouragement and day-to-day help, editing, and advanced cooking skills, this book would have been impossible.

To my daughter, Ellen, who so generously shared her intuitive insights, wit, and wisdom with me.

To my son, Steve, who rescued the computer from my beginner's touch more times than I care to admit, and who was always there to give me his loving, expert help.

To my brother, Carl, whose insightful philosophical thoughts helped clarify my thinking.

To my friend, Dr. Arthur Bernard, who introduced me to the wisdom of dreams and gave me so much of his time as well as his extraordinary insights.

And to my editor, the extraordinary Karen Speerstra, whose encouragement, skill, and intuition is so very much appreciated. A warm thank-you to Bryan Mattimore and George Prince, for their enormous input of time and invaluable editorial advice. And to Deborah McConchie and Dr. Laurie Nadel, whose suggestions were also right on target and much appreciated.

A special thanks to Floyd Ragsdale, Joseph Killough, Lauren Berger, Riza Federman, and Kari Danziger for sharing their remarkable dreams. To all of those who gave so generously of their time to be interviewed, many thanks. Also to friends and business associates who contributed in so many different ways to this work: Audrey Wu, Robert Taraschi, Ilene McCuen, Tom Samples, Arthur Ganson, Roberta Leviton, Jay Vogt, Francine and Len Solomon, Simone Lottor, Mike Snell, Katherine Logan Prince, Arthur LaGace, Laura Hart, John Pehrson, Marilyn Bentov, Wes Anderson,

David Tanner, Gabriella and Mickey Krochmalnic, Bob Gill, Robert Hanig, Mark Sebell, Sharona Ben Tov, Fran Shiffman, June Levinson, Julie Ross, Nancy Rosenzweig, Maria Keesling, Gloria and Stan Rosenzweig, Tim Allen, John Brandt, Marsha and Jerry Weinberg, Sandra and Harvey Kupferman, Margo Golder, Nancy Kane, and Roger Driben. Thank you.

# Introduction

After I was abruptly dismissed from a short interview for the position of Manager of Training at a well-known high-tech company, I thought, now I know how Typhoid Mary must have felt. Or perhaps the feeling was more like what the "untouchables" feel in India.

It began when I sent a resume to the company. Shortly thereafter the Manager of Human Resources called and said, "Your resume is very impressive." His tone of voice was soothing, yet professional. I was flattered by his remark and murmured a shy, "Thank you."

Then he asked, "Do you have time for a phone interview right now?" While I hadn't prepared myself to be suddenly thrust into the interview mode, I gingerly agreed. Although my intuition sensed that he was anxious to speak with me, it never warned me of the trap that lay ahead. Apparently that facet of my intuition was temporarily out of order and on the disabled list. I had no inkling of what was to follow. "Yes, of course," I said gamely.

His next question was "How do you begin to create your management training programs?" This inquiry caught me by surprise. While I had been quickly reviewing in my mind all of my past accomplishments that I would recount to him in clever detail, he caught me off guard when he asked about my *method* for developing the courses. I thought for a moment and then said something like, "After I understand what a particular group would like to achieve, I begin to design the course intuitively." As soon as the word "intuitively" left my lips, he said, "Thank you," and bang went the telephone. He probably regarded the word "intuitive" as a code word for being on the fringe of lunacy. Many people find that "confronting the nonrational is unnerving," says Marilyn Ferguson, author of *The Aquarian Conspiracy*. Call it unnerving, unsettling, or annoying, whatever it was, the slam of the telephone said it all: "No job!"

Too bad the questioning ended there. Had he been a bit more inquisitive, he could have learned the value of intuition. He could have asked a few more questions such as, "How successful is this approach?" or, "Is there any advantage to using this process?" or, "What are some of the outcomes that you can tell me about using this method?" However, he asked none of these questions because the word "intuition" had apparently turned him off.

What he did not realize is that at times the logical and the intuitive may be one and the same and have the same result. And, when they are not the same, the intuitive may actually work better. The reason: an intuitive approach may be able to get to the core of the problem far more quickly than logic alone—and is frequently more accurate.

If a survey were taken today, I suspect the results would show that it would be more detrimental than helpful when applying for a job to admit to having intuitive skills. Of course, there might well be exceptions to that if one is seeking a creative position in a public relations or advertising agency, or as an ideation consultant. Science, research, and predictability is valued in our culture, but intuition is regarded as unpredictable, if not "flaky," therefore, of little or questionable value. The irony, however, is that as much as we would like to live in a predictable world, chaos is more descriptive of the current reality. This was brought home to me in a bumper sticker I saw recently that said, "Get Used to Chaos." I realized that the writer of this message knows something that makes many people feel uncomfortable: nothing is predictable; anything can happen and we had better learn to live with it.

If that is our future, it is a bit unsettling. True, chaos has become a more deeply felt presence than ever before, but how do we get used to it? Given a choice, most of us would prefer the sure, the eternal, and the dependable. To confront the new and chaotic tells us that the learning process must begin all over again. It's like when you finally got the hang of being twelve years old and then suddenly you were a teenager at thirteen, and just when you got that under control, bam—you were fourteen. To seek the innovative would seem to be deliberately enticing more chaos into our already stress-filled lives.

At the same time, we are barraged with the call to be innovative and generate new and creative ideas that may then become breeding grounds for more chaos. It seems like a no-win situation. If we increase our own creative ability, we may be simultaneously bringing more chaos into our lives. How do we find the balance, then, between becoming more innovative and creative and still keeping in check those anxieties that are aroused by the new? The answer: Ask your intuition. Intuition is that often invisible element that is nearly always present when the creative idea suddenly erupts. It let's you know that the creative idea is worthwhile, and that it will work, and ultimately it will give the surrounding, encompassing chaos a shape, a feel, and lead to a surprise revelation. Intuition is a function of your mind—your hidden intelligence.

Why is it hidden? Although it is an intelligence common to everyone, few people recognize its existence and even fewer know how powerful it can be. While some rely on this intelligence as a guiding compass, others are oblivious to its presence. If you would like to become more aware of your own intuitive power to become the catalyst for creativity, this book will offer ideas and techniques to recognize and summon your own intuition when needed so that when it speaks, you will know how to listen. This hidden intelligence, our intuition, can make sense out of the chaos; it can become our personal servant who has only our best interest at heart.

Those who recognize its value are, not so coincidentally, the leaders in their fields. I have interviewed several senior executives, from multilevel corporations, such as American Greetings and 3M Companies, to owners of entrepreneurial start-ups like Tender Loving Things and ideation consultants whose major focus is creativity and innovation. They all have made it quite clear that relying on their intuition has been an important factor in their success. In every case, each person interviewed said his or her intuition is an *active* partner in good decision-making and creativity.

Like stripping the leaves of the artichoke to reach its succulent heart, we will begin to peel away the perceptions and misperceptions of intuition in order to reveal it's hiding place and learn how to summon it when a crisis looms ahead. Like money, intuition isn't everything, but it does come in handy when you need it.

Why learn to tap into your intuition? Because a chaotic marketplace requires constant innovation; without it, businesses will not survive. DuPont is a company that has heeded the call by requiring that 30 percent of its sales must be received from products developed within the last four years.

If intuition leads to innovation, then what is intuition and how do we know when we are being intuitive? A dictionary defines intuition as "a quick and ready insight; or immediate apprehension; or cognition, knowledge or conviction gained without evident rational thought and inference; or knowing without knowing how we know." Innovators are by definition "intuitors," because often the innovative idea emerges from a "quick and ready insight" that seems to know the correct answer without any apparent logical thinking involved.

Some theorists believe that when this occurs, the intuitor actually does think logically, but it happens so quickly that the logic is understood only on a subconscious level and is processed instantaneously to reveal a solution. The intuitor frequently gets the answer first and then explains the logic of it, working backwards from the solution, whereas the logical thinker begins with the facts and builds on them to deduce the logical answer.

How do we know when we are being intuitive? Intuition happens when we get a sudden insight to guide our most important decisions. It leaps out at us from some secret place to protect us from harm. Just as it informs animals as to which creatures are its natural predators, intuition does the same for us. It is hidden, yet always there. It is unseen, yet dependable, because it can be the wise prophet that answers difficult questions. Discerning executives have learned how to listen to it; smart managers know how to court it.

Sometimes intuition speaks with a such a soft voice that you barely hear it, such as when you begin to cross a street and do not hear or see that truck bearing down on you, but you hesitate to cross for a reason you cannot say. Or, when a client calls and asks you to train his people in time management and you know somehow that this is just the tip of the iceberg, that the company has systemic problems that this type of training alone will not cure.

It may speak at times with a very tiny voice, almost imperceptibly, as it whispers to let you know that you are angry with the wrong person. You may bellow or complain to someone over trivial matters, while your intuition is informing you that the petty, albeit hurtful event may have been triggered by an unconscious childhood memory. It speaks by causing your stomach and throat to tighten, but you disregard these signs and scream anyway, because your emotions have overtaken your intuitive wisdom.

And there are times when this intelligence shouts at you. It tells you when you have negotiated a terrific deal and when you have come up with a great new product idea. It whoops at you when you hear another person's unique marketing plan and you know instantly that it will work. It roars so loud at times that you want to jump up and down and scream "YES!"

What is this intelligence that has so many voices and such an enormous range in volume, that has so much influence in some areas of your life and so little in others? It is your intuition. Yet, it is hidden from those who do not recognize its value or accessibility. Relatively few people admit to using this intelligence in their business lives because it is seen as "soft," not as something reliable or having value. In contrast, we call that which has value "hard," suggesting that it is solid and something that can be depended upon, like statistical projections and numbers.

We know, however, that statistics can be arranged to say almost anything and that numbers can be deceiving, such as when the books are "cooked," both of which render statistics and numbers undependable, hence soft. In contrast, many intuitive people say that their intuition is correct for them 80 to 90 percent of the time. Which is "hard" and which is "soft"? If hard is reliable and soft is not, then hard would be useful data that would have a high probability of accurately predicting the future. Soft would not have this quality. If the numbers have been finagled, or based on educated guesses with no solid data available, then they cannot always offer a reliable forecast. However, if your intuition can accurately predict the future 80 to 90 percent of the time, which would be more useful to you?

Because this intelligence is neither logic nor emotion, it can transcend all other intellectual abilities to help us make wise judgments when there is not enough data. It is something that comes to us from we know not where, yet we know it is true, that it is correct. It makes its wisdom felt when you get a very strong impression that the person you just spoke with on the telephone is untrustworthy. Or when you are contemplating buying a business whose numbers add up to say "buy," but you cannot overpower that little voice inside that tells you to "wait," and you hesitate—only to discover that the books you had been shown were the faux version of the real thing.

What is intuition? It is knowing that something is right or wrong by a gut feeling. It is not emotional, although at times it is related to emotions. For example, fear is an emotion, and sometimes when we meet someone we are instinctively afraid. Why? Because our intuition is telling us there is something about this individual to fear. When you see a new gizmo and you suddenly think it could be something very big, it is your intuition that sees the vision of a business opportunity. Yes, the gizmo may have generated excitement, but the initial flash of knowing was your intuition.

"We need a new way of thinking to deal with our present reality, which is sensed more sensitively through intuition than by our capacity to observe and reason objectively," said Jonas Salk, the discoverer of the polio vaccine. "Our subjective responses . . . are more sensitive and more rapid than our objective responses . . . intuition must be allowed full rein and allowed to play."

# PART ONE

## *What is Intuition?*

> Like the wolf, intuition has claws that pry things open and pin things down, it has eyes that can see through the shields of the persona, it has ears that hear beyond the range of mundane human understanding.
>
> ...CLARISSA PINKOLA ESTES, *Women Who Run with the Wolves*

Irma Schretter has always been aware of her uncanny intuition. While it has been consistently useful, it became indispensable when she began a property management company several years ago. Like the ceiling fan in *Casablanca*, her intuition is always "on." Her antennas seem to be forever reaching out in every direction and have seldom failed her. When she interviews candidates for a position with the company, her intuition tells her who will work out and who will not. When she takes on property to manage, her intuition lets her know which will be profitable. And when buyers come to negotiate the purchase of a property, let them beware, because her intuition may discover something that they'd prefer she didn't know. This happened when two sisters came into Ms. Schretter's office ready to purchase a condominium for their brother. No irregularities showed up in the application they had filled out. There was no question as to their financial ability to pay for the property. Still, she had a nagging feeling that something was not right. She stalled and decided to investigate their backgrounds a bit more. Nothing turned up. So they signed a purchase and sales agreement, although she was still uncomfortable about the impending deal. Then she stalled some more. Considering that property managers like to make sales, especially to buyers who have certified checks in hand, this is not a likely scenario. The stalling could easily have cost her a sale. What was going on?

Despite the apparent information that the buyers were qualified, Schretter could not shake the feeling that something was not quite right. So she continued to investigate. Finally, she learned that the brother who was to live in the condo that the sisters were purchasing for him had just been released from jail and was not likely to be a well-received neighbor at these luxury condominiums. At this point, she refused to go through with the sale, despite the threat of a lawsuit for reneging on the agreement. The matter was finally settled out of court. Although Schretter had never met the brother during these negotiations, she, like the wolf, used her intuitive "claws" to pry things open. We are all capable of such knowing.

For example, when we meet someone for the first time, we form an impression of that person in the first 30 seconds. Upon what is this quick impression based? It certainly cannot be the result of logical or deliberate thought, because there wasn't enough time. It may be formed intuitively. If we judge another person in a 30-second time frame, there must be a multitude of sensory perceptions that bombard us to create what we think is a reliable impression, whether we're aware of it or not.

If you speak to people who say that they get impressions this quickly, and for the most part they prove to be accurate later on, their intuition is usually credited as the knowledge server. However, we sometimes hear people say that "I misjudged him when we first met." This judgment may have been based more on expectations and culturally acquired cues than on intuition.

For example, we often judge people by outward appearance. A well-dressed person gives certain impressions that are opposite from a person in unimpressive clothes and poorly groomed. If we allow outward appearance alone to determine our opinion, then we are not listening to the information that our intuition could offer.

If you have ever asked your doctor why she prescribes one medication over another, her answer might reflect the thoughts of several physicians who told me that for any given ailment, such as high blood pressure, there could be as many as 200 possible medications. Why do they prescribe one for one person and another for someone else? Is it based on experience? Possibly. But when pressed, they say it's intuition. With enough practice, perhaps bits and pieces of information are stored in their brain and they are unconsciously tapping into that to predict which medication will work best for any particular patient. How often is it the correct choice? Their reply: between 80 and 100 percent of the time. We have known all along that the practice of medicine is not only a science but an art, and physicians need to rely on intuition as well as knowledge to write the best prescription.

When these doctors spoke of intuition, what did intuition mean for them? It is when answers do not spring from logical deductions or emotions but is simply there. It is as though their own boundaries are extended, and they are receiving information that they have no logical way of knowing.

The root of the word intuition comes from the Latin verb *tuere*, meaning "to guard, to protect." If this is the function of our intuition, as it was in Irma Schretter's case, then it always works for our good because it guards us from making poor decisions and protects us not only from outside forces that would want to harm us, but also from our internal dialogues that may precede decision-making.

In Gavin de Becker's book, the *Gift of Fear*, he describes intuition as a "cognitive process that works faster than we recognize and far different from the familiar step-by-step thinking we rely on so willingly. We think conscious thought is somehow better, when in fact, *intuition is soaring flight compared to the plodding of logic.* [emphasis added]" When we are aware of our intuition, we just know something—and we know it in an instant. For the intuitive, it may require long and painstaking explanations to convince the nonintuitive of something that she grasps instantly.

Gavin de Becker believes that our bodies and minds have built-in radar detectors for fearful situations. While animals instinctively know who their predators are, as human beings, we sometimes allow our thinking brains to interfere with the reception of this same knowledge, and we ignore these feelings. One reason may be that we do not want to seem irrational and prone to groundless fear. If we see no overt signs or evidence of someone's evil intent, such as a gun or a knife, we may not trust our own instincts. Yet, unless we have an emotional problem with being overly fearful and afraid of many things, when we suddenly feel afraid, our intuition is telling us there is something to fear. When this occurs, it should be listened to, not explained away by discounting one's own impressions. "If your intuition is informed accurately, the danger signal will sound when it should," says de Becker. Gary Zukav, in *The Seat of the Soul,* defines intuition as "perception beyond the physical sense that is meant to assist you." Your mission: to allow your own intuition's wisdom to have a greater impact in your life.

# **1**

# *Understanding Intelligence*

To define intuition as the hidden intelligence, it may be useful to understand what we mean by intelligence and why intuition is one of several different types of intellectual abilities. A dictionary definition of intelligence says it is "the ability to learn or understand or to deal with new or trying situations" and "is revealing or reflecting of good judgment or sound thought." However, when most of us think about intelligence, we think about those grade school IQ tests that produced a number to inform our teachers of whether we would be quick learners. Over the past twenty or so years, many researchers have questioned the validity of these tests, pointing out that they are often culturally biased, measure only one kind of intelligence, and disregard other types of intelligence that would predict success in life.

Professor Ellen Langer of Harvard University has another view of intelligence tests. She writes, "I do not mean to suggest that intelligence tests do not measure something, but the dimension the tests measure may be a neutral trait. The abilities measured by intelligence tests may be useful in certain situations, much as it is sometimes useful to be tall." If the world were built to accommodate short people, however, with low ceilings and chairs and tables reduced in size to suit the short person's needs, tallness or shortness may be neutral traits, but it is more useful in such a situation to be short. Being tall, then, would not be a negative trait; it would be neutral but less convenient. Likewise, the present measures of IQ are valuable for predicting scholastic success, but scholastic success does not translate necessarily into success in life. Nor can IQ measures predict, for example, whether a person will be a musical genius or gifted in art, invention, or management.

One aspect of intelligence, which perhaps may be a better predictor of success in life, is emotional intelligence, if it could be measured as the standard IQ tests are today. In his book *Emotional Intelligence,* Dan Goleman illustrates that having a very high IQ alone is not necessarily a predictor of success in life, especially if that person has what he terms a low emotional intelligence. Goleman relates the story of a high school student who had an A+ average over four years, but one day received an 80, equivalent to a B, on a test in physics. His reaction to this grade was to stab the teacher. He probably aced the standard IQ test, but failed abysmally in emotional intelligence, which suggests that he is likely to find it tough coping in the world, despite his high scholastic achievement. Another example of high IQ combined with a low EQ (emotional intelligence) is Ted Kaczinski, the convicted "unabomber" who allegedly killed several people by sending them packaged bombs in the mail. Scoring high on the conventional IQ test cannot predict how "intelligently" one will handle life. While these cases are extreme, we may all be familiar with more frequently encountered, yet less dramatic examples of people who have the best academic credentials and a personality that finds it difficult to establish emotionally satisfying relationships.

Another problem with IQ tests is that they measure the speed with which one solves a problem; the quicker one answers the questions, the higher the score, hence the higher the intelligence. While this may be a useful skill in some cases, there are times when it is better to let the problem simmer in one's brain overnight, as for example, when trying to work out a creative solution to a problem. Sometimes a problem requires noodling in the brain for several days or even years before a brilliant solution emerges. Dyslexics, such as former New York Governor Nelson Rockefeller, often fare poorly on these timed IQ tests because they do not read quickly. In their life's work, however, they may be very successful, perhaps because their brains require more time to nurture creativity.

Intelligence tests, then, are not necessarily a predictor of success in life, nor can they reveal the existence of any specialized talent. Rather, they seem limited to forecasting success in scholastic studies, the neutral dimension they measure. Like having a musical or artistic intelligence, intuition is another aspect of our intellectual skills.

What is intuitive intelligence? At this moment we have no quantifiable tests to measure it, as we do for the standard intelligence tests. Also, there seems to be a wide variation between individuals in being able to tap into this skill. Some people are more intuitive than others, or at least are tuned into it more frequently. One reason for this may have to do with a difference in brain waves, and the firing of neurons in the brain. When some psychics' brains were scanned at a Stanford Research Laboratory (more about this in Chapter 19 on psychics) they were found to have a different brain wave pattern than non-psychic people.

However, for the past twenty years or so, there has been a great deal of attention paid to the differences between the attributes of the left and right brain. In 1978, sponsored by General Electric, Ned Herrmann created the Herrmann Participant Survey Form to profile thinking styles and learning preferences in accordance with brain dominance theory. Continuing research led him to develop a comprehensive four part Whole Brain model, the Herrmann Brain Dominance Instrument (HBDI). The HBDI defines four different thinking functions or preferences and locates them in four quadrant areas of the brain. Recently there has been some controversy over where thinking and emotions are located in the brain, which will be discussed more fully in Chapters 10 and 11. For convenience, I will use these designations because they have become part of our language as a short hand way to describe thinking or personality preferences—with the left brain being the place where analytical skills live, and the right brain being the repository for intuition and emotion, implying that those people who score as highly intuitive would have a more actively engaged right brain. Yet, when it comes to intelligence testing, it raises some interesting questions. For example, is there a correlation between those whose right brain is dominant and who score lower on a standard IQ test because they do not rely on logic as much as intuition, or do those whose left brain is more dominant score higher? Or, taking an entirely different tack, do intuitive people intuitively "know" the answers on examination questions irrespective of logic and, therefore, score higher? In other words, is the standard IQ test measuring thinking skills or intuiting skills or some combination of the two?

## RIGHT BRAIN, LEFT BRAIN, WHOLE BRAIN

When Mark Twain said, "Never let formal education get in the way of learning," perhaps he was on to something that we have recently begun to study. Some theorists have noted an inverse correlation between loss of intuitive capability and scholastic achievement. Dr. Paul Torrance of the University of Minnesota has shown in many cases that imagination tends to contract as knowledge expands. His studies suggest that the more we concentrate on left brain learning, the more our right brain intuitive perceptions decrease in intensity until we no longer believe that they exist.

Marvin Camras, the inventor of magnetic recording and the holder of more than 500 patents, observed that "little children tend to be creative, but the more education you get, the more the inventive spark is educated out of you. In our educational process, you have to conform. Educators don't like you to go off the beaten path. After you've gone through more and more education, you conform more and more. You might even say that you're discouraged from inventing. Of course, different people have different natures. Some people can invent in spite of their education" (Hall, 1995).

If we take a look at people whose cultures emphasize left brain learning far less than ours, their right brain intuition appears to serve them quite well. For example, it informs the inhabitants of the rain forests as to what herbs and plants offer medicinal cures. There are hundreds of plant species found in the rain forests of South America whose curative properties are now being explained by the intuitive medicine man, or shaman, to the university-trained scientists. True, they have had hundreds if not thousands of years for trial and error experimentation, and an oral tradition for passing knowledge down to each generation, but often the shaman says that his knowledge comes from the spirit world (like intuition?). If these far less formally educated people have the ability to know which plants are beneficial for specific maladies, then why is it that our logical processes, which are thought to be superior, do not give us the same information? It seems rather paradoxical that our best and most highly educated minds need to learn from a native shaman, a "traditional" medicine man if you will, how to use the various forms of plant life to treat illnesses.

The Naskapi Indians of Labrador survive on a daily basis by the intuitive guidance they receive each night in their dreams, which directs them where to hunt the next day, or to stay where they are because a winter storm is approaching. To survive in a harsh climate, they find that relying on their intuition derived from dreams is indispensable.

# 2

# *Intuition and Creativity*

Innovation begins within the embryo of intuition, is nourished by imagination and breathed into life with ingenuity and hard work. In the beginning, there is intuition. The dictionary definition of creativity is "having the quality of being creative as opposed to imitative," which is a rather circular definition. For most professional practitioners, creativity is defined as making novel, useful connections that allow one to arrive at a unique or innovative solution.

Gutenberg's printing press is an example of this kind of connection-making. He got the idea for the movable-type printing press when he combined the functions of the punch that was used to imprint coins with those of the wine press, a powerful method used to squeeze grapes. The purpose of the coin punch was to leave an image on small coins. The purpose of the wine press was to exert much more pressure to squeeze grapes. In order to arrive at that insight, Gutenberg had to combine two disparate thoughts: printing a mark on a coin, which could also be used to print a mark on paper, and the added force of a wine press, which would allow the printing to be done on large pieces of paper rather than on small coins. Combining the two, he was able to press small squares onto paper, and soon came the printing press with movable type.

His creative leap was the thought that said, "If I put this combination of presses together, it could be useful in printing words on paper." However, it is likely that the intuitive flash said, "If I put these two presses together, I know it will work!"

Jean Houston believes that "our deep mind is making associations all the time. It's just that we generally don't inhabit enough of ourselves to become aware of them." When ideation consultants use connection-making methods like Gutenberg's to generate ideas in their workshops, they are attempting to bring forth the invisible connections that are already there, by gently nudging their clients to reach deeper into themselves. They stimulate connection-making by juxtaposing similar or dissimilar objects or thoughts with the problem to be solved, thus, engaging the mind to think in divergent ways. These systems work very well for opening up thinking processes and generating a multitude of ideas. They also work to stimulate intuition, because very often when viable answers to problems seem to come out of nowhere, our intuition has delivered them.

Dr. Arthur Van Gundy, a Professor at the University of Oklahoma, compared the effectiveness of using two different approaches for eliciting creative ideas. The first process, which did not actively stimulate intuition, he labeled the "brain drain" method. It was conducted by asking a group of students who sat around a table in a plain undecorated room to come up with as many ideas as possible for new products.

Van Gundy's comparison group of students were also asked to come up with as many ideas as possible for new products within the same time frame. However, for the second group the atmosphere was highly stimulated. The students were bombarded with a variety of experiences, such as touching product samples and looking at magazine photos. In addition to the visual prompts, they worked at their problem in a spontaneous and less formal environment, with loud music, abundant food, and Nerf guns, presumably to bring them back to the "innocence" of childhood. In 45 minutes, the first group came up with about 29 ideas. The "stimulated" group turned out 310 ideas in the same time.

Not only was there a difference in quantity between the two groups, but also in quality. To ascertain the quality of the generated ideas, Van Gundy had them scored by evaluators who worked in industry and who would base their judgments on marketplace potential. The lists were scrambled so that the outside judges had no idea which group had generated which idea. The result was that the stimulated group put forth 36.3 marketable ideas, whereas the "brain drain" group produced only 6.5. ideas with potential market value. (The frationated ideas are a bit mysterious, but I presume they have something to do with mathematical calculations.)

If we look at why the second group was more creative than the first, we can see that exposing the students to pictures and products while trying to solve the problem at hand lent itself to spurring connection-making that tapped on intuition. In most idea-generating workshops, participants are encouraged to come up with as many ideas as possible, whether they have any market value or not. Once they have been generated, they get narrowed down to the workable, the probable, and the potentially profitable. How do we know whether intuition is present in these idea-generating sessions? Often we see it by the group reaction. If an idea is proposed and nearly everyone responds with a, "Yes, that's it; that's brilliant; why didn't I think of that," then you will know it is very likely a winner and that intuition played a role in achieving the solution as well as the immediate recognition that it would be successful.

It will be apparent as you read this book that many successful ideas have intuitive components. Although one can have hundreds of ideas, when the right idea strikes, the intuitor knows it will work. She does not need the validation of testing or market research: the intuitive person just knows.

**3**

# *Executive Intuition*

When Richard Whiteley, Vice Chairman of the Forum Corporation, a training and development firm based in Boston with over 600 corporate clients, said that he uses pendulums and Tarot cards, I knew he didn't learn that while getting his MBA at Harvard Business School. He was one of the founders of The Forum in 1971, and has learned that the decision-making techniques using left brain analysis acquired in graduate school do not always predict success. When he uses intuitive techniques, he says, the decisions they impart are invariably correct.

Using a pendulum and Tarot cards are two methods Whiteley uses to receive the wisdom of his intuitive mind; they often reveal information that he already knows but is unaware of. In 1997, for example, he used a pendulum as a guide in the development of a seminar. He and the co-developer knew they had too much material to be included but were unsure of which sections to leave out. So Whiteley made a pendulum with a weight at the end of a string and swung it over each section, asking it to tell him yes or no, does this part stay or does it go? The pendulum expressed itself as requested. Both course developers examined the pendulum's decisions and found that it led to a viable design they had not previously seen. They felt that all of the pendulum's recommendations were sound and made the necessary cuts. The result: a successful course was produced.

Does Whiteley believe that the pendulum has supernatural power? Not at all. He does believe that he knows the answers, but that sometimes it is only his body that knows, and it is slow to communicate this information to his brain. When he uses the pendulum, it picks up what his body already understands and allows that insight to sift into his conscious awareness. The same holds true for the Tarot cards. When he chooses a card at random and then looks at it to see whether it has any meaning for him, invariably it does. He realizes that there is nothing supernatural here either. He could take any picture and look at it and try to find a connection and meaning for himself. However, he finds the Tarot cards especially useful because their pictures are somewhat ambiguous and can lend themselves to many different interpretations.

Laura Mather, Whiteley's executive assistant is also intuitive, to the point where others believe she has radar receptors in her brain. She feels that she is very much on the same wave length as Whiteley, which makes him in her words, "a pleasure to work with."

Philosopher Andre Sonnet offers one explanation for why a pendulum or a Tarot card can tell us what we need to know: "Conscious and subconscious are separated by a perceptive threshold. It separates what we are able to perceive. The weaker stimuli stay beneath this threshold; that is, within the domain where the psychic forces are the most intimately effective." In this case, Whiteley's subconscious mind knew something that his conscious mind did not; it was beneath the threshold. The pendulum was able to cross the barrier to perception. "Clearly, then," says Sonnet, "our psychic faculty has the capacity to perceive stimuli that go unnoticed by our conscious."

Is Harvard Business School, or most business schools for that matter, missing out on recognizing that there is an intelligence that can be developed as another source for information retrieval? If they ignore the information that can be derived from the right brain, they are overlooking an important source. While the high-tech Internet has enormous left brain value, the vast Internet scanned by the right brain can go far beyond the present boundaries of knowledge. The left brain knows what is, but the right brain knows what can be. The right brain reads the future and makes connections to the present via its intuitive network.

Despite the absence of courses on intuition in most formal educational settings, a recent study by Jagdish Parikh at Harvard Business School found that business executives in a cross-cultural study attribute 80 percent of their success to acting on intuitive insights. Parikh received over 13,000 responses to his questionnaire and found that over 75 percent of those respondents felt they used intuition and logic about equally. Some 48 percent of female respondents said that they use *more* intuition than logic in their personal lives. Between 52 and 79 percent of respondents agreed or strongly agreed with the following statements:

1. Many senior managers use intuition in making decisions, at least to some extent.
2. Higher intuitive capabilities would contribute to greater success in business.
3. Intuition has a role to play in almost every facet of life.
4. Intuition is a characteristic associated more with women than with men.
5. Few managers who use intuition would openly admit to the same.

It is this last statement that creates the fundamental paradox. If 52 to 75 percent of people in the sample agreed to all of the above statements, including not wishing to admit to the use of intuition, then there is a problem. It is agreed that higher intuitive capabilities would contribute to greater success in business, yet few managers will admit to using it. The question is why?

The reason could be that intuition remains the "secret" no one will talk about in our culture. In Parikh's cross-cultural study of nine countries, the United States ranked far below the United Kingdom and Japan in their acknowledged use of intuition in business decision-making. Thus, intuition appears to be something that our culture not only does not support but perhaps sees as either nonexistent or unreliable.

If most executives in the survey agreed that higher intuitive abilities would contribute to greater success, why does the word intuition seem to be anathema in the American culture? It is likely that those whose jobs are accountable to others cannot afford to trust information based on intuition, because their supervisors need hard data, not what is perceived as probability. Another reason may be that we live in a left brain culture, one dependent on logic and analysis. Since intuition, pattern recognition, and holistic understanding are located in the right brain, they are culturally invisible. In other words, the right brain grasps the forest, sees the big picture, and the overall configuration, while the left brain counts the trees and notes the details. For most people, counting the trees is easier than seeing the forest. The number of trees in the forest is exact; the shape and contents of the forest is not. Relying on what can be seen and verified is more comforting for most people than trying to relate to a muddled big picture that cannot be seen with any type of precision.

Professor Howard Stevenson at Harvard Business School defines intuition as seeing patterns, and he suspects that the highly intuitive person has a more developed right brain and sees patterns that others do not. This may be one reason why intuitive CEOs are successful. They can use both their left and right brains and extrapolate from the patterns they see to make good predictions and decisions.

Stock market analysts also watch for patterns in social trends. Many believe that they can predict whether the market will rise or fall according to the degree of optimism felt by people who are influenced by the positives or negatives in their lives.

These analysts observe social patterns rather than statistics. They contend that everything that happens, whether it's the latest *Seinfeld* episode, an increase or decrease in crime, a landing on Mars, the latest pop songs and magazine covers, and so forth, are all factors that can affect the public mood—and the market.

One analyst, Robert Preschter of the Elliott Wave Theorist newsletter, has made a career of studying the relation of movies, sports attendance, and coffee house openings to the stock market. He says that horror movies and divisive social trends predominate during bear markets, while upbeat movies and new social gathering places correspond to bull markets. Preschter is convinced that there is a general "knowledge" that we can learn by being attuned to the popular culture that helps to determine stock market swings.

This theory is very similar to the theory of Carl Jung, who believed that there is a collective unconscious surrounding and enveloping us and that everyone can tap into it. For example, Jung's theory suggests that everything that has been and will be invented is already there, and the inventor need only learn how to tap into this collective unconscious to invent something "new." Edgar Cayce, the mystic who was able to diagnose and cure many illnesses, had a similar theory he called "the superconscious mind." He envisioned this to be a universal mind that anyone, anywhere, could tap into by deepening his or her intuitive or psychic abilities.

For stock traders, catching the wave means perceiving social trends and making their moves quickly. Drawing inferences from social trends is one method businesses use to predict the future in terms of what new items will be hot next year and the year after. An example of this is intuiting fashion trends that designers must predict seasons if not years away from production. If they are wrong in their forecasts they may find themselves deep into red ink even though they may have predicted that basic black would be here forever.

Seeing patterns is one thing; interpreting them correctly is another. If you speak to some people who have been involved with the stock market for a number of years, they may say that they can find no absolutely reliable predictive pattern. Others, who claim to use their intuition when selecting a particular stock, contend their intuition is infallible, because they can look at that pattern and determine fairly accurately what it means. Whatever their system, it would be interesting to know whether those who choose stocks on some intuitive basis do better than those who rely on careful analysis.

For many executives who rely on intuition, it is likely that their decisions are arrived at by a method similar to that used by Conrad Hilton, who received many intuitive insights in his career: "I know when I have a problem and have done all I can—thinking, figuring, planning—I keep listening in a sort of inside silence until something clicks and I feel a right answer." If it worked for this hotel magnate, why not you?

# 4

# *I Do What I Think*

What we do is based on what we think. If we believe that we are logical, then all of our actions must have a logical reason or else we would not engage in them. That familiar phrase from Descartes intrudes a philosophic stumbling block into this reasoning, because it may keep us from knowing how to access our intuition. He wrote, I think therefore I am. And, if what I think determines who I am, it also determines what I do.

For example, if I see a company whose patterns of business practice look sound, I may choose to invest in this company because it has all the positive elements that I have learned will be important to its future. However, my judgment of any pattern is based on what I have been taught to look for and how to think, so that this trained thinking will precede my investment. Sometimes, trained thinking processes lead to fortuitous moves; other times, what seems to be logical is visible only on the surface, and the answer as to whether I should in fact invest lies hidden, open only to intuition. What I do will reflect what I think. If I allow my intuition to inform me, I may act upon it; if I negate its existence, then I may take another course of action.

Thinking precedes action. If I think that I can be intuitive then I am more likely to have intuitive insights than if I believe I

am not open to intuition. However, some beliefs are unconscious. We may not be aware that we do not believe we can be
intuitive. Some theorists suggest that up to 80 percent of our
actions are based on unconscious motives. Therefore, we may
seldom be aware of the thoughts that precede our behavior. If
this is the case, our unconscious mind then directs our life far
more than conscious awareness. If we are unaware of having
intuition, then we could be leaving some of the most important
actions of our lives to be determined by unconscious processes!

When we are unaware of our thinking, our actions may
belie our intentions. For example, a mother who hits her young
daughter may say that she does not believe it is right to strike
her child, but she cannot stop it, it is out of her control. This is a
situation where she is unaware of holding the belief that it is
permissible to hit a child. It is likely that she was an abused
child, and her emotional memory tells her abuse is justified, but
her conscious, logical mind says it is not.

Being unaware of our beliefs is not knowing that at times
we may be acting in our own worst interests, as in the above
example. Yet there are other situations when we are quite aware
of the divergence between our thinking and our doing, our
heads and our hearts, and this split is often forced upon us by
the workplace. Loyalty to the corporation says that we must do
its bidding and abide by its thought processes, which in turn
dictates our behavior. In this case we do not do what we think,
but what our boss thinks. If there is a divergence between doing
what the boss wants done and what we think is right, it can
become a major stressor in our lives. A recent study that
involved 2,534 postal workers concluded that most people who
complain of backache are actually reflecting being unhappy at
work. When two groups of workers were compared, those who
went to "back school" to learn to take care of their backs, and
those who did not, there was no significant difference in their
rate of injury. In fact, among those who went to back school,
injury rates were slightly higher. The conclusion: backache is a
result of job dissatisfaction. People who hate their jobs are more

likely to strain their backs or see no value in taking back-protecting precautions.

Furthermore, when there is animosity toward one's superiors, the worker may resent doing anything the boss suggests, such as being careful while lifting, because it was the boss's idea. John Gray, in *Men are from Mars, Women from Venus*, makes a similar point: men do not like to do what they are asked to do by their wives because it feels like it's their mothers telling them what to do. It is not hard to see that many men may also make this same type of connection to their bosses; they see them as being like their fathers or mothers, and they resent doing whatever it is that they ask.

Another common stressor that is bred from a disparity between what I think and what I am asked to do, is competition that is in-house bred. If our own abilities and achievements can be valued without measuring them against others, then we are encouraged to be the best that we can be without competing against coworkers. But, when our work is pitted against others and internal rivalry becomes more intense, it results in a terrible morale problem. Yet, this kind of misguided competition is still encouraged in large organizations, based on the premise that competition is good and makes people try harder. It is a concept that has not been proven to be successful; in fact, just the opposite occurs. People do not try harder. They put less effort into the job, or they quit.

Stephen Covey, in *7 Habits of Highly Effective People*, illustrates the difficulty that this type of competition creates when he tells the story of a company president who brought him in to consult on what he viewed as the lack of cooperation among his salespeople. He told Covey their basic problem is that "they are selfish." He wanted Covey to develop a human relations system that would solve the problem. When Covey looked into it further, he discovered that in the president's office, behind a curtain was a photograph of horses in a race with the pictures of his salespeople placed over the faces of the horses. Winning this "horse race" meant winning a trip to Bermuda. Once a week, the president called his salespeople into this room and asked who would be going to Bermuda. As Covey said, "It was like telling one flower to grow and watering another. . . . one manager's success meant failure for the others."

It seems to me that if the executive had used his intuition, he would have perceived that this commonly accepted "logical" practice was extremely detrimental to everyone's morale. My intuition asks, "Why would the president want to reward one person as a winner by branding the rest of his people losers? Wouldn't he want everyone to be a winner?" If he wants the entire sales team to perform, it seems painfully logical to reward them all, or punish them all; but rewarding one and punishing the rest suggests that not only are they losers in not winning the trip, but whatever their accomplishments, they too are devalued. For example, suppose the average salesperson sells 100 products a month and the winner sells 150. Is there something wrong with selling 100? Didn't that 100 contribute to the profits of the business? To call these people losers is to negate their worth, to discount their performance and belittle their abilities. The result: people are reluctant to cooperate and become frustrated, angry, and stressed out.

Intuition can inform the executive where to look if he wants to know why some salespeople perform better than others, such as checking out each person's potential number of clients, territory, experience, training, and personality. If these factors are not addressed, no trip to Bermuda will solve the problem.

While it may take some intuitive understanding to be clear on what you think versus what you are told to think, there is another kind of knowing that is also intuitive: knowing when the right opportunity is there for you or if the person you recently met was someone it was important for you to know. When we become aware of the significance of these events, we may refer to it as a synchronous experience. A true life example is given in the next chapter to better understand this concept.

**5**

# *Synchronicity*

Synchronicity is a term that is being heard more frequently today. It is similar to what we mean by "luck" or being alert to recognize an opportunity and take advantage of it. Synchronicity may be present when an uncanny coincidence occurs, or when events happen, whether fortunate or not, that are not accidental but meant to guide us. Arthur Koestler, paraphrasing Jung, defined synchronicity as "the seemingly accidental meeting of two unrelated causal chains in a coincidental event which appears both highly improbable and highly significant. The people who come to you are the very people you need in relation to your commitment. Doors open, a sense of flow develops, and you find you are acting in a coherent field of people who may not even be aware of one another. You are not acting individually any longer, but out of the unfolding generative order. . . . At this point, your life becomes a series of predictable miracles" (Jaworsky, 1996).

Skeptics may or may not agree with this belief, but the word "miracle" may definitely raise a red flag. Let's take a look, however, at one recent success story that could be applied to this definition of synchronicity. Watch how it did, indeed, end in a miracle—if we define a miracle, in this example, as an unexpected business opportunity that generated more income than was ever imagined possible.

This is the story of Jeff Larkin. Larkin had completed four years of college as a computer science major. When he graduated in 1991, he found few jobs available to test his skills. After searching for several months, he settled for a low-level entry position at Digital Equipment Corporation; when the company began their massive layoffs, he was one of the first to go. Jeff could not find professional work anywhere in the area and was forced to look for a job at fast food restaurants or other places that hired nonskilled workers. He found nothing. For nearly two years, he borrowed money from friends to live on while his spirits sunk with each job rejection. Finally, not being able to borrow any longer, he was forced to move back to his parents' home in another city, broke, deep in debt, and jobless.

Then, a daughter of one of his parents' friends heard about his situation and asked him to send her a resume. Her employer, Artful Finance, offered bonuses to its employees to bring in referrals for new hires, so she was as motivated to get him in the door as he was to be there. Jeff was hired on a temporary basis, because his resume showed very little work experience. About a year later he was hired as a permanent employee. In another year, he received a raise and was earning enough money now to rent his own apartment.

While working at Allied Finance, Jeff met Tom, a coworker in the same department, and they became good friends. Both men were feeling frustrated with the job because their supervisor was very difficult: vindictive, dishonest, and scheming were a few words they felt described him most accurately. Their day-to-day work was filled with anxiety; they never knew whether they would be bad-mouthed behind their backs to their coworkers, chewed out directly in front of them, or forced to lie about their time sheets.

Meanwhile, Jeff had been sent for specialized training in a unique software skill, a $10,000 expense that the firm picked up, on the condition that he would remain with the company for at least six months. One day, Tom had a particularly difficult time with the supervisor and abruptly offered his resignation. Tom arranged to receive the same specialized software training Jeff had been given. He paid for it on his own, making the decision to be a consultant rather than to continue working for this company. He was fed up with their mutual boss as well as the lack of opportunity to make a substantially higher salary. When his training was completed and he began consulting, Tom doubled his former salary.

At this point, Tom had the vision to see how he and Jeff could pool their specialized training and talents into a business of their own and suggested that they eventually become business partners. Tom urged Jeff to leave, but Jeff was not the risk-taker that Tom was. He had suffered for almost two years without being able to get any kind of a job, and those memories froze whatever entrepreneurial zeal he might have otherwise had. Finally, after much soul searching, he decided to let his intuition guide him, and he "heard" something tell him to leave. Several months later, Jeff resigned and again borrowed money, this time to finance further training in the specialized software in order to become additionally qualified to consult with Tom's firm. One month later he began consulting. In three months he earned more than what he would have earned in a year at his previous job. Not only has he tripled his former salary, he has also vastly improved his working relationships with his mentors, who are far more reasonable and pleasant than his former boss.

In partnership, Jeff and Tom have not only become more financially successful than Jeff had ever anticipated, but they have established a new business that will create work for others as well. Let's look at the synchronicity of events.

Event #1: Because he had no job opportunities in the city where he lived and was deeply in debt, Jeff Larkin was forced to relocate to his parents' home.

Event #2: His parents had a friend whose daughter worked for a company looking for programmers.

Event #3: Hired by this company, Larkin was sent for the first part of specialized training with a large software vendor; the company paid for his training costs of $10,000.

Event #4: He met Tom at the company and they became friends. It is most unlikely that he would have met Tom had he not worked at this company.

Event #5: Tom, the risk-taker, left the company to become a consultant and suggested to Jeff, the risk-avoider, that he think about a business partnership.

Event #6: Larkin, using his intuition, decided to take the risk of leaving, along with the added risk of borrowing more money to finance advanced training to become a qualified software consultant with the new company.

Event # 7: Within three months, he incorporated a business with Tom. He is now earning more money than he had ever anticipated. (The miracle.)

If Jeff had not been unemployed and so deeply in debt that he was forced to move back to his parent's home, this chain of events leading to his success might never have happened. Apparent negative events, such as losing a job and not being able to find even the most menial work, turned out to be fortuitous. Jeff's story is reminiscent of a Chinese folktale that emerged hundreds of years ago. It tells of how fortune and misfortune may be difficult to distinguish at first glance.

A man who lived on the northern frontier of China was skilled in interpreting events. One day, for no reason, his horse ran away to the nomads across the border. Everyone tried to console him, but his father said, "What makes you so sure this isn't a blessing?" Some months later his horse returned, bringing a splendid nomad stallion. Everyone congratulated him, but his father said, "What makes you so sure this isn't a disaster?" Their household was richer by a fine horse that his son loved to ride, but one day he fell and broke his hip. Everyone tried to console him, but his father said, "What makes you so sure this isn't a blessing?"

A year later the nomads came in force across the border, and every able-bodied man took his bow and went into battle. The Chinese frontiersmen lost nine of every ten men. Only because the son was too lame to fight did the father and son survive to take care of each other. Truly, blessing turns to disaster, and disaster to blessing; the changes have no end, nor can the mystery be fathomed.

*The Lost Horse*

In this folktale, "disaster" ultimately works to the father and son's advantage, fortune to their disadvantage. Those who believe in fate or synchronicity feel that there is a purpose to whatever happens to us. It is not coincidence, and it is destined to be for our ultimate good, even if it does not seem that way at first. For example, a common experience many people have suffered is losing a job from downsizing or being fired. Either way, it feels like a disaster. However, executives at Drake Beam Morin, an outplacement firm, say that over 80 percent of those who were let go ultimately found a much better position and are happier with their new jobs. The ancient wisdom of the Chinese tale still remains wise and true.

Many people may feel that a more accurate depiction of synchronicity is when events happen simultaneously or thereabouts. I had a recent experience that would fall into this category. I had been trying to locate an educational group for several months and could not find its address or telephone number through any of my contacts. Then one day I called someone who said he could find the telephone number for me and would get back to me the next day. The next day, at 11 A.M. he called to give me the number. At 10:55 A.M., just five minutes earlier, I had received a letter in the mail from this same organization. The letter was sent to a person who had lived in my house over twenty-five years earlier, and it arrived within minutes of my friend's call. Considering that I had been living at this same address for fifteen years and had never received a mailing from this organization before, it was a remarkable coincidence.

# 6

# *Gender Matters*

It is said that women are more intuitive than men, and this may have some validity when it is applied to interpersonal relationships. For example, one married couple may be with another couple who are old friends, yet the woman is generally the first to sense that there is something very wrong with their friends even though nothing seems amiss. If she shares this presentiment with her husband, he may tell her she is (a) imagining things, (b) dreaming, or (c) nuts. Later they learn that this couple is on the verge of divorce. Generally, although not always, women seem to be better tuned in to relationships than men. Carol Gilligan's research over 15 years ago showed that girls as young children were more interested than young boys in maintaining relationships rather than in competitiveness, and that these same values carry into adulthood as well, for both genders (Gilligan, 1982).

In other matters, however, both women and men are more or less equal in their intuitive knowing and creativity, but their interests may have a slightly different focus. Although it is not politically correct to say that men and women are different, in fact, many of their interests are. No, the differences do not apply across the board because there are exceptions to any generality; there are some women at MIT, but relatively few, just as there are some men at Vassar, but also very few. When men and women have somewhat different interests and foci to their lives, this may be reflected in how they use their intuition. However, when they are both involved in developing similar new products, their methods are the same in terms of making connections, but each person draws upon what has been in his or her experience, and often, because of the different roles that men and women take on, their connections may be different.

For example, a man who is charged with designing better cleaning products for the home—let's say a new machine that will clean the kitchen floor—may envision a robot carrying some form of a pail and mop; he may see it as an imitation of what a human being would look like performing this function. A woman charged with the same assignment might relate the new invention to the windshield cleaning mechanism in cars, where it sprays a fluid on the windshield and then wipes it off. Perhaps her machine would spray the cleaning liquid on the floor and then have a hot dryer mop it up, where she makes the connection between her hair dryer and drying the floor. Both products might work, and work equally well.

In both examples each has used the same intuitive technique of connection-making; the difference may be in what they make connections with. She connects to things she knows or uses every day, such as a car and a hair dryer. He, too, connects with what he presumably knows; how robots work and what they could be programmed to do. The principle is the same: both genders make connections to what each know and relates it to whatever is the task at hand. The difference may be based on their experiential backgrounds, which may differ according to their perceived role in the culture. Thus, when differences occur between the genders, it may be more influenced by their cultural domain and not the creative process.

At MIT's Media Lab, for example, women and men are working together to create unique sound and light systems with high tech gadgetry that is pushing the envelope to what may be a giant leap in digital and laser sound technology. Perhaps one reason for their extraordinary advances is that they have combined the brain power as well as domain differences of both genders. New product developers, take note. There is an obvious advantage to men and women working together from a wide variety of backgrounds to create something new: it works.

Laura Day, in *Practical Intuition*, says that intuition is

> about receiving and interpreting information. As you gain control over your intuition, it's important to keep these two steps distinct. The first step is receiving intuitive data in response to a question. Intuitive information usually presents itself as symbols. This step is non-linear.
>
> The second step is both linear and non-linear. At this stage you are both interpreting, or translating the symbols and piecing them together. It's linear in the sense that you use your logical mind to fill in and make sense of the gaps. . . . It's in the translation process that useful and applicable information is created. I use the word "translation" because intuitive data are often received in the symbolic language of the unconscious, and the practitioner then has to find the meaning or significance of the messages.

We see symbols every day. When we can relate these symbols to a problem at hand, they often lead to a solution. One example is the traffic standard that holds red, green, and yellow lights. These symbols mean stop, go, and proceed with caution. When used in other contexts, the colored lights may solve another problem, such as how to get an advertising message across to the public. Stop & Shop Companies, a major grocery chain, uses the traffic light symbol as part of its logo in signs and letterheads. If you can become aware of the symbols you encounter every day, it can expand your creative ideas for new services and products: it requires only a little interpretation to make the intuitive leap!

# Conclusion

There was one question that I posed to nearly everyone I interviewed for this book: Is intuition always correct? The answers varied. Some intuitive practitioners said that nothing is 100 percent correct. If that is so, I asked, then why should one rely on any intuitive insight? One answer was, "You just have to go with your best feel." Others said, "intuition is correct for that moment, but may be incorrect for the next." And still others said, "If it is intuition, the real thing, then it is always correct." The attitude generally expressed was that genuine intuition comes from a higher place and is meant for our good, therefore, it is always correct. A higher place indicates a spiritual context.

Masoru Ibuka, founder and the late honorary Chairman of Sony Corporation, also felt that creativity comes from a mystical place: "There is a spiritual side of the world that is very unpredictable and vague that is the source of human creativity." This source of creativity that he referred to, I believe, is intuition.

If intuition is given to us and is meant for our good, then the ultimate challenge becomes learning how to distinguish between emotion, wishful thinking, and intuition. It is helpful to have a teacher, someone who is experienced in receiving intuitive information, to help us sort out the emotional or wishful from the genuinely intuitive. Then, we must figure out the meaning of the intuitive message if it comes to us in symbols. Eventually, with practice, we will learn how to spot the differences and know when and if the signals we receive are actually in our best interest.

Although some people seem to be better at being intuitive than others, it is an ability we can all acquire. Being intuitive is like learning how to swim or play a musical instrument. Some musicians are virtuosos, but the rest of us with a little experimentation and practice (and earplugs?) could, at minimum, hack out a simple tune. In the following chapters you will learn how to coax your intuition out of night dreams, daydreams, and a variety of other places that intuitive practitioners have suggested. The result: your own creativity will be far more available than ever!

Many years ago, Oliver Wendell Holmes recognized that many of us never explore our latent talents. He offered us a wake-up call: "Alas for those who never sing but die with all their music still inside of them." Your intuition may be the key to discovering how to let your own music burst forth . . . and, well, you aren't getting any younger.

# PART TWO

# *Techniques and Tools to Spark Corporate Creativity*

Ideas are like rabbits. You get a couple and learn how to handle them, and pretty soon you have a dozen.

...JOHN STEINBECK

How do you move people from being comfortable with sitting on whatever is obvious and relatively certain to flying off into fanciful "what ifs"? Can you turn a person who doesn't trust anything invented after 1950 into someone who can come up with innovative ideas? The short answer is maybe. Experts in ideation skills attempt to convert the I-never-had-an-original-idea-in-my-life-and-never-want-to-type person to the exact opposite: someone who can experience his or her native intuition through a variety of techniques that stimulate whole brain thinking. It is not an easy task, in large part because of our cultural adaptation.

This problem is encountered, for example, when attempting to change a workplace culture that has ensured a worker's job security by rewarding mediocrity and playing it safe by confining people to specific roles and thinking patterns. Most of those who survive in the politics of the conventional organization probably did well in schools that rewarded them for getting the correct answers and being politically savvy, while discouraging creativity and resourcefulness. One of the first lessons many kindergartners learn is that they must color inside the lines, a restriction intended to help them develop better dexterity with hand-eye coordination. It results, though, in reigning in their previous anything-is-possible world view to conform to adult values. The teachers also often insist that the colors the youngsters choose should reflect an adult's reality, so grass must always be colored green, not orange or purple, or the children are in danger of being sent to a psychologist for an evaluation. Invisible walls define acceptable behavior throughout our lives; not to adapt to their presence is flirting with quiet ostracism or worse, being perceived as a misfit within the community. Ironically, it is often those very misfits who come up with the most brilliant and innovative ideas.

# 7

# Are Creative People Different?

There is a widespread cultural notion that creative people are, well, odd. Studies of the traits ascribed to creative people by conventional wisdom, according to the research of Mihaly Czikszentmihali, includes being impulsive, nonconformist, making up the rules as he or she goes along, liking to be alone, and tending not to know their own limitations. These qualities are seen in a negative way by those who do the judging, which suggests that they are thinking, "They are not like me, therefore, they're not to be trusted."

The studies also revealed that another common belief about creative people is that their least typical traits would include "being practical, dependable, responsible, logical, or sincere." This misperception that creative people are lacking in basic character values in fact has nothing to do with their creativity and may be as true for people who choose to be less creative as well. If this perception is pervasive, that creative people cannot be depended upon and are not practical, responsible, logical, or sincere, any methods devised to get past this erroneous belief would need to be extraordinarily powerful. When a mindset is this rigid, something comparable to the megatons of dynamite needed to implode a building may be necessary to dislodge it.

Professor Howard Gardner observed that "most cultures throughout human history have not liked creative individuals. They ignored them or they killed them. It was a very effective way of stopping creativity." Being ignored is one thing. Killing, on the other hand, may be closer to the way we handle new ideas today, while we mercifully spare their creators. How did we come to reward mediocrity and punish the creative person? One theory is that from the industrial revolution to the 1980s the implied rule for career success was that certain people would invent new products and processes, and the rest of us were meant to work within the systems that others put into place. The better you were at doing precisely what you were told, the more rewards you would receive from the organization. Since the 1980s, there has been a sweeping cultural shift reflected in the number of books, articles, and seminars devoted to how to become more creative and become a better leader, which implies that we should not be following procedures, but rather conceiving of new ones. Now everyone is exhorted to be a leader, and followers have suddenly become a disenfranchised class, or so it would seem.

If leadership and innovation is "in," and "followership" and maintaining the status quo is "out," then here's the rub. How can you become an innovator without the risk of others seeing you as having those negative characteristics, such as being impractical, undependable, and irresponsible, as described earlier? If one becomes an innovator, it may risk credibility, respect, or affection among your peers! If you are not an innovator, it means stagnation, which may lead to financial loss. It is a difficult choice: be more creative and risk being ostracized, or maintain the status quo and risk losing your job. As Paul Torrance once noted, "It takes courage to be creative. Just as soon as you have a new idea, you are a minority of one." The books that push us to be more creative are already out there with frightening titles that spin fear into the heart, such as, *Innovate or Evaporate, Swim with the Sharks, Do Lunch or Be Lunch, Competing for the Future, The Fourth Wave,* and so on. Thus, the rush toward innovation escalates to a frantic pace.

# 8

# *Idea-Generating Techniques*

Since many older corporations have set procedures that make creativity from within difficult, except in some very notable exceptions such as the 3M Company and Motorola, it is the consultants who are now coming to the rescue. By conducting their creativity sessions in groups, there is peer pressure to probe the intuitive and creative part of the brain; if the group is involved in the same push toward creativity, then no one individual loses social acceptance, which the lone inventor in years gone by was willing to sacrifice.

Ideation experts use their own intuition and a variety of techniques to penetrate that childlike part of us that we thought was buried forever when we learned how to conform to acceptable patterns of thinking. The following is a description of a few of their tools. This is not meant to cover every method used today because, as ideas, they are being developed and refined continuously. However, this will give an overview of some of the most successful ones.

Coincidentally, many techniques developed to stimulate different areas in the brain are mirrored in Howard Gardner's explanation of multiple intelligences. Many of the following exercises were created independently by ideation practitioners. Yet, with a quick look you can see that they tap into the verbal/ linguistic, logical/mathematical, body/kinesthetic, visual/spatial, musical/rhythmic, and interpersonal as well as intrapersonal areas that comprise Gardner's research on the various types of intelligence that each of us has to a greater or lesser extent.

Some exercises that concentrate on the interpersonal and intrapersonal provide interesting insights into the self and others' behavior. For example, they can help you see why one person loves to tackle details while another finds being immersed in details as comfortable as being trapped in a mosquito infested hammock. Some people look at the forest, the big picture, while others are fascinated by the minutiae that comprise the forest but are slower to grasp the meaning of the whole picture. Clues as to why the behavior of others can be irritating (not our own, of course) can be learned with the Myers Briggs Type Indicator and other similar brain or personality mapping systems.

Those techniques that tap into the verbal/linguistic area use metaphors and analogies to stir the creative connections, such as the well-known Synectics® method. The body/kinesthetic intelligence is most frequently tapped into using the hands, by playing with a substance such as PLAY DOH, or building models of the new product idea, or taking part in ropes courses, such as the outward bound types. Many people find that using their whole bodies with simple physical movements, such as going for a walk or a run, also leads to new ideas.

Then there is the visual/spatial intelligence, that is tapped into by many consultants in the form of Picture Prompts™, a system trademarked by the Mattimore Group. This procedure will be explained in more detail later, but essentially it is the presentation of a series of pictures to a group to use as a metaphor for their problem. Other visual techniques include picturing events or places in one's mind, or using the images received in dreams as metaphors for the problem. Music may also accompany many of the creative games, and several studies have shown that while listening to the music of Mozart, one's intelligence and creativity are at least temporarily enhanced. The following are descriptions of some of the most effective and widely used systems that successfully elicit intuition as they spark creativity.

## SYNECTICS

During the 1950s and 1960s, after the austerity of the war years, there was a widespread interest in developing new products and new processes, and in general appealing to the attraction of "New." Creativity was not as common a concept as it is today. The only "system" for stimulating creativity was something called "Brainstorming," which was a relatively simple, straight-forward process originated by Alex Osborn of the advertising firm of BBDO (Batton, Barton, Durstin, and Osborn) in the late 1940s.

Arthur D. Little, a large industrial research firm based in Cambridge, Massachusetts, was active in helping companies develop new products and processes. In 1960, four members of one of their invention groups left ADL to start their own invention service. William Gordon, Carl Marden, George Prince, and Richard Sperry believed they had developed a system that was far more effective than brainstorming. The new company offering this service, as well as the invention process itself, was called Synectics—a name derived from Greek *syn*, which means together, and *ectics*, which is an arbitrary suffix derived from eclectic. The Greek may have been faulty, but the process proved to be very effective. Another translation of the word could be *syn*, bringing together, and *ectics*, the diverse.

The young company soon faced a difficulty it had not envisioned. The senior managers who hired Synectics were hungry for inventions, but the rank and file who had to make the new, crude working models into finished products ready for the market were not invested in the inventions of outsiders.

This attitude, which was becoming more and more common, was referred to as the N.I.H. factor: Not Invented Here.

To overcome this resistance, as well as to avoid bankruptcy, Synectics changed their approach. It became the first company to offer to train its clients' employees to be more creative. Companies sent their new-product developers to Synectics where they learned the system for creating ideas. However, this new strategy was not without its own problems. When companies seek to develop or name new products, or come up with clever marketing strategies, they have a relatively small percentage of the workforce who are naturally creative or intuitive from which to draw their talent.

According to the surveys of personality type decoded by the Myers Briggs Type Indicator, which will be explained in more depth later, only 25 percent of the population in the United States score as intuitors. And only 2 percent of the population combine intuition and thinking with introversion, a trait that is most commonly found in scientists and inventors, and only 20 percent of the population combine intuition, thinking, and extroversion, the most common traits for innovators.

While being intuitive is not precisely the same as being creative, most creative people feel that intuition plays a strong role in the creative process. Creativity is often defined as making conscious trials connecting disparate thoughts until a new combination offers a solution, whereas, intuition is unconscious and doesn't need the trial connection-making; it just "knows" the answer. Some think intuitives work backwards; that is, they get the idea first and then they figure out why it works.

## The Mind-Free Excursion

The challenge: how do you teach people to be more creative and intuitive if that is not the natural inclination for more than 75 percent of the population? One answer was delivered brilliantly by Synectics when it devised a group process, the Mind-Free Excursion. With this system, a group of people who wanted to come up with a new product would gather around a table and first define the objective or problem as carefully as possible. Once the goal was explained by the client, the group went into a wishing mode where each person stated his "wishes" for the product, be it practical or outrageous, on an anything-goes basis. The client then selects one of the wishes to pursue and the fun-filled excursion begins. This is a brain-stimulating event that asks participants to find connections between unlike entities, stimulating neural network connections between the left and right brain.

To get an idea of how this works, the following is an example of a problem posed by The Bell Telephone Company, then affectionately known as Ma Bell. The problem was, how to prevent their pay telephones from being vandalized. After the group defined the problem, it came up with two desired characteristics that evolved from the wishing process: the wish was that the telephone be enduring and indestructible.

In the next phase, the group chose two words from a list of "worlds" such as the world of the "Wild West" and the world of "politics." Each person then connected the word "enduring" with the concept of the Wild West or politics. For example, someone said that cowboys and Indians are enduring reminders of the Wild West. Another offered the large stone monoliths standing like pillars in the desert that she had seen on a recent visit. Each connection was recorded on a flip chart. At this point, the group was asked how to take all of these connections and suggest an idea for the telephone. Several ideas were offered and recorded. Again, the client was asked to take one idea to pursue further. In this case, the client chose "pillars in the desert" and from this evolved the idea of building pay telephones into "pillars" or walls in order to avoid vandalism. Within a year of this "excursion" the telephone company began installing phones into walls. Today we rarely see a public telephone that has not been implanted into its surroundings.

This system elicits ideas by forcing connections between unlike entities. In the above example, the thought of "enduring" was juxtaposed to the concept of the Wild West. It could have been used with the worlds of oceanography or comedy. Choosing from the list of worlds was completely arbitrary and *apparently* by chance. The connections made between the two worlds would seem to be random as well. However, something intuitive happened when the thought of juxtaposing "enduring" with "pillars in the desert" was mentioned. Although the solution could not have been articulated at that moment, that is, the thought of building the telephone into walls, it was an intuitive insight that grasped the significance of pillars in the desert as being helpful in solving the problem. From thinking about pillars, the concept of building telephones into walls to keep them from being vandalized emerged. This, while seemingly accidental and unplanned, is actually an example of how the intuitive knowledge of the participants was being stimulated to verbalize what their unconscious minds knew all along, that if they built a telephone into a wall, it would make them more enduring and less destructible by making it more difficult to vandalize.

At the time, building a telephone into a wall was a new solution to a difficult problem. While it seemed like a breakthrough idea then, all new discoveries in retrospect seem obvious. How often do we say "Why didn't I think of that?" when we see a clever new idea, because the answer usually looks so obvious, so simple. It is just that no one saw the obvious before. A genius is sometimes described as someone who sees what has always been there and makes it usable in ways that have a profound impact upon our lives, such as the harnessing of electricity. Intuition is also seeing the obvious: all new product development and scientific discoveries are based on seeing the possibilities of what was always there that no one had noticed. For the intuitive person who leaps to insights such as these, the answer is obvious and usually correct, but may not be obvious or even understandable to others who do not grasp the insight and require being brought along step by step to understand its significance.

How does Synectics® draw on intuitive insights? By creating the opportunity to make seemingly irrelevant connections that may not have any relation to solving the problem at hand. However, when a connection is made that relates to the problem, the intuitive brain will know it. When the intuitive heard the word "pillars," he instantly jumped to the concept of walls without knowing why, and then takes another leap to "seeing" the telephone implanted in the pillar. It prompts a word association that connects to something we already know, but were not aware of knowing, which is the solution to the problem.

If this method draws out what we already knew, then where was this information hiding? According to Carl Jung and Edgar Cayce, there is a vast cache of universal knowledge out there where the answers to everything exists. Jung called it the collective unconscious, a reservoir of knowledge that we can tap into in quiet moments or in our dreams; Cayce called it the universal mind, which has the potential to be known by everyone. Polio vaccine discoverer Jonas Salk felt that everything that can be known is known and that our intuition will lead us to its discovery. Synectics is one method for tapping into our intuitive unconscious. Here are some others.

## SIX HATS

Alex Osborn noted early on that moods usually do not mix to explain why the judgmental and the creative tend to clash. "Each may mar the working of the other. The right mood for judicial thinking is largely negative, 'What's wrong with this?', 'No, that won't work.' Such reflexes are right and proper when trying to judge. In contrast, creative thinking calls for a positive attitude."

Edward De Bono, author of several books on creativity, reflects this wisdom in constructing a process that very diligently separates the judicial from the creative. In the "Six Hats" system it compartmentalizes the process for eliciting creative ideas by separating the various approaches toward solving a problem. His method is to assign the group to imagine wearing six color-coded hats at various times in the creative problem-solving process. Each hat designates a different thinking process.

The White hat is neutral and simply carries information. It looks to see what information we have and what the mission consists of, that is, what we would like to have and how to get the information we need. Everyone puts on this hat at the beginning to look at the facts and the information at hand, without any emotional or logical input allowed. Just the facts.

The Green hat is for creative thinking and new ideas. It represents the search for additional alternatives. When everyone wears the Green hat, it is possible to ask for and generate ideas.

The Yellow hat is for optimism and the logical positive view of things; it looks for feasibility and how something can be done. It also looks for benefits, but they must be logically based. While wearing the Yellow hat, no criticism of the idea is acceptable. The group simply tries to ferret out all of the good points of an idea. If it looks like it would cost too much to make, this comment is reserved for the Black hat part of the procedure.

The Red hat has to do with feelings, intuition, hunches, and emotions. I personally disagree that emotions fall into the same category as intuition, because intuition is knowing without knowing how you know; most often, it has nothing to do with emotion, which is how you feel about something. However, when the Red hat is worn, it tells others that "I am in my emotional mode and this is the way I feel about this project." For example, "I don't trust this information," or "I don't like it," or "my gut feeling says its great," and so on. However, if we understand the Red hat as representing anything other than logic and judgment, then intuition may be included here.

The Blue hat represents the blue sky and an overview. It is for process control and looks at the thinking process itself. The Blue hat sets the agenda for thinking, suggests the next step, asks for other hats, asks for summaries, conclusions, and decisions, and can comment on the thinking being used.

The Black hat elicits the image of the judge wearing black robes who comes down heavy in judgment. The Black hat is caution, meant to prevent us from making mistakes, doing silly things, and acting unlawfully. The Black hat is for critical judgment and points out why something can or cannot be done. It also may be used to troubleshoot an idea or locate obstacles. This is usually worn in the last step of the process when the final decision is being made as to whether to go or not go with a specific idea.

The advantage of this system is that while members of the group have their Green hats on and are in the creative mode, they cannot switch hats and put a damper on the process by being critical (which is the job for the Black hat) or emotional (the Red hat). This keeps everyone on track and together in stimulating ideas without knocking them down. It also prevents the game of winning and losing, wherein if two people disagree each takes a position and then becomes more interested in winning than in exploring the subject. The six hats allow them to get away from argument in order to become more objective. When everyone is wearing the same color hat, they can be more productive rather than talking at cross-hat purposes. Also, in many companies, it is not natural to allow time for creativity, but the presence of Yellow and Green hats makes it possible to allocate time for deliberate creativity and intuitive ideas to be expressed without having them shot down immediately.

It should be noted that these processes are also used in most brainstorming courses, including a Synectics excursion in which the criticism of ideas is discouraged until the final phase of evaluating the idea and arriving at a decision.

# 9

# *Shortcuts to Stimulating Big Ideas*

The following methods can be used more rapidly than those previously mentioned. While some methods work better with groups, others, such as mindmapping, can be very successful for an individual or a group. Some people have received an answer to a difficult problem in as little as twenty minutes using mindmapping, whereas, the typical brainstorming processes may take several days. Discontinuous problem solving may offer answers in a short period of time also. Each of these activities can generate new insights both within an individual and a group.

## MINDMAPPING

Mindmapping is a system created and popularized by Tony Buzan. It begins with writing the problem or drawing an image of the problem in a circle in the middle of a large piece of paper. From there the mind freely associates with any thoughts that emanate from the word or pictures in the center. Drawing branches in different directions out of the circle to express a variety of thoughts leads to more thoughts. For example, the words in the center could be, "New Toy for Five-Year-Old." In lines flowing out from the center one could write, "existing toys," "favorite toys," and so on. Each of these lines can generate more and more ideas, until the final new product ideas emerge. Twenty minutes into the exercise we may eventually pry ideas out of our unconscious mind and intuitive wisdom to reveal something we were not aware that we knew. When mindmapping is done with a group, the number of ideas generated increases rapidly, and a number of divergent ideas are brought together by everyone building on one another's thoughts.

Awareness Mapping is an expanded version of mindmapping. It was suggested by Michael Munn in his essay that appeared in *Intuition at Work*. He describes it as a two-dimensional map of associations around any central idea, question, word, or image. The associations can be words, phrases, pictures, or feelings. If you are working with feelings, you can describe how one feeling leads to another and then another, or how a feeling has led to an action, and so on. In his experience, this has been a powerful personal or group brainstorming tool.

## DISCONTINUOUS PROBLEM SOLVING

Discontinuous problem solving is the opposite of logical sequential problem solving. A familiar example of the discontinuous method is the game often played by families on a long car trip where someone begins a story with one or two sentences and then the next family member continues the story for another one or two sentences and so on. The object is to tell a story, having no idea where it will go.

In an ideation session discontinuous problem solving could begin with writing something at the top of a page, such as, "The best way to position our edible jewelry, such as chocolate earrings and mint necklaces is to . . . " The paper is passed around and each person in the group writes an answer to this, either building on the previous answers or adding his or her own unique slant on the subject. By the time twenty people have finished writing their ideas, many useful concepts often emerge. This can also be done verbally, with people in the group offering ideas as someone writes them on a flip chart. In a variation on this theme, several pieces of paper may be placed on the wall with different leading questions; each person then goes from one chart to the next, adding ideas by building on those already there. This may lead to some bizarre ideas, but from these often wild beginnings, viable solutions frequently explode. By forcing connections, even those that may seem far-fetched, we will be expressing our unconscious knowledge, otherwise known as natural intuition.

## PICTURE PROMPTS™

This method involves collecting a large number of pictures, perhaps thirty or more, such as advertisements in magazines, reproductions of artists' works, or photographs. Each person in the group is asked to choose a picture that suggests a solution to the problem at hand. Because the right brain tends to think in pictures, this is a powerful method for eliciting the natural ability of the right brain. When forced to select a picture, you are not consciously aware of what is leading you to select one particular image over another. Yet, as the exercise continues, you begin to understand that it was your intuitive wisdom that actually did the choosing. When you begin to explain why this picture relates to the problem, you suddenly realize how your intuition came to select it. This requires your left brain to figure out what the right brain knew all along.

For example, suppose the problem is, "How do I convince my boss to bring an ideation session into the company?" You scan through thirty-odd pictures, and you find that it is the picture of the glass of ruby-red wine that seems to beckon you.

When asked why you chose this picture you may say, "I think I could use a drink right now"; or, "If I wine and dine my boss, I'll soften him up and show him the pleasures of ideation like the pleasure of a fine wine"; or, "wine is made from fruit, and I'll show him how fruitful new ideas can be." Once the participant looks at all of these potential solutions prompted by the picture of the glass of wine, he can elect to pursue the most viable option. The right intuitive brain selected the picture based on information that it already had but was unaware of, and the left brain's logic verbalizes this knowledge. Bryan Mattimore, the consultant who trademarked this technique, frequently uses Picture Prompts™. He says that it is very useful for about 75 percent of his session participants. There are some people, however, who simply cannot relate to the picture prompt at all and do better with the verbal and written exercises.

Chris Miller, founder of Innovation Focus, uses another visual exercise that asks each person in the group to look out the window and focus on some object, or to select a dream image from childhood. The group then does word associations with that image or object, or builds a story around it, or recommends a vacation spot based on the image. This process takes the mind away from the issue or problem on which they had been previously focused, leading it into another realm for awhile. Later, when they are pulled back to address the problem once again, more clarity and fresh insights suddenly emerge.

Richard Feder, a founder of The Marketing Group, uses a technique that asks the group to draw a picture of a particular situation and then exchange it with another person. Each person then draws her comments or changes on everyone else's picture. Finally, they combine all of the thoughts and draw a picture of the resolution.

Collage-making is another visual technique used by several consultants to solve problems. Pictures either on a specific theme, such as photos of nature, or on a variety of themes, are given to a team to cut and paste into a collage. In the process of creating the collage, the team's collective intuition may guide the outcome when new ideas emerge that were not previously anticipated.

## KINESTHETIC EXERCISES

Some consultants like to involve their clients in kinesthetic exercises, such as using their hands to build models with pipe cleaners or Lego® sets, or to construct prototypes with a variety of materials. The mind-hand coordination elicits intuitive answers as we begin to build something with no particular model to follow.

After watching a group of people construct "hats" out of pipe cleaners, I understood how hands could unlock enormously creative talent. Their "hats" ranged from beanie types to regal crowns to upside-down and inside-out arrangements; many were far more original than the typical output from a conventional hat factory. However, this exercise was not universally successful. Some people were not comfortable working with their hands and were far less creative than they might have been using verbal or visual techniques. As Howard Gardner points out, we seem to have varying intelligences insofar as our creativity is concerned, and these appear to impact our response to exercises that would dip into our imagination. Those who like working with their hands will respond well to kinesthetic prompts; those who are visual work best with visual prompts. Given a group of fifteen to twenty people, it is probably wise to try a variety of techniques to see which ones are best at bringing out each individual's unique intuitive qualities.

Other types of kinesthetic exercises are games in which groups of people move around in teams against one another in an effort to get the ball. This exercise is comparable to basketball, but less strenuous. Or, for a bit more use of brawn to stimulate the brain, they may try outward-bound ropes-type courses.

Some consultants use kinesthetic exercises with variously textured materials, such as silk, satin, fur, and roughly-textured objects, that participants touch as they listen to classical music and quiet their minds. In one experiment, a coffee bar wanted to come up with some interesting and profitable ideas on how to position itself against its competitors. As the group listened to the music and touched the satin and fur, they found that erotic feelings were aroused, which led to the thought of sex, which then led to the question of how do we appeal to both genders in the advertising. When they touched something with a rough texture, they found it appealing in a different way. This led to the suggestion that the image for the coffee bar should be somewhat rough, that is, not sharply defined, but hazy enough to allow for imaginations to create whatever concrete idea occurred to them. The result is still top secret, but using these materials has led to some unique advertising and decorating ideas that will become an interesting counterpoint to today's versions of the coffee bar.

Still, the most commonly used kinesthetic experience that stimulates many intuitive insights is running or taking long walks. During this time the moving body permits a relaxation of alertness within the left brain, allowing the right brain to become aware of its knowledge. It is a way of quieting the left brain to allow the right brain to "speak." The intuitive insight is also stimulated by the production of endorphins, known as pleasure centers, which are known to be increased during running. Is there a connection between stimulating the pleasure centers of the brain and intuition? This may be an interesting study for a brain researcher to explore.

Recent experimental work on where intuition is located in the brain was reported in the *New York Times*. It concluded that "people have a covert system in their brains for telling them when decisions are good or bad and that the system, which draws upon emotional memories, is activated long before people are consciously aware that they have decided anything" (Blakeslee, 1997). The author of the study, Dr. Antonio Damasio, created a card game that tested the subject's intuition. "While people use facts, logic, and pure reasoning to make decisions, these inputs are not enough," he said. "Decisions are also influenced by what has happened to a person in previous situations." He speculates that "stored emotional memories come percolating up through a circuit in the prefrontal lobes, the region of the brain involved in decision-making."

If Damasio's theory is correct, then those people who say that their intuition improves with age are saying, in effect, that since they have lived longer and have acquired more emotional memories to draw upon, this makes their intuition better. Dr. Damasio says that these emotional memories are covert, but that they become intuitions that help guide decision-making on an unconscious level. "If covert memories make it into consciousness," he said, "they remain enigmatic but are given a name: gut feelings."

However, many intuitive people would disagree that intuition is nothing more than emotional memories, because it would seem that intuitive problem solving has little to do with emotions when a connection is made to solve a problem that has not been experienced before. For example, how does a scientist discover a vaccine for the first time, if nothing like it existed before? Where did the idea come from that suggested he take dead viruses and inject them into people to protect them from disease? It was not emotion. It had to be an intuitive insight that connected dead viruses with protection. Further, children who presumably have a smaller "bank" of emotional memories because they have not lived as long as an adult should have less ability to be intuitive according to this theory. Yet we know that children can be very intuitive, and we sometimes describe this phenomenon as being "wise beyond their years."

For many people, another route to elicit intuition is through their dreams. The relationship of dreams to emotions is acknowledged by most researchers. However, the expression of emotions, whether conscious or unconscious, is only one function of dreaming. Another function that dreams perform is house-cleaning the shards and remnants of the day's activities, which are often quickly forgotten. Yet another function for our dreams is problem solving, or finding a solution to nearly any kind of problem, whether it's "How much should I bid for that building?" or "What is the next product that I should manufacture?" Answers to these questions and hundreds of others have been revealed in dreams.

## DREAM INCUBATION

Because dreams express intuitive insights naturally, consultants are beginning to turn to dream incubation as an adjunct to their ideation sessions. These may begin with a variety of mind games that tap into the visual and logical connection-making intelligences during daytime hours, and which use a variety of exercises similar to those described earlier. In the evening, when the participant's minds have received far more information (and possible solutions) than before, the group is coached to experience the answer to the problem in their dreams. In a recent session that I led for *Industry Week Magazine,* a vice president of marketing at a chair manufacturing company had a vivid dream that took place on a college campus. In the dream he saw himself on the top of a building, swinging a wood and metal beer keg that he used to successfully fend off attackers. When the dream was interpreted, he learned that targeting more college campuses would be a good way to expand the market for his product. Since the wood and aluminum beer keg in the dream worked so well in keeping his "enemies" at bay (competitors?), he thought that he should consider adding metal or aluminum elements to the wooden chairs to make them more attractive to his customers.

While these are short descriptions of several techniques, all of them have one thing in common: any one or a combination of several of these approaches can take the person who is not inclined to be intuitive and bring out that latent side of his or her thinking. Although all of these techniques do not work for everyone, many are successful for a high percentage of the ideation consultants and their clients. If one technique doesn't click, they quickly switch to another until they can tap into that part of the collective thinking that can release the intuitive flash. The success of this process gives one pause when invoking the maxim that you can't make a silk purse out of a sow's ear. They have had a lot of "sow's ears" to play with in terms of seemingly nonintuitive clients, and they have produced hundreds of "silk purses" in the form of successful new products or services.

# 10

# Thinking Style Instruments

The idea for developing instruments that would measure creativity evolved after World War II, when the Air Force commissioned J. P. Guilford, a psychologist at the University of Southern California, to study the subject. The Air Force wanted to select pilots who would respond well in an emergency, such as the unexpected failure of a gear or instrument, with appropriately original behavior to save themselves and the plane. The usual IQ tests were not designed to test originality or quick thinking resourcefulness, hence Guilford was funded to develop what later became known as tests for divergent thinking. In 1968 he published a book on this subject, *Intelligence, Creativity, and Their Educational Implications*. This was one of the first research efforts to make the distinction between intelligence and creativity, and it included suggestions for the education of both characteristics. Since then, many instruments have been devised to measure one's proclivity toward creative thinking; a description of the most popular ones in use today follows.

# THE MYERS BRIGGS TYPE INDICATOR

The Myers Briggs Type Indicator (MBTI) is based on the work of Carl Jung and constructed by a mother-daughter team, Katherine Cook Briggs and Isabell Briggs Myers. The instrument reveals behavioral and personality preferences with four letters. The four-letter score will indicate that you are either an **E** for extrovert or an **I** for introvert; an **N** for intuitive or an **S** for Sensor; a **T** for thinker or an **F** for feeler; and a **P** for perceiver or a **J** for judger. Scores can be high, medium, or low in each category. For example, if a test score suggests that you are introverted, it may also fall close to the low score for an extrovert, suggesting that at times you would feel equally comfortable in either role, but more often would prefer the introvert's view of the world. Of course, we do not always behave in the style that our MBTI score would suggest. For example, you may score as an intuitive, but there may be situations when you choose to behave as a sensing person, and vice versa. Whatever the score, it does not indicate that your behavior is consistently predictable.

However, the Myers Briggs indicator does point in those directions where specific tendencies and talents would be useful, as well as where trouble spots would occur. It also explains how one person may be extremely annoying to his opposite type who may, by fate or choice, share space in his cubicle at work—and more likely in his bed. Talk about strange bedfellows! Many people tend to marry someone with qualities quite unlike their own, perhaps with a conscious or unconscious need to balance out their own shortcomings. For example, when a painfully shy introverted woman is married to a gregarious, friendly extrovert, the couple gain the best of both worlds. She will be brought into social interactions far more readily than when she is on her own, and he will experience more control of his flamboyant behavior and the pleasures of solitude in her presence. The variety of instruments available to learn how personality influences behavior will be discussed later in this chapter.

There is a frequent misunderstanding that the extrovert is always a very gregarious person. That is not always the case. What distinguishes her behavior from the opposite type is that she is someone who takes action and sees things very concretely. An extroverted child may say, "The sky is very blue and the grass is so green today!" The introverted child may say, "I see the trees pushing against the sky." This contrast is an example of concrete thinking versus abstract thinking. This attitude, whether extroverted or introverted, has little to do with being gregarious. Both extroverts and introverts may like to be around people; that is a function of upbringing or nurture, not nature, as Carl Jung would say. The extrovert can sometimes be found talking to himself when he is alone, because speaking clarifies ideas in his mind. The introvert would rarely engage in outward expression when she is alone. Generally, but not consistently, people who seek public office, salespeople, and some entertainers may score high on the extrovert scale. Inventors, scientists, writers, artists, and those who like to work alone frequently score on the introvert side. To determine whether you are more **E**, extroverted, or **I**, introverted, check which characteristics in the following columns more accurately describe you. The descriptions in Tables 10.1 through 10.4 are from the American Management Association's course, *Intuitive Leadership: Turning Gut Feelings into Competitive Advantage*

If you find that you have checked off substantially more in one column than the other, then you can assume that indicates you lean strongly toward either introversion or extroversion. If you see yourself as an introvert, you may tend to criticize some of the qualities of an extrovert as lacking in-depth thought and being too spontaneous. Likewise, the extrovert may be critical of the introvert, who may not act quickly enough because he still hasn't come to a definite decision, having seen a number of possibilities. If you need to hire someone who must make quick decisions, then look for an extrovert-leaning applicant for the

## TABLE 10.1  Attitudes/Orientations to Life

| EXTROVERSION | INTROVERSION |
|---|---|
| Directs energy toward people, activities, and things | Directs energy inward towards concepts and ideas |
| Says what's on his or her mind | May not say what he or she is thinking |
| Wants to create organizations and systems | Wants to create mental frameworks |
| Appears to be relaxed and confident with people | Appears reserved and questioning to others |
| Acts-Thinks-Acts | Thinks-Acts-Thinks |
| Sometimes Thinks-Acts-Thinks | Sometimes fails to act |
| Prefers a busy active workplace | Prefers a quiet workplace |
| Enjoys a wide range of interests | Enjoys a depth of interest |
| Likes to talk on the telephone | Dislikes telephone interruptions |
| Focuses on the present | Does not always live in the here and now |

position. On the other hand, if you need someone who will give thoughtful consideration before any move is made, then look for an introvert. And, if you want someone who will be thoughtful and analytical as well as quick to act, look for someone who combines thinker (explanation follows) with extrovert.

Another function measured by Myers Briggs is the perceiving function. In this area, one scores as either a sensor or an intuitor. A sensor is someone who experiences the world through the five senses, as well as senses what needs to be done and acts upon it. He sees a call to action constantly and feels most comfortable when he is actively doing something and making things happen. On the plus side, strong sensors get things done and move the world along a little faster. When not at their best, they will be impatient and sometimes act in haste, not giving enough thought to the outcome. The sensor also does not like to deal with ambiguity. For example, he may regard people as either good or bad, rather than see them as a mixture of many traits, some admirable, some less so. When confronted with a person who may be a mixed bag of good and not-so-good qualities, the sensor will choose only one of those characteristics to judge the person and rely on that.

On the other hand, the intuitor learns through indirect perception by way of the unconscious. She incorporates ideas or associations provided by the unconscious that may range from the merest hunch to brilliant examples of creative art or scientific discovery. To get an idea of your perceiving function, look at the columns in Table 10.2 and see whether you are more likely to be an **S**, sensor, or an **N**, intuitor, as the second letter in your four-letter description.

As you can see, the intuitive is comfortable with ambiguity to the point of being able to take the time to sort out the best course to take for herself, something the sensor is often unlikely to attempt. On the down side, the intuitive may take too much time to reach a decision, see too many sides to an issue, remain in an ambiguous state, and delay action. Career choices where a sensor would excel would be in sales, accounting and finance,

**TABLE 10.2  Perceiving Functions**

| SENSING | INTUITION |
| --- | --- |
| Practical, detail-oriented | Innovative and imaginative |
| Accepts life as it is | Tends to question life |
| Sees and is attentive to details | Sees how details form a pattern |
| Learns a skill and improves it with time | Learns new skills and changes careers |
| Needs facts and data | Looks for the "whole picture" |
| Values realism and common sense | Values imagination and creativity |
| Focuses on the concrete | Focuses on the abstract |
| Lives in the present | Lives in the future |

leading a platoon into war, and running a fast food or gourmet restaurant. For the upscale chic bistro, an excellent partnership can be achieved by combining the talent and temperament of an intuitive chef who can create unusual and imaginative recipes with that of a sensor, who would have the sergeant's call to action to manage the help and the many picky details.

Although there is a definite place for the sensor, and according to several studies our population is 75 percent sensor, Weston Agor, in an article that appeared in the *Futurist Magazine,* said that intuitive talent is enormously important to cultivate, especially since they are only 25 percent of the population.

> Extensive research on brain skills indicates that those who score as highly intuitive on such test instruments as the Myers Briggs Type Indicator tend to be the most innovative in strategic planning and decision-making. They tend to be more insightful and better at finding new ways of doing things. In business, they are the people who can sense whether a new product idea will "fly" in the marketplace. They are the people who will generate ingenious new solutions to old problems that may have festered for years. These are the executives that all organizations would love to find.

Another characteristic measured by the Myers Briggs is the judging function, where you are scored as either a thinker or a feeler. Whichever way you score does not mean of course, that you don't think or you don't feel. What it does mean is that the thinker draws his highest sense of accomplishment from using logical analysis and looking for consistency within a given set of facts, whereas, the feeler first feels whether the information is pleasing or displeasing, whether it's supportive or threatening. The feeler needs to feel empathic with others. The score indicates your thinking preference and is not necessarily based on skills in either direction; yet, having a strong interest in either one or the other, the skills would tend to develop in those directions. For example, if one's sense of self-worth is based on being an excellent logician, then that is the skill that you would hone most highly. On the other hand, if it is of value to you to be empathic and helpful to others, that is something that you would cultivate and perfect. Look at the columns in Table 10.3 and find out whether you tend to favor being a **T**, thinker or an **F**, feeler.

The thinking type individual is generally found in scientific research, mechanical engineering, law, and medicine. Feelers often gravitate towards working as psychologists, physicians, human resources managers, advertising creators, writers, artists, actors, and musicians.

The fourth and final dimension measured is the judging and perceiving function. The judger tends to form a judgment quickly, whereas, the perceiver may hold off judgment until more information has been received. When pushed to make a decision, judgers turn on their judging function immediately and turn off the perceiving function. If the perceiver is pushed to make a decision, she will most likely become anxious, shut off the judgment function, and wait until all the facts are in before

**TABLE 10.3   Judging Functions**

| THINKING | FEELING |
| --- | --- |
| Uses objective criteria to evaluate data | Seeks to increase harmony |
| Looks for the logic in a given situation | Looks for the "heart" of a given situation |
| Tends to be direct and truthful | Prefers to be tactful |
| Has a gift for intellectual criticism | Has a gift for empathizing with others |
| Treats people fairly | Treats people gently |
| Can be impersonal when hiring or firing | Finds it difficult to fire people |
| Likes to save time, especially on the phone | Finds it hard to interact without being friendly, especially on the phone. |

making a decision. The judger will judge whether an idea is good or bad instantly; in fact, he rarely holds off judgment, making an assessment of something as soon as possible—otherwise it will stir anxiety. The perceiver, on the other hand, is more open to a variety of ideas and more information before making a decision. She is far more comfortable waiting to get the entire story and is more apt to come up with many ideas to solve a problem. The judger, on the other hand, when he hears something that seems right, will say, "Yes, let's go with it, end of discussion," which may or may not be the correct course to take. Table 10.4 will help to determine if are you more like a **J**, judger, or a **P**, perceiver.

What characteristics are the most common? In the United States, the extrovert is most common, accounting for 75 percent of the population, while the introvert accounts for only 25 percent. Likewise, 75 percent of the population are sensors while only 25 percent are intuitives. In Japan, however, the statistics are just the reverse, 75 percent of the population are intuitive and 25 percent are sensors. This would indicate that the preference for extroversion and sensing is either culturally based or

**TABLE 10.4  Orientation to the Outer World**

| JUDGMENT | PERCEPTION |
|---|---|
| Likes to plan his work and his plan | Likes to be spontaneous |
| Needs to be organized and scheduled | Often procrastinates |
| Likes to start on time | Tends to run out of time |
| Needs to be right | Prefers to be tolerant |
| Tends to be purposeful, goal directed, and goal oriented | Likes flexible schedules |
| Has anxiety until a decision is made | Has anxiety about having to make a decision |

found in the genes, perhaps owing to racial differences. We cannot say school systems that encourage only left brain thinking are responsible for this cultural bias, because the schools in Japan are far more rigid and require more left-brain attention to math and other hard-knowledge skills than do American schools.

Perhaps the reason intuition is so pervasive in Japan can be traced to Buddhism, the country's most widespread religion. Unlike the Judeo-Christian tradition, which directs the individual to read and study the scriptures so that we will learn how to live the good life, Buddhism encourages its followers to acquire wisdom from within. When the individual reaches the highest plane of knowing and understanding, or nirvana, this is an intrinsic form of knowing that stems from one's own thoughts: the objective is to reach the god that resides within each of us. In western religious traditions, our values are shaped by extrinsic knowing; we are counseled to follow Biblical teachings so that we may be rewarded, if not in this life, then in the hereafter. This mindset closely matches the sensor's sensibilities.

A typical sensor, for example, is very happy to be told what to do by someone in authority and will do it to the best of his or her ability as quickly and thoroughly as possible. This is one reason why a sensor would charge intuitors (his opposite type) with "making up the rules as they go along." The sensor is oriented to an outer directive; the creative or intuitive person generally responds to an inner call, much like the Buddhists.

Another possible reason for the strong sensor population in this country is that it could have evolved from our country's early years in the days of the Wild West, when being quick on the trigger and following orders (both actions are a response to requests or threats from others) was the only way to survive. Being action-oriented seems to be the all-American way. This has been consistently reinforced in our popular culture, which shows a vast preference for action movies, beginning with the cowboy and Indian films of the 1940s and 1950s and then the war dramas of the 1970s and 1980s. At the same time, themes of violent action have evolved, ranging from the rumbles of street gangs to the violence of the Mafia, from the spy thrillers of the CIA and espionage to interplanetary warfare, and ultimately to films of nearly total destruction, such as *Independence Day*. However, some critics feel that the total destruction film genre has already become passé, so it will be interesting to see where the craving for action takes us next. Will it ever burn out? Unlikely, unless the burning takes place in a massive inferno caused by a worldwide earthquake!

Extroversion is the other most popular temperament type, and for good reason: to be an extrovert is generally to be well-liked. In fact, extroverts can become so well-liked that we have had politicians, such as the legendary Mayor, James Michael Curley of Boston, voted into office in 1947 while being tried for fraud and corruption. He spent five months in jail and then resumed his job as mayor and served out the term. In a recent survey in Korea, where the participants were asked who they would most like to see cloned, a small percentage suggested the names of politicians who were in jail on a variety of corruption charges. Apparently, likability can win over morality to a greater or lesser extent nearly everywhere.

## THUMBNAIL SKETCHES OF THE MOST AND LEAST COMMON TYPES

Although there are a total of sixteen temperament types described in the Myers Briggs, a full description of each would be superfluous here because there are several books you may refer to that offer extensive descriptions of each personality type. The four most common types, which each make up 13 percent of the population, are ESTJs, ESFJs, ESTPs, and ESFPs: in other words, each is both extroverted and a sensor, then also either a thinker or feeler, and either a judger or a perceiver.

However, I think it would be useful to describe two of these four most common types, each being 13 percent of the population, and two of the least common, each being only 1 percent of the population. It is interesting to note that the most common types tend to be the least intuitive, and the least common types are the most creative—which is probably one reason why we have so many books on how to be creative. This suggests that although you may score as a sensor, the opposite of intuitive, you still have intuitive ability but choose to use it less often. When you become aware that it can be a valid and useful option at times, it is likely to increase your success with creative problem solving.

The following descriptions can be found in *Please Understand Me*, by David Keirsey and Marilyn Bates, which includes a detailed analysis of all sixteen types.

### ESTJs

ESTJs are social people who are very much in touch with the external environment. They are quite responsible and generally outstanding at organizing procedures, rules, and regulations. They tend to be impatient with those who do not carry out procedures with sufficient attention to details. They are systematic, organized, detail-oriented, punctual, and prepared. They prefer hierarchy, authority, and routine and often find success in traditional organizations such as the armed services or businesses with layered levels of authority. ESTJs are comfortable in evaluating others and tend to judge how a person is doing in terms of standard operating procedures. They are generally loyal to their institutions, their work, and their communities, and they make excellent, faithful mates and parents.

On the down side, ESTJs may not always be responsive to contrary points of view and the emotions of others, and they may have a tendency to jump to conclusions too quickly. They may not be willing to listen patiently to opposing views. ESTJs are so in tune with the established, time-honored institutions and ways of behaving within those institutions that they cannot understand why others might wish to abandon or radically change them. Yet ESTJs can often hurt others by their indifference. They follow routines well both at home and at work. They also tend to approach human relations through family traditions and rituals that have a special meaning for them and in which they willingly participate. ESTJs do not confuse people by sending mixed messages; what you see is what you get.

### ESFPs

ESFPs, on the other hand, radiate attractive warmth and optimism. Smooth, witty, charming, clever, and open, they also represent about 13 percent of the general population. They are great fun to be with and are the most generous of all types. ESFPs will avoid being alone, seeking the company of others whenever possible. They love excitement and create it wherever they are. Their joy of living is contagious, as are their happy faces. They have an air of sophistication and are likely to be dressed in the latest fashion, displaying an enjoyment of all the good things of life: dress, food, physical comfort, and happy times. They create a mood of eat, drink, and be merry wherever they go.

These ESFPs make exciting if somewhat unpredictable mates, which can generate anxiety in their quieter spouses; they seem to be always living on the edge of adventure. Yet, ESFPs can be generous to a fault. What is theirs is yours, and what is yours is yours. They love freely, without expecting anything in return. On the down side, however, their talent for enjoying life may make them more subject to temptation than others. They are inclined to be impulsive, and, thus, both male and female ESFPs are vulnerable to psychological if not physical seduction, giving in easily and agreeably to the demands of others. Because an ESFPs tolerance for anxiety is the lowest of all types, they tend to avoid it by ignoring the dark side of a situation as long as possible.

ESFPs tend to gravitate toward business and are adept at selling, although they can also be very effective in education and nursing. They are good at working with people in crisis, which sometimes draws them into social work or psychology, and they are also attracted to the performing arts, where they thrive on the excitement of being in the limelight.

### INTPs

We have just looked at two of the Extrovert (E)-Sensor (S) types. Their direct opposites are the Introvert (I)-Intuitives (N). Each of these four types make up only 1 percent of the American population. They are INTPs, INTJs, INFPs, and INFJs for a total of 4 percent of the population. While each of these types can be very creative, the INTPs tend to exhibit the greatest precision in thought and language of all sixteen types. They can detect contradictions in statements no matter how distant in space or time the contradictory statements were made, and their minds seem to be constantly searching for whatever is relevant and pertinent to the issue at hand. Consequently, they can concentrate better than any other type. Authority derived from office, position, or wide acceptance does not impress INTPs. Only statements that are logical and coherent carry weight. External authority per se is irrelevant.

INTPs prize intelligence in themselves and in others, but can become intellectual dilettantes as a result of their need to amass ideas, principles, or understanding of behavior. For INTPs, the world exists primarily to be understood. They can become obsessed with analysis and will persevere until the issue is comprehended in all its complexity. INTPs can be intellectual snobs, often showing impatience with others less endowed intellectually, which can generate hostility and defensive behavior from others. They tend to be reflective, independent, low-key, complex, and curious. Career choices for the INTP often include inventor, designer, architect, or writer. If the organization is to use the talents of an INTP appropriately, he or she must be given an efficient support staff who can capture ideas as they emerge and before the INTP loses interest, becomes bored with the project, and moves on to explore other ideas.

As mates, INTPs take their marriage relationships seriously and are usually faithful and devoted. INTPs are willing, compliant, and easy to live with—albeit preoccupied at times. They may have difficulty expressing their emotions verbally, and the mate of an INTP may believe that he or she is somewhat taken for granted. They deal with the environment primarily through intuition, and their strongest quality, the thinking function, remains relatively hidden except in close associations. For that reason, INTPs are often misunderstood and perceived as difficult to know. They are inclined to be shy except when with close friends, their reserve being difficult to penetrate. Because their feeling qualities may be underdeveloped, they may be somewhat insensitive to the wants and needs of others, often unaware of the existence of these needs. INTPs are logical, analytical, philosophical, and scientific, and they enjoy the redesign of systems. They like to engage in debate so that they can develop a deeper understanding of concepts and ideas, while avoiding routine and small talk.

### INFJs

The INFJ, who has an unusually strong drive to contribute to the welfare of others and who genuinely enjoys helping people, is another one percent of the population. This type has great depth of personality, exhibiting a good understanding of and ability to deal with complex issues and people. An INFJ is likely to have visions of human events, past, present, or future, and demonstrate an ability to understand psychic phenomenon better than most others. They have strong empathic abilities and can be aware of another's emotions or feelings even before that person is conscious of them himself. They are usually good students, achievers who exhibit a quiet creativity. They can have qualities of perfectionism and put more into a task than is perhaps required. Generally, they will not be visible leaders, but will quietly exert influence behind the scenes.

For some people, INFJs are hard to get to know. They are reserved and tend not to share their thoughts except with those they trust. INFJs like to please others and tend to contribute their own best efforts in all situations. They prefer and enjoy agreeing with others, and find conflict disagreeable and destructive. What is known as esp (extra sensory perception) is likely to be found in an INFJ more than in any other type, although other types are capable of this also. INFJs have vivid imaginations, exercised both as memory and intuition, seeming to amount to genius at times, and others may view an INFJ as mystical.

For careers, INFJs may choose counseling, clinical psychology or psychiatry, or they may teach in these fields. They make outstanding therapists who have the ability to get in touch with the archetypes of their patients in a way some other types do not. They often select liberal arts as a college major and opt for occupations that involve interacting with people, but on a one-to-one basis. They may also be attracted to writing as a profession and often use the language of imagery, being masters of the metaphor, in both their verbal and written communications, which tend to be elegant and complex. They are futuristic, empathetic, creative, and reserved. Integrity is a strong value.

INFJs may also like to work at jobs that require solitude and concentration, but also do well when in contact with people. They enjoy problem-solving and can understand and use human systems creatively and humanistically. INFJs listen well and are willing to consult and cooperate with others. They are also generally good at public relations and have good interpersonal relations. However, they can be crushed by too much criticism and their feelings are easily hurt. Rather than criticism, they respond well to praise and use approval as a means of motivating others. If they are subjected to hostile, unfriendly working conditions or constant criticism, they tend to lose confidence, become unhappy and immobilized, and may even become physically ill.

This is just a short overview of the Myers Briggs typology. Most people find it useful not only for gaining a better understanding of their own strengths and weaknesses, but also to learn how others may see them in a positive or negative way. We may become more aware of how to adapt our "natural" inclinations to the requirements of the workplace. This would mean, for instance, that if one is a strong J, or judger, one has a tendency to be less open and understanding of new ideas and may come to judgment too quickly. Learning how to wait until all the facts are in could be useful for both the short and long term when it comes to important decisions.

These personality descriptions may also be useful in the hiring process. If the qualities needed to fill a particular position can be defined, then knowing an applicant's temperament type will be helpful for placing her in the right position, not only as far as the work itself is concerned, but also in terms of her relationship with her supervisor. For example, you would not want to put an INFP in a position under an ESTJ, because the tendency of the latter to be hypercritical would discourage the INFP from doing her best work. And, if there are a lot of details involved in the work, it would be best not to place an intuitor in that position; instead, seek a sensor.

## WHOLE BRAIN DOMINANCE PROFILE

Ned Herrmann, author of *The Creative Brain,* is the founder of Herrmann International in Lake Lure, North Carolina, with franchises in 18 countries. He has devised a different type of questionnaire, already translated in 12 languages, that measures the strengths and weaknesses of each of four functions of the brain.

In the HBDI, the brain's functions are divided into four quadrants. On the right side is the upper and lower cerebral, having the intuitor/feeling functions, and the left side, upper and lower limbic, has the thinker/sensor functions.

In Herrmann's terminology, which coincides with Jung's personality descriptions, if you score as a strong *Thinker,* which he locates on the left upper cerebral part of the brain, then you would be someone who prefers logical analysis and tends to be mathematical, technical, and a problem solver. If you received a high score on the lower left limbic side of the brain, the *Sensor,* you would be someone who is controlled, conservative, a planner, organizer, administrator, and a doer. Scoring high on the lower right limbic part of the brain is the *Feeler*, someone who is emotional, musical, spiritual, and a talker. Those who score high on the upper right cerebral side of the brain are the *Intuitors*, people Herrmann describes as creative, synthesizers, artistic, holistic, and conceptualizers. To illustrate how one type dominates another, he offers some well-known people as representing examples of excellence in each of the quadrants.

For example, he suggests that Descartes, Marilyn Vos Savant, Adam Smith, Aristotle, and Kant are (or were) strong thinking types. Sensor types include J. Edgar Hoover, Phyllis Schlafly, Susan B. Anthony, Julius Caesar. Some feeling types are Gloria Steinem, Betty Friedan, Eleanor Roosevelt, Maya Angelou, Louis Armstrong, Princess Diana, Mother Theresa, and Martin Luther King. And, on the intuitive quadrant, there is Leonardo DaVinci, Picasso, Einstein, Steve Spielberg, Amelia Earhart, Spike Lee, Madame Curie, Margaret Mead, and Mozart.

There are some personalities, however, that straddle the four quadrants, scoring about equally in all four areas of the brain. These include Albert Schweitzer, Thomas Jefferson, Golda Meir, Lech Walensa, and Winston Churchill. It would also appear that President Bill Clinton has strong leanings in each of the four quadrants. He is a logical thinker; he is a doer; he expresses his emotions easily; and he is perceived as being intuitive with people. He is also very much an extrovert, yet with an introvert's ability to analyze a problem in depth. Having the ability to use each side of the brain equally well is probably a major factor in his becoming president, because nearly everyone can choose an aspect of Clinton's personality with which to identify. The feelers empathize with Clinton's expression of emotion; the thinkers relate to his analytic ability and background as a Rhodes scholar; the sensors relate to his ability to take action; and the intuitors perceive his seemingly deeper reflection on issues, although one may disagree with his conclusions.

Most people who take the HBDI come out fairly strong in one quadrant, and to different degrees weaker in each of the others: this reveals where strengths and weaknesses are located. Herrmann notes, however, that 5 percent of those who have taken this assessment have scored more or less equally in each quadrant. Many CEOs who were tested also scored fairly equally in each quadrant, although many frequently edged into the intuitive quadrant a bit more than others in the general population. This suggests, perhaps, that an ideal or typical CEO would be a man or woman for all seasons, one who feels as comfortable with logical analysis as with imaginative "blue-skying," as comfortable with interpersonal skills as with routine and the discipline to get things done. This analysis is corroborated by many consultants who work with CEOs and who noted that, for the most part, senior executive officers are extremely quick to grasp ideas and have strong abilities in all four thinking areas. It is interesting to note that the scores of executive secretaries are very much like the CEO's, where they too score fairly evenly in all four areas. In fact, Herrmann believes that,

> . . . women are, on average, more whole-brain oriented, more intuitive, and less fact based, more open to new ideas than to the status quo, more people-oriented than thing-oriented. Therefore, they perceive their surroundings more sensitively, manage the innovative process more comfortably and respond more rapidly to changing environmental circumstances.

He concludes by saying that,

> . . . on average, (please note these are averages) men have clear advantages in rational, fact-based functioning and women have clear advantages in intuitive, emotionally-oriented functioning. Put the two together in a cooperative way, rather than in competition or conflict, and you have the potential for tremendous iteration and, therefore, genuine synergy.

When Herrmann wants to expand the right brain potential for some of his clients (usually executives) who have high scores on the left side of the brain and significantly lower scores on the right, suggesting that they tend to avoid their intuitive or emotional sides, he might take them for a boat ride on a lake and ask them to search for metaphors in nature that have to do with the problem at hand. By bringing them back to nature in a relaxing environment, he allows their left brains to relax while visual cues stimulate their less used right brains. Further, when they are asked to see a metaphor in nature that relates to their problem, it requires the use of the right brain, because the right brain understands metaphors, whereas, the left brain cannot. As Herrmann explained,

> I took them to a dam, I took them to a waterfall, to a sand bar. I even took them up on top of a mountain and had them look back on the lake to see things from a holistic perspective. Out of that came some metaphoric insight that enabled them to get a better grasp of the problem they were struggling with. They came out of it with a positive feeling.

## I SPEAK YOUR LANGUAGE

A similar diagnostic tool, called "I Speak Your Language," was developed by Drake Beam and Associates. It, too, is an instrument that measures the personality on the same four axes as the Herrmann Brain Dominance Instrument, noting the highest and then second highest scores in two of the four quadrants. The highest score represents the individual's first choice of behavior for use in everyday activity, and the second highest score becomes their back-up style if the first doesn't accomplish its objectives. The two lowest scores represent the least used aspects of the personality.

This instrument defines the sensor, thinker, feeler, and intuitor personalities in much the same way as the others do. In addition to this baseline information, this instrument also reveals how one would behave under stress. For example, suppose your scores were:

Intuitor = 15

Thinker = 27

Feeler = 18

Sensor = 30

This would indicate that your primary style of learning and behavior would be sensor and that thinker would be your back-up style. Under normal conditions, you would behave in a pragmatic, results-oriented, logical way. This type of individual would find it important to see concrete and tangible results and probably would seek activities that allow him realistic and immediate feedback.

On a secondary scale, however, which measures behavior under stress, this same individual might score:

Intuitor = 7

Thinker = 21

Feeler = 24

Sensor = 28

Thus, under stressful conditions, this individual still uses the sensor type as primary, but the back-up style now shifts to feeler rather than thinker. This means that under normal conditions this person is likely to be seen as down-to-earth, logical, controlled, and somewhat impersonal. Yet under stress, he or she is likely to convey a less impersonal and more emotional attitude, being less or more concerned about the feelings of others. Under stress, this individual would also rely even less on intuition than under normal circumstances. This would suggest that if you get a group of sensors in an ideation program and they feel stressed, their intuitive response may zip down to near oblivion, making creative problem solving difficult, if not impossible.

To give this questionnaire to a group of people before undertaking any creativity program would help the individual to understand why he or she may feel some reluctance toward getting involved in brainstorming games designed to elicit intuition. Sensors, for example, may feel challenged beyond their own perceived capabilities; this may result in their feeling stressed, emotionally charged, and angry with the facilitation process. It is also useful for the facilitator to know in advance who is likely to fly off the handle in anger or will fly off the wall—with creative ideas.

## THE PREDICTIVE INDEX

Praendex, Inc., located in Wellesley, Massachusetts, has created another instrument, the Predictive Index, that will reveal personalities from another perspective. Their assessments are more concerned with social behaviors rather than with brain patterns. The four axes that are measured are A for dominance, B for extroversion, C for patience, and D for formality.

The A axis measures dominance, or how much or little one likes to exert one's influence on other people and events. Someone who scores high in this area may be seen by others as confident, independent, innovative, and venturesome. However, those with a super high score may be perceived as domineering, controlling, or even belligerent, while those with a low score would be considered unassuming, unselfish, and possibly mild. Those with a particularly low score would be seen as meek and submissive.

The B axis measures extroversion. Like the Myers Briggs, this factor assesses the degree to which a person is driven to interact socially with other people. Thus, someone who scores high in this area would be considered friendly, outgoing, sociable, talkative, and socially skilled. Scoring very high in this area would indicate that the person is quite gregarious and exudes a great deal of charm. A low score, on the other hand, would suggest that the person is considered reserved, quiet, serious, and, perhaps, shy, similar to the description of an introvert. A very low score would suggest that this person is withdrawn and secretive.

Patience, axis C, is the measure of the intensity of a person's energy and tension level. Someone with a high score is relaxed, patient, deliberate, and calm. A very high C may be perceived as lethargic and unresponsive. A low C, on the other hand, is tense, impatient, restless, and driving, similar to the sensor. A very low C may even be perceived as volatile. If you combine a low C or volatile personality with a high A, the dominance factor, you will most likely have a potential criminal, someone who can lose control and at the same time has a need to dominate others, a typical pattern for spousal abuse.

The fourth dimension, D, is formality. This factor measures the degree to which individuals are driven to conform to formal rules and structure. This drive leads to an emphasis on thoroughness and detail, not unlike the Thinker on the Myers Briggs and others. A high D would be careful, cautious, precise, detail-oriented, and formal. A very high D might be considered a perfectionist and inflexible. A low D, on the other hand, would be thought of as casual, free-wheeling, and uninhibited, something like the extrovert-feeler-perceiver type. However, a very low D might be considered rebellious, undisciplined, and sloppy, sometimes the description of a highly creative individual. After analyzing how these four scores come together, one may be termed a "venturer," a "specialist," an "authoritative salesperson," a "scientific professional," or another description that includes each aspect of the personality as they work together in the individual. This is similar to the four-letter description of personality types of the Myers Briggs.

One of the advantages of this system is to show how personality styles may or may not fit a job description. For example, conventional wisdom says to put a strong extrovert in a sales position. So the company gives the Predictive Index to its employees and finds that one of its successful salespeople is leaning more toward introversion than extroversion. What to do. First, you may want to look at what it is he sells. If he sells highly technical products, he needs to have a good understanding of how to explain the technical attributes of the product to clients. This trait is usually not found in an extreme extrovert. Perhaps the job qualifications should be looked at more carefully in terms of what the client prefers in a salesperson. Who is the client-buyer for this high-tech product? She is most likely to be highly technical herself and prefers to deal with someone who can "speak her language." If the salesman exhibits less extroverted behavior and seems more introverted, as the client is apt to be, they may actually build a mutual respect and trust by sensing their similarities. To put the extreme extrovert in this position, then, would seem counterproductive. Conventional wisdom in this case would fail by not taking into account the needs of the customer in the client-server relationship.

Another important value of the Predictive Index would be to see how a given personality type would enhance a particular job or be unsuited to it, not only in relation to the job itself but also in relation to coworkers. For example, if most of the employees are high Cs, it would mean that they have a strong need for social support, especially from their boss. They will not do well with an extreme introvert who does not lavish much attention on them. What this instrument does is supply the "intuitive" insights into personality, strengths, weaknesses, and needs to allow managers to place people in the best positions, given their natural inclinations, and pair supervisors to subordinates with personality profiles that will not clash. For instance, placing two high As together would be a recipe for disaster, because they would each be fighting for dominance.

In 1983, two psychologists at the Harvard Medical School studied The Predictive Index to see whether there was internal consistency, stability, reliability, and accuracy. The doctors validated it as being free from sexual bias and racial discrimination. However, I found that when taking this instrument, I answered each question according to how I felt at the moment, and knew, on reflection that had I been engaged in another type of work, I would have answered it somewhat differently. Also, I felt that a few of my answers were far more common for women than for men, and that there was a very slight bias in that regard.

## THE KEYS INSTRUMENT

Unlike the instruments described above, which measure the individual's propensity toward intuition and creativity, the Keys Instrument measures the factors that encourage or discourage creativity within the organization. Because creativity is closely linked to intuitive insights, a look at how an organization either encourages or discourages creativity can be very useful for many companies. Theresa Amabile, a professor at Harvard University, has developed an instrument that will give an organization an overall score as to how and where creativity is encouraged and where it is discouraged. Her research has documented a link between the social environment surrounding an individual and the creativity of the individual's work output. While Dr. Amabile concedes that intrinsic motivation is necessary for high levels of creativity, and that even when the workplace may contain discouraging factors, the highly gifted creative person will nevertheless succeed.

She also believes that better work output and satisfaction with the job can be achieved for most companies if they are sensitive to the needs of their people. For example, employees are more successful and productive when they know that rewards and recognition will follow from good, creative efforts—without being promised specific rewards for specific results. An example of how a specific reward may be detrimental is telling the salesperson he must achieve a certain dollar amount in sales to get the reward. Because this feels like one's behavior in performing the job is controlled by others, it often inhibits his or her creativity in learning how to increase sales.

While many managers seem to hold onto the carrot-and-stick method for motivation, it has been shown in study after study that this method succeeds only in the short-term. The stick or threat of punishment works to keep people doing only what is safe, not creative, because to be creative one must take risks. If the risk fails, the threat of job loss is an overwhelming fear that will inhibit the slightest expression of original thought. If the prospect for reward is bestowed only for specific results, it will diminish the inner drive to become all that we can be. In the long-term, the system fails because it keeps people in a noncreative state in order to hold onto their jobs. In other words, one does one's most creative work when we are motivated by the enjoyment of the task itself, not extrinsic motivators, such as competitive races to gain a monetary reward.

This point was also made by Alfie Kohn in his book, *Punished by Rewards*, which researched how rewards affect behavior. Kohn concluded that when extrinsically motivated, people will not continue the behavior for its own sake. For example, if you pay a child to read a book in order to get the child interested in reading, it will work for a while, but once the rewards end, the child is more likely to not read any longer because the intrinsic enjoyment of reading for its own sake was subjugated by a well-intentioned form of bribery. In Kohn's book, *No Contest: The Case against Competition*, he shows that when internal competition was encouraged within a company, it resulted in producing less creative work.

Amabile has found that the organization can increase the employee's creativity if the social environment is shaped to encourage a person's inner motivation to emerge without being discouraged. She created the Keys Instrument to assess the six factors crucial to the social climate that would encourage creativity. These are:

1.  Organizational systems should provide an open atmosphere where new ideas are encouraged and judged fairly, and where people are recognized for their creative work and encouraged to take risks and solve problems creatively—without fear of punishment if the idea does not work.

2.  A manager should offer support to subordinates and communicate this support effectively, setting clear expectations and goals.

3.  There should be work-group support with teamwork, in which everyone is willing to help each other with a commitment to the work, and there is mutual trust among fellow workers.

4.  There should also be sufficient resources with access to appropriate needs, including facilities, equipment, information, funds, and people.

5.  Perhaps most importantly, there should be challenging work that has importance to the organization.

6.  Finally, there should be the freedom to decide how to accomplish the task; in other words, a sense of control over how one works.

Along with these six stimulants to creativity, there are two areas where obstacles are found in many organizations that are factored into the analysis. One obstacle is experiencing destructive criticism, "turfism," rigidity, and resistance to change. The second is workload pressure, with unrealistic expectations for what people can achieve in the organization, or too many distractions from project work, or insufficient time to complete the project.

When a large corporation gives this instrument company-wide, the results reveal which areas in the organization offer employees the opportunity for being creative, which areas are the weakest, and whether the existence of impediments to creativity outweigh the encouraging factors that may be present. Once they have the results of this survey, the organization is encouraged to work with its employees in small groups so that each person can voice suggestions on how to make the work more rewarding and creative. In short, when managers understand the variety of human motivations and the subtle ways the work environment influences it, they can begin to restructure the system to encourage the highest levels of intuition in the service of creativity.

James Higgins, author of *Innovate or Evaporate*, offers some examples of companies that have already learned these lessons:

> Innovative firms actively promote risk taking and the pursuit of new ideas. They don't squelch ideas or punish risk taking. Rather, the organization's culture, its myths, policies and procedures convey the message that having new ideas and taking risks are desired behaviors. Royal Dutch Shell, Rubbermaid, and Johnson & Johnson have so inspired their workers that at some of these companies a mistake is now regarded as a badge of honor (Higgins, 1995)!

## A WORD ABOUT THE BRAIN

In the previous examples of correlating thinking or personality styles to different areas of the brain, several studies mapping the brain's functions stemming from work done in the 1960s and 1970s had suggested that separate functions could be assigned to the four quadrants of the brain. This model correlates well with Jung's four psychological functions and becomes a convenient way to explain personality or thinking preferences. However, some newer studies on the brain suggest that the emotions are not necessarily in the limbic part of the brain, but rather centered in the amygdala—almond-shaped clusters of interconnected structures located above the brain stem on either side of the brain near the bottom of the limbic ring.

In his book *Emotional Intelligence*, Daniel Goleman cites the work of Joseph LeDoux, a neuroscientist at the Center for Neural Science at New York University. LeDoux believes that the amygdala is the specialist for emotional matters. "If it is severed from the rest of the brain, the result is a striking inability to gauge emotional significance of events, sometimes called affective blindness."

LeDoux regards the amygdala as something like an alarm center; when an alarm of fear hits it, it sends urgent messages to every part of the brain and triggers the flight or fight response in the hormones, sending its signals out over a very complex circuitry to other parts of the brain.

Current thinking today is that there is not a single defined "emotional" brain, but rather "several systems of circuits that disperse the regulation of a given emotion to far-flung but coordinated parts of the brain. Further, scientists believe that when full brainmapping of emotions is accomplished, each emotion will have its own topography, a distinct map of neuronal pathways determining its unique qualities, though many of the circuits are likely to be interlinked at the key junctures in the limbic system, like the amygdala and prefrontal cortex" (Goleman, 1995).

If we accept this, that there is no one location for emotions, then perhaps there is no one location for intuition, as well, and that our scores tell us less about the physiology of our brains and more about personality and thinking style preferences. Further, how we score seems to have its roots either in the genes as an inherited predisposition, or as a product of one's upbringing and/or culture. One argument for "nature" rather than "nurture" can be seen in Herrmann's studies where he found that on average, women scored differently than men; more women had stronger scores on the right brain and men on the left. That these same types of predispositions may be inherited with the genes also can be seen in noting that creativity often seems to run in families, as, for example, the Bach family of four composers. And, in many studies of twins who were reared apart, many interests were found common to both, suggesting that our intellectual or vocational interests may, indeed, reside in the genes.

On the other hand, looking at how nurture affects personality, we know that the sensor type, for example, is someone who needs to have more control in his life than the others and may become obsessed with perfectionism, not only in himself, but may impose it on others as well. And, we know that this personality can be created by growing up in a home where faults and mistakes were constantly criticized and accomplishments seldom praised. Thus, a sensor can be created by his upbringing, and this personality trait is not necessarily in the genes.

So where does that leave us? That we can be people for all seasons; that is, if given the motivation we can increase and integrate all four brain or personality functions to balance our shortcomings and increase our creative potential. By understanding the positive as well as the less than positive traits associated with each personality, we are better able to understand others, not only how they think, but how they may think of us, possibly their opposite type. Relating this to the brain and having a name for it perhaps makes communicating about it easier. It has become a shorthand way to describe someone: when we say "he is left brained," most of us know generally what this means. It saves us the trouble of going into the details of an in-depth description. Thus, if the left brain/right brain terminology has become part of our language, perhaps there is no need now to revise it when we are speaking of personality or thinking styles, even though it may not be a physically accurate description of our brain pattern.

# Conclusion

We have traveled from the brain games that ideation people play to personality profiles, and to creativity measures for organizations in search of tools to stimulate our own as well as organizational intuitive power. The underlying theme here is that while a relatively small percentage of people come by creative traits naturally in this country, anyone can become more creative and intuitive. To begin the process, it may be helpful to take a personality or thinking-style assessment instrument and see whether your type is intuitor or sensor, and then learn how to incorporate intuitive-sensing into your everyday life. It is also useful to see whether the workplace culture serves to discourage your natural need to express creativity by its subtle or overt disapproval of the free expression of ideas.

In the next section, we will look at executives who use their intuition and creativity every day and by their actions create a workplace that encourages creativity. As I have found in interviews with the people who work for intuitive managers, the general consensus is that working with these people is an exciting and rewarding experience. Intuitive executives seem to encourage creative work environments naturally. When asked the question, "How do you like working for your intuitive boss?" most employees replied with palpable excitement in their voice, "I *love* working here!" It required no put-on to please the inquiring mind. It was real, it was genuine, it was refreshing.

# PART THREE

## *Executive Intuition*

> People with high levels of personal mastery do not set out to inte-
> grate reason and intuition. Rather, they achieve it naturally—as a
> bi-product of their commitment to use all resources at their dis-
> posal. They cannot afford to choose between reason and intu-
> ition, or head and heart, any more than they would choose to
> walk on one leg or see with one eye.
>
> …PETER M. SENGE, The Fifth Discipline

Eighty percent of the CEOs whose profits doubled over a five-
year period were found to have above-average intuitive powers,
according to research by John Mihalsky and E. Douglas Dean at
the New Jersey Institute of Technology. The reason: it is believed
that intuitive people develop superior insight, which enables
them to perceive whole situations in sudden leaps of logic
(Michalko, 1991).

From my interviews with several CEOs and other levels of
upper management in entrepreneurial businesses, nurturing the
intuition of their employees as well as their own is a strong
value. Still, there is an interesting twist on this: some companies
prefer *not* to encourage intuitive thinking at the lower levels.
That kind of thinking is reserved for upper management only; at

a lower level, the employee is relied upon to perform the basic needs of the workplace, whether it's keeping the books, stitching the garments, or keeping the customer happy. Perhaps these executives are overlooking the fact that it can take a heightened intuitive ability to better understand the customer in order to make him happy, whether it's a direct relationship, as in sales, or an indirect one, such as knowing how people would appreciate fine tailoring. Encouraging an employee's use of intuition could have a meaningful impact on the bottom line.

If we accept that being intuitive is present in 80 percent of CEO's, then the question is why many people, who are aware of the role that intuition plays in their business judgments, consider it politically incorrect to mention or even suggest that they have this skill to anyone other than a trusted friend? In fact, a common experience job seekers report is that the hiring person interviewing them has no interest in their intuition, unless it is in an industry that values this trait.

Even so, this is the one tool that is most frequently cited by people who must plan on future needs for their companies, such as Ron Kubinski at the 3M Company, or Violet Frayne at American Greetings. But they don't talk about it publicly. Where do their ideas come from? First, it's an intuitive flash, then there's the research to back it up, and finally they mount a demonstration of the idea with charts, drawings, life-like models, or whatever it takes to help the decision-makers understand the future, grasp it, feel it, and see it as though it were a *fait accompli*. This makes it easier for decision-makers to give the go ahead to the new product that their intuitive "future-readers" could have accurately predicted from the beginning. The intuitive mind doesn't need to see it, touch it, feel it, smell it. It just knows it.

John Mowen, author of *Judgment Calls*, feels that the intuitive decisions "are best made by experts when time is short, a unique high stakes decision is required, and a rational analysis has resulted in two or more essentially equivalent options." Still, there are some CEOs who are not concerned with intuiting the market or sensing a vision for the future. When Lou Gerstner was recruited in the early 1990s to rescue IBM, he declared, "The last thing IBM needs now is a vision: it needs lower costs and better market focus in every division." Microsoft's Bill Gates echoed a similar sentiment: "Being a visionary is trivial. Being a CEO is hard." No doubt being a CEO is difficult, and perhaps for Gates, being a visionary is easy. However, the skills required for both CEO and visionary are often found residing in the same body, although it could be that the most successful CEOs begin, like Bill Gates, as a visionary.

A year after arriving at IBM, Gerstner spoke differently. His left brain approach was not working well and he learned perhaps through failing that, "Changing a culture is not something you do by writing memos. You've got to appeal to people's emotions. They've got to buy in with their hearts and their beliefs, not just their minds" (Gardner, 1996). It seems that Gerstner had learned that number crunching is only one aspect of a company's success, and that if you want to get the most out of people, you must know who they are and how to reach them. To accomplish this, the CEO must tap into his own right brain intuition and empathy to reach his employees.

Tom Peters appears to have just such an intuitive feel for people. He is probably the best known intuitive-bordering-on-psychic business leader today. In his book, *The Pursuit of Wow,* he tells of how he can walk into a room in the wee hours of the morning, long before the meeting is to begin, and know by its feel how the crowd that will assemble there the next morning will respond. Is it the vapors in the empty room that distill a future energy that only he can sense, or is he actually psychic?

## A HARVARD BUSINESS SCHOOL STUDY OF INTUITION

Daniel J. Isenberg, a professor at the Harvard Business School, studied sixteen senior managers in major corporations. He spent days observing them as they worked. Then he interviewed them and had them perform various exercises designed to discover what made them successful. He identified five different ways that successful managers use intuition:

1. Successful managers use intuition to sense when a problem exists.

2. Intuition assists in rapidly performing well-learned behavior patterns. Once managers are "fluent" at performing specific tasks, they can execute programs without conscious effort. Isenberg defines intuition as the smooth automatic performance of learned behavior.

3. Intuition is used to synthesize isolated bits of data and experience into an integrated picture, often with an "aha" experience.

4. Intuition is used to check on the results of rational analysis. In practice, executives work on an issue until they find a match between feelings and logic; they search until their "gut" clicks with their intellect.

5. Intuition is used to bypass in-depth analysis and come up with a quick solution.

"The higher you go in a company, the more important it is that you combine intuition and rationality, and see problems as interrelated," Dr. Isenberg concluded. This verifies the casual observations of consultants who work with senior executives, as well as studies performed by several others: the higher up you go, the greater the role played by intuition in decision-making (Isenberg, 1984).

Charles Merrill, of the Merrill Lynch brokerage firm, once said that if he made decisions fast—intuitively?—he was right 60 percent of the time. If he took his time and analyzed a situation carefully before reaching a decision, he would be right 70 percent of the time. However, the extra 10 percent was "seldom worth the time."

# 11

# *Intuition in Multilevel Corporations*

As part of my research for this book I interviewed several managers at large multilevel corporations to see whether intuition played a role in their work. What follows are the views of those managers who were very much aware of how intuition played an important role in the company's success.

## INLAND PAPERBOARD & PACKAGING

Tom Graves is Manager of Marketing Strategy at Inland Paperboard & Packaging Corporation, one of the world's largest corrugated box makers, based in Indianapolis. Seventy years ago the company began manufacturing corrugated boxes with a singular mission: make them fast and make them cheap. That was the past. Today the market demands more, much more. Packaging has to perform on automated equipment, move products through an unforgiving distribution network, and

even help marketers sell their products in the store. As Graves
puts it,

> We must understand our customers' world and solve their prob-
> lems before they even know the have them. To do that, we must
> find new ways of looking and seeing. We must find new
> approaches. And that is where intuition and creativity come in.
> The role of intuition in corporate decision-making is poorly
> understood and vastly underrated.

As the company grew, they found that their business profoundly changed from making plain simple corrugated boxes to
making containers to order for a variety of products. Now the
business is evolving to require more complex creativity, such as
incorporating inventive advertising on the outside of the box.
Some of their clever new creations include a box shaped like a
suitcase covered with graphics for Coors beer, or the boxes for
Hewlett Packard that promote movies. Another innovation they
developed is being able to see the product while it is in the corrugated box and still keep it sturdy enough for shipping. This
type is sold to the wholesale clubs, such as Sams, to allow them
to sell the product directly out of the box.

Graves says he is an INFP, according to Myers Briggs, that
is, an introvert-intuitive-feeler-perceiver (see Chapter 10).

> Historically, most business decisions have been made by manag-
> ers with analytical, concrete personalities. Their Myers Briggs
> personality type is STJ. They make their decisions based on facts
> and their past experience. Once a decision is made, it is a closed
> matter and they move on. Their linear thinking style is predict-
> able and trusted. For most problems, the STJ process produces
> excellent results. But there is a percentage—let's say 15 percent—
> of the decisions that need to be made and would be better solved
> using a different style. And because American business has filled
> its managerial ranks with STJs, we have the possibility of a fair
> number of wrong decisions.
>    Now the problem is two-fold. First, I think that 15 percent of
> poor decision-making is growing, because the complexity of most
> business environments is increasing along with the workloads

and rapid change felt everywhere. Second, those 15 percent of incorrect decisions made five years ago didn't go away. They had consequences. Each of those poor decisions had a cause and effect relationship with the entire business system. These "offspring" of earlier problems multiply in our complex environment and effectively hide from the STJ manager who is not equipped to recognize and deal with them because his "genetic" make-up requires a different kind of thinking . . . intuitive thinking. When you look at all of these factors, there's no question that in order to survive today's chaotic business environment, we must have both systemic and intuitive decision making.

More and more of our most successful business icons are, in fact, of the Myers Briggs type NFP. They are managers who use their natural ability to see things differently. They trust their NFP process, which is so very different from the traditional business STJ thinking style. Although every business should understand the value of plugging more NFP thinking types into their decision-making process, unfortunately, in most corporate environments, this is not the case. In fact, it is a bit dangerous to expose oneself as one who relies on intuition and feeling. I have learned that it is better to use my NFP process to get results, and then explain these in STJ fashion.

Graves believes that:

intuition only works well when you use it confidently. You must practice using it until it becomes mastered. Practice will help you to tell the difference between true intuition and false hunches. While STJ thinking makes excellent use of the information that is in the brain, NFP thinking is capable of also using information that comes from sources outside the brain. When I use intuition, I often start with the sensation that the answer is just outside my consciousness, just beyond my grasp, but still very near. There is a feeling that the entire solution lies there, ready-made, waiting to be accessed.

What blocks intuition?

Prejudice, suspicion, denial. Sources both inside and outside of you, and you may not be able to tell the difference between a wish and a need or emotional reaction.

My dexterity involves learning how to access it, how to bring it into focus, and how to interpret. The STJ believes that he himself manufactures the solution. His work is analysis. In contrast, the intuitive person believes that the solutions already exist and that he needs only to discover them, or be aware when they are being bestowed upon him. *Neither process is superior, but in today's business environment, both are essential.*

His advice to others:

You must believe that intuition is real and have faith that you are someone who can receive it. The thinking skills of the NFP and the STJ are different. Both are useful in discovering a solution to a problem, but the thought processes for reaching solutions are quite different. Yet there are some problems that simply won't yield to the STJ process, just as other problems cannot be solved with an intuitive process. The trick is to know which process to use, when to use it, and have the flexibility and courage to use both, as needed.

## QUAKER OATS

Lynette Barnes Hinch, Director of Marketing Development for The Quaker Oats Company, Worldwide Food Service Division in Chicago, is intuitively involved in developing new products. How does Quaker Oats come up with new products? "One way," Hinch says,

is line extensions. This means taking the oatmeal and finding another reincarnation for it, such as putting the cereal in individual cups that can be microwaved in one minute. A second way to develop totally new ideas is by talking to customers, to understand their needs. One new product that resulted from this approach was an oatmeal cookie in a vending machine. Listening to the consumer is basic to our improvisations.

When asked what she does when she comes up with an intuitive insight for a new product, she replied,

In the food service industry, there is usually not much quantitative research available, or if we take the time to do it, it will prolong getting the product to market. Then it becomes intuition versus risk taking. The intuitive idea is supported if it can be test-marketed. For example, we had the idea that a generic line of ready-to-eat cereal would do better if it were restaged to look like a branded line by improving product quality and changing the packaging. After restaging the line, it is now holding market share in the ready-to-eat cereal category, which demonstrates that the product was not the problem; it was the way the product was perceived. It needed to be presented as more upscale. Because there is very little data available in food service, for most decisions you still have to make the gut judgment.

Hinch is also intuitive when hiring new people. "All of my new employees are strong performers," she says. "I believe that I am good at assessing people as potential peers and coworkers. Every person that I have been responsible for hiring has worked out well."

## REEBOK

Patricia Hambrick is Vice President of Global Marketing at the Reebok Company, based in Massachusetts. Her mission: to drive the brand image in worldwide sales. Hambrick reports directly to Paul Fireman, CEO of Reebok, who encourages his people to tap into their own intuition, whether in the creation of new products, marketing, or internal systems. Hambrick describes Fireman as a great intuitive thinker. "He has a wonderful feel for the business, encourages and rewards thinking that's out there, and encourages you to trust yourself. In fact, when he bought Reebok, a British company, that decision was almost completely intuitive."

Although Hambrick gets information on future trends from Sputnick, a market research firm in New York City that goes out on the street and talks to kids to see what they are thinking and buying, she must take it from there. "No one can give you all the answers, and it is up to your gut to put it together," she says. Is her intuition always correct? "I'd say my percentage of being correct is between 80 and 90 percent."(I offered to accompany her to the race track anytime.)

When asked, is intuition the same as creativity? She replied:

> I don't think that you can be intuitive without being creative. For example, fashion designers need to tap into their intuition and creativity when they are creating new styles. Although they tend to approach problems more creatively than others, they also need to have a feel for business. It requires using both sides of your brain. The CFO? He ignores intuition. It's something that doesn't interest him.

When speaking to other employees at Reebok and asking how they liked working for intuitive managers, their most frequent answers sounded like some version of "I love it! It's the best job I've ever had! I am allowed the space and freedom to make a mistake and be creative!

When intuitive CEOs surround themselves with intuitive employees, it appears to breed a very high morale in the work force—as well as a successful business.

## AMERICAN GREETINGS

At American Greetings, creativity is encouraged everywhere. Violet Frayne, Product Manager at the company's headquarters in Cleveland, has an intuitive feel for people, which she regards as the source of her talent for producing winning new product ideas. When asked what intuition is, she replied, "it's flashes of lightning . . . you feel it in your gut. Some things are so clear it just strikes you. You know the answer. You really feel it. You get excited." American Greetings makes greeting cards, party goods, gifts, and novelties, and is the largest publicly traded company of its kind with $2 billion in sales. Frayne works in the Discovery Department, where incubation of ideas for new products is centered. The focus there is to make money by creating things that people want to buy.

"I have oddball, unbidden instincts for what people want," she says:

I listen to my heart, although the men here talk about feeling it in the gut. I accept things that I know without knowing why. I think I am very empathetic, and nonjudgmental. I believe in the Golden Rule. I don't lie, and I come to situations with an open mind to stay in tune with my intuition.

I asked Frayne how was she able to develop this intuitive mind set. She thinks that at least part of this skill was developed from growing up in a family where all the children had to do everything. They had lessons in painting, playing musical instruments, writing fiction, and acting. It seems their family's motto was "Creativity R Us." Frayne began her career at American Greetings as a joke writer and later became an art director. Eventually, she learned that the people who had the highest paying jobs were not there to create but to be financial analysts. That discovery led her to get an MBA in finance and, indeed, a more remunerative position in the operations department. But full-time number crunching did not dry up her intuition and strong empathic feelings. When she became involved in product development she created the popular "caregiver" cards, to be sent to nurses, teachers, and other support people. That creation evolved to "life event" cards including a line of cards that a child might send to a stepmother expressing the thought, "you are like a mother to me." Frayne seems to have a rare breed of talent: she combines mathematical ability with creativity. It is like scoring 800 on both the verbal and math SAT!

When Frayne was asked how she selects a new product idea, she said it was important to "visualize the final outcome of a product or it's not going to happen." When someone walks in with an idea,

I see a vision of it right away, and I encourage him to visualize it in the store. If he can do that, it's 60 percent more apt to happen. We then build a strategy to present to the company. We show visuals which make it real, with an artist drawing the cards. Then, we make the business plans and demonstrate how it would be displayed in a store, carefully orchestrating the presentation to get the decision-makers into the concept. For them, this lessens their risk. We need to be persuasive and compelling.

Apparently, the power to persuade is an aspect of the job that is of equal importance to the idea. "An idea is worth nothing if it doesn't get to the marketplace," says Frayne.

As the Director of Creative Resources and Development at American Greetings, Steven Tatar's most visible role is recruiter of artists and editors. Tatar says that, although the hiring process includes looking at their art portfolios and résumés and, during the interview, assessing their personality, he relies on his intuition to make the final cut in selecting employees. He can recall instances when the portfolios were impressive and there was nothing wrong with the applicant's personality, but something didn't click, so the person was not hired. "How does that work?" I asked. "It's everything melding together that is intuitive, like sudden recognition. I know it just feels right, beyond questioning. It feels like experiencing something profound."

Tatar is also a professional sculptor. He taught art and card design for two years before taking a one-year leave of absence to design and create a fountain commissioned by the Cleveland Institute of Art. He defines two types of intuition. The first is the accumulation of past experiences up to the present that relies on what has accrued in the brain that can be put together. It is the creative act of making sometimes unlikely connections. The second type of intuition, he feels, is the more powerful: "It can be found on the right side of the brain where image-making lives. It gives form to an image or thought, and you get a profound sense of rightness—and best of all, it's testable." His creative juices begin when his mind quiets down, after a long working session. "I get myself out of the way and innovation comes from what is out there in different ways. We don't own ideas. *Intuition allows ideas to come to you.*" Gerald Jampolsky reflected this feeling when he wrote, "To awaken is to accept direction from our inner, intuitive voice which is your guide to knowing" (Jampolsky and Cirincione, 1992).

For many people, intuition is closely related to what some may call psychic experiences. A definition of the word psychic, as supplied by Belleruth Naparstek in *Your Sixth Sense,* is a "sudden pop of information that comes all of a piece, seemingly from nowhere." Although this may be how most people would define intuition as well, there is, perhaps, a difference in the type of information that is received. Perhaps this difference can be illustrated by an experience Tatar relates, one which seems to be more psychic than intuitive. He tells of a time when he was riding in a car with a group of friends and sleeping in the backseat. The driver spotted another car on the highway that had broken down and stopped to see if he could offer some help. While they had the hood up and were searching for clues as to what could be wrong, Steve, still groggy with sleep, shouted out what the problem was and how it could be fixed. His friend checked it out, agreed with his diagnosis executed from the back seat of another car, and made the repair. This leads us to wonder whether, if one suddenly knows, simply knows, that a new product idea will be successful, and it proves to be successful, was it an intuitive or a psychic kind of knowing?

# 12

# *Entrepreneurial Intuition*

The following interviews reflect the view of CEOs who began their companies within the past six to fifteen years and attribute at least part of their success to their intuitive instincts.

## TENDER LOVING THINGS

Mark Juarez is an entrepreneur who habitually tunes into his intuition to create new products and accurately predicts which will sell and which will not. He is president and CEO of Tender Loving Things, a company he founded in 1992 that creates, among other things, wooden hand massagers with a line of products called "The Happy Massager."

Where did Mark get the idea for a massage tool? The story begins much earlier, actually. Several years before starting the business, he had gone from one job to another working in sales. First he sold energy efficient windows, then wine and service products. Knowing that none of this was right for him, Juarez began a fifteen-year odyssey of travel around the world. He worked odd jobs in pubs and bars in Europe, finding shelter in hotels whose ambiance ranged from luxurious to "I'm glad my mother can't see me now." Bicycling around the world eventually wore his knees down to the point of his being almost unable to walk, and he became desperate for anything to restore them to their precycling condition. After trying several types of knee repair therapies, he found that massage was the most effective, which influenced him to learn the skill of the masseuse. Today, he can run up to five to six miles at a clip.

Tender Loving Things first began with an invention:

> I had been working for several months on trying to develop a wooden massage tool for people with carpal tunnel syndrome in their hands. Then, I had a flash on how to do it. In a dream, I was playing with sticks and balls in my mind, and I saw the massager taking shape as a molecule-type figure. It had four legs with a round ball center. The next morning I drew it up and then made a prototype. Almost everything comes to me when I am in a dreamlike state.

Juarez realized that he had to get a patent on this idea and began the process by reading a do-it-yourself book on how to obtain one. Then he went to the patent office for some expert help and literally began massaging people there with his new massage tool. From this he quickly learned that there are not many people who can resist a good rub. The patent office employees were so helpful that he was able to file the patent without the costly services of an attorney. (You, too, can try this technique at the patent office, but be careful you don't rub them the wrong way!)

After developing the product, Juarez needed a name for it. In another dream state he saw it floating through the air and felt it could be developed as a playful character. It became the "Happy Massager," with a happy face painted in the round ball in the center. In yet another dream, he received a message that he should develop a community and create a place where people could work and grow, and so began his manufacturing plant. He founded the business in 1992. By 1996, he had sold 7 million massage tools, hired a workforce of 300 people and sales grossed $20 million! Juarez gives a generous portion of his product to numerous charities for children, senior citizens, and people with AIDS, and he encourages his employees to donate 5 percent of their time working in the community. It would seem that his products reflect his attitudes about creating a meaningful life. While the products are meant to heal aching hands, his company contributes toward healing the community.

Juarez had two years of college and was 35 years old when he started his business with virtually nothing. Although he had no prior experience in managing people, he experienced no turnover in the first two and a half years. However, the company has recently experienced sharp growth and rapid change. They now have twenty new products, including an entire line of bath products, massage tools, and a rice-filled fleece neck wrap that is heated in the microwave and then releases a moist heat to stimulate and warm the muscles.

There is very little structure at Tender Loving Things, and Juarez admits that the bean counters whose job it is to exert financial control have problems with this lack of structure. When asked how he operates his company, Juarez replies, "Mostly intuitively."

At Tender Loving Things, there are a group of people who are responsible for new product development, and Juarez is one of them. How do they know if a new idea will sell? "I know it intuitively and I am correct 100 percent of the time," he says. While this may seem to border on braggadocio, Juarez defends his intuition by relating the story of a customer who wanted him to make a tool that the company had developed experimentally. Mark had already decided it wouldn't sell, so declined to manufacture it. The customer insisted that it was marketable and requested that he make 150 pieces for her. As Juarez predicted, it flopped.

Creativity is encouraged at Tender Loving Things. When employees offer ideas that Juarez doesn't think will fly, he has them answer a five-page questionnaire on the feasibility of production, which serves to clarify in the idea-proposer's mind whether the idea will work. It also saves Juarez from becoming a discouraging influence toward their highly valued creative thinking. While his intuition has been extraordinarily accurate thus far in predicting sales, Juarez recognizes the need for hiring firms to do market research studies. Predictably, lenders want to see facts, figures, and projections. At the bank, intuition doesn't fly.

When I asked Cara Pike, the environmental coordinator and public relations officer at Tender Loving Things, what it is like working with Juarez, the first word that flew out of her mouth was,

> Exciting! He intuitively understands what I am about. It is usually difficult to convince a CEO at most corporations of the importance of being environmentally responsible, but Mark has given me carte blanche to come up with new ideas. I am self-managed, which allows me to be as creative as I can. He sees me as an entrepreneur working within the company. I feel I have opportunities here that I wouldn't have in other organizations.

Intuition for Mark Juarez is more than getting a sudden insight about a new product or a new marketing strategy. It is also being able to have an empathic understanding of what it is like to be an employee and to support and inspire those in his employ to express their innate creativity. It is having a feel for the needs, wants, and desires of the consumer to get a sense of what will sell. His world is part of a growing movement where businesses are becoming more in touch with the community. One mutually beneficial spinoff of this is a greater ability to develop useful products that people want to buy, and at the same time they are giving something back in terms of charitable donations and community projects.

Similarly, there is a growing trend among many entrepreneurs and executives that they must bring a vibrant new feeling to the workplace. They regard their mission as more than making a profit; they want to make a difference in the world. This is reflected in the philosophy of a number of firms such as Ben & Jerry's Homemade, Tom's of Maine, StrideRite Shoes, and even the *Harvard Business Review*. The *Review* recently sent a letter to potential subscribers that begins, "Your career isn't about money, is it? I didn't think so. It's about something deeper." The *Review* knows that the letter is most likely sent to CEOs and managers who would like to reflect these values in their work. No, today, it isn't just about making money.

These are some of the high ideals that prompted Tom Chappell, president of Tom's of Maine. Tom had a strong intuitive feeling that natural toothpaste would sell. Tom's wife and co-owner, Kate Chappell, also seems to know intuitively what flavors of toothpaste will find buyers. Not long ago, she had an idea for making fennel flavored paste and commissioned a market research study on it. The data from the survey suggested that it would be a loser. She disregarded the data, manufactured it anyway, and it has become a winner.

## BELIEVING IN THE HIGHER SELF

How do intuitive leaders accomplish so much in so short a time? Mark Juarez says, "We can do almost anything if we believe it's possible." Steve DeVore, founder and CEO of SyberVision Systems, Inc., speaks of his company's study on what it is that motivates high achievers: "One of the spiritual characteristics of the high achiever that we have identified is what we call 'the sense of higher self.'" He views high achievers as those who believe that they have almost godlike abilities and that nothing is impossible. They are convinced that just by being present, they can control their environment and their circumstances.

DeVore allows that this could be seen as possessing a huge ego, but it's a healthy way of being. It is as if they are saying, "Nothing is impossible for me—I possess the intelligence of a god." This same kind of self-confidence in an ability that some may envy is reflected, too, by Sandra Kurtzig, founder and CEO of ASK Computer Systems: "I never gave it [failure] any thought. I just seemed to say, 'This is what I'm going to do.' . . . I never thought that I couldn't do it." (Ray and Myers, 1986).

Whether you call this "ego" or a "sense of the higher self" or "intuition," there is obviously something important working here that is uncommon. And perhaps, because it is so uncommon, it gets dismissed as having no substance by those who rarely if ever experience its power. Charles Housen, CEO of Erving Paper Mills in Erving, Massachusetts began recycling paper over thirty years ago, before recycling was "in." He also seems to have this "can do" attitude when it comes to handling unforeseen problems. He recalls the time that he received a freight-car load of old telephone books to recycle, only to discover that he had been sent the yellow pages instead of the white. At the time, there was no technology for recycling yellow paper because they did not know how to get rid of the yellow color.

Handed the proverbial lemon, he was determined to find a solution for releasing the yellow dye. After many months of research, his chemists finally solved the problem. As a result, he was able to expand his production significantly by having more raw material available. Today, his company's products, bath tissue and paper towels, are commonly found in restaurants and hotel bathrooms, while its damask-like recycled dinner napkins have found a place next to the sterling silver at many dinner tables.

## HANDSONTOYS

When Andy Farrar, CEO of HandsOnToys, an entrepreneurial start-up begun in1994, heard about a toy idea from his sculptor/ artist/partner Arthur Ganson, he knew immediately that it would be successful. The toy, Toobers & Zots,™ is a collection of bendable plastic tubes that hold their shape, along with foam cutout pieces that children can put together and make into different constructions and configurations. Like Mark Juarez, Farrar and Ganson did no formal market research to see whether the toy would fly; they simply knew it would. In fact, two of their partners actually quit their day jobs to join the business, on the strength of Ganson's idea.

In the fall of 1994 the company displayed Toobers & Zots at the New York Gift Show. It received not only instant favorable press, but also orders for 17,000 toys. There was just one problem. They did not have the financial or technical resources to manufacture them. The partners had not anticipated the tremendous response their product would receive and had no experience in manufacturing anything like this. No established manufacturer was willing to take the risk and spend the time and money needed to solve the sophisticated technical problems on an untested idea. It was left to Arthur Ganson, the toys' inventor, to design and construct machines that could manufacture them. To fulfill their orders, all of the partners were forced to work.

For a year and a half the toy was manufactured with Ganson-designed machinery. And although the process was time consuming and not as efficient as they knew it could be, they were able to turn out over 1,000,000 Toobers for their waiting customers. The company had been founded on $20,000 of credit card debt, then funded with loans from friends and relatives. After the toy became a success, the owners were able to raise one and a half million dollars in equity. Since their company's difficult first years, Farrar and Ganson have located a manufacturer who has the capability of turning the product out quickly and economically, but only after the investment of some $2 million to produce this seemingly simple toy.

Farrar says he is intuitive, but when overloaded with specifics and details, his intuition tends to shut down. He is most creative when alternating between focused problem solving and open-ended brainstorming. Sometimes his best solutions arrive while daydreaming. He feels that intuition and creativity are clearly connected. Is his intuition always correct? "No," he says, "emotion gets in the way and sometimes puts filters onto the clarity that you might otherwise have. When I meet people, I get a lot of nonverbal clues to understanding them, even with people I know. I don't make important deals over the phone, only in person."

The next incarnation of Toobers & Zots will be Wrapsters, plush-covered Toobers with wonderful faces and elaborate tails in brilliant colors that can be wrapped around the neck or wrist, as well as played with like puppets. The chief idea generator for new products is sculptor Arthur Ganson, who builds moving sculptures that are machines, or are they really machines that are actually sculptures? The *Smithsonian Magazine* described his work as kinetic art:

> Ganson's machines hurl knives, spurt grease, unfold Chinese fans and make a chicken's wishbone walk. They chirp like birds, dust frantically, breathe deeply and talk back via handwritten notes. They pose existential questions, plumb spiritual depths, make elegant jokes and stupid puns. These machines do "nothing" yet work extraordinarily well, particularly at making people laugh.

This sounds very much like the Seinfeld shows which were about "nothing;" the actors worked well together and also made people laugh.

One of Ganson's more sensuous pieces is a machine that moves a precariously positioned arm to dip into a vat of oil and then spill it on itself, with a constant slow motion of dipping down to the vat and then oiling itself. At first it elicits a chuckle from the spectator. Then you find yourself identifying with the machine and somehow, almost against your will, identifying with the feeling the machine must be experiencing, of having this nice warm oil spilled gently and lovingly over one's body to keep it moist and supple for all eternity.

Ganson says that his intuition not only leads him to the idea but is also present at each stage of the creation. If his trial and error methods aren't working in the building stage, his intuition tells him how to fix it. It would seem that at HandsOnToys everyone's intuition is working well, from Ganson's first concept of the toy to Farrar's recognition that "we've got something big here." Future ideas run the gamut from toys that whirr to toys that purr, their fluffy nonmechanical creations. The whirring will come from copies of Arthur Ganson's extraordinary machines, which are on permanent exhibition at an MIT museum.

## DRAGON SYSTEMS

Janet and James Baker began Dragon Systems in 1982 to make speech and technology recognition systems for use with a computer. Janet is President and her husband James is Chairman and CEO. Their only competitors in the United States are IBM and Kurzweil, but Dragon leads both in sales. To date they have provided most of the world's PC-based speech recognition systems. The machine will record your words as you speak them into a microphone, spell them correctly, and, if necessary, adjust the grammar. Their systems are fluent in French, Italian, German, Spanish, Swedish, American English, and British English.

To what does Dragon Systems owe its considerable accomplishments? After speaking with Janet Baker, it became obvious that both Bakers have brilliant minds, with Ph.D.'s in Computer Science from Carnegie Mellon University. But brilliance isn't everything; Baker also taps into her intuition. She starts her day between 5 or 6 A.M., preferring to work in the quiet early morning hours when she gets many new insights. Often, she wakes up with more clarity on whatever was the problem of the moment, probably the result of dreams that have sorted through the day's issues, and revealed a new insight. Her mind is always working and always making connections. She cautions, however, that dozens of decisions need to be made on a daily basis. "some I make quickly, but I've learned that I should not make them precipitously. I'll do my homework. But there are some things that we cannot have known, such as chance events. Yes, I make mistakes, but I try not to make big mistakes."

Baker did not always listen to intuitive feelings, but says, "I trust it more now." This theme was repeated by nearly everyone

I interviewed. They learned to trust their intuition more as they got older and more experienced. "I'm a good judge of character," Baker said. "I can judge people pretty well when it comes to hiring them. I think I am better attuned to people than my husband, but he is better in other ways."

In 1982 Dragon started with four employees, all of whom worked without a salary until they got the business off the ground. By 1990, they had fifteen employees. As of this writing, they have 250 people on staff with offices in Germany and England. Who uses Dragon Systems? Currently, doctors, lawyers, business people, writers, and handicapped people, among others. Doctors dictate their diagnoses and histories of their patients; lawyers read their notes or briefs into the machine; the physically impaired find this a convenient way to write and communicate with others. One of their best known clients is the actor Christopher Reeve, who uses it to record his thoughts and maintain both his personal and business correspondence. At the moment, Dragon Systems has products with a price range from $99 to $299. The difference in price reflects the convenience desired in speaking. If you want to speak slowly, the $99 version will do. If you want to speak at a conversational pace, then the more costly model will fill that need. Baker predicts enormous growth in this technology in the next few years, and we will most likely see speech-breathing Dragons everywhere.

# 13

# Intuition in Advertising, Food, and Manufacturing

## INGALLS

In the advertising business, intuition is everything. It is the precursor of rampant creativity, the founding force for acquiring new clients and the rock formation underlying their success. According to Bink Garrison, Chairman and CEO of Ingalls, an advertising and public relations agency headquartered in Boston, he encourages anyone and everyone to use his or her intuition to come up with creative ideas. Garrison sees intuition as part of the creative process. His own intuition is central to understanding the client and the client's objectives, which then gets translated into ad campaigns to which the potential consumer will enthusiastically respond. Intuition comes into play for Garrison not only in creating the ad but also in knowing whether the ad will succeed in fulfilling its purpose: enticing sales. "If the ad doesn't grab you, then it's not intuitive," he says. "You don't promote what *you* want necessarily, but what the consumers give you permission to do." Garrison also relies on his intuition by learning how to "read" and then respond to the needs of potential clients when he presents his services to them.

What are the best qualities for a CEO of a multifaceted agency? Garrison's reply: "Being highly intuitive, not only with people but with their business needs and their customer's needs"—although he grants that many people who are successful in similar positions and are not particularly intuitive. He finds the Myers Briggs Type Indicator, however, very helpful in understanding others. (For an in-depth explanation of the Myers Briggs see Chapter 10.) He says that he is an ENFJ, indicating that he is an Extrovert, INtuitive, Feeler, and Judger, which suggests that he may base many of his actions on how he feels and intuits, as contrasted to a strong ST (Sensor/Thinker), someone who bases actions mostly on the logic of analysis. As a Judger, Garrison is someone who needs closure, who often feels uncomfortable when he has to wrestle with ambiguity. Being an EN, Carl Jung would say, suggests that he is ideally suited to his position. The following is Jung's description of the EN personality:

> The extroverted-intuitive is uncommonly important both economically and culturally . . . he can render exceptional service as the initiator or promoter of new enterprises. He brings vision to life, presents it convincingly, and with dramatic fire, he embodies it.

Considering that business at Ingalls is up over 20 percent in 1997, his ENFJ seems to be working quite well. When I asked Garrison what he does as chairman and CEO on a daily basis, his reply was, "There is no job. I make it up each day." Sometimes it is coming up with ideas for new products that he will recommend to a client. This happened with one client recently. As a result, two weeks after proposing it, the client began the production process. It appears that advertising agencies not only create ads for products, they create products for ads, and presumably, if the new product is their brainchild, the resulting ad for it will be very successful!

Steve Connelly, President and Executive Creative Director at Ingalls says that he tends to "let my gut handle most decisions." He defined intuition as your gut reaction to any decision. Is it always right? "No, it's not right all the time, but it gets better as I get older." When it is wrong? "When the initial assessment is not well-understood. Sometimes, if I don't understand the problem well enough, I make a bad decision. I work with a lot of creative people and they are by nature intuitive. They know how to create something that people will respond to." When he is creating an ad, it is important for Connelly to be briefed on the mindset of the customer, "so that I can hit a trigger for them to react to. It requires empathy for the customer."

For example, the *Boston Globe* was looking for an agency to promote its Olympic coverage for the 1996 Winter Olympics in Lillehammer, and they gave several agencies one month to present samples of their work. "We knew intuitively that they were looking for an agency that could provide a quick response," Connelly told me.

> To demonstrate our ability to move fast, which we felt was one of their criteria in choosing an agency, we prepared everything except the creative work until the Sunday before our deadline. Then we read a front-page story in the *Boston Sunday Globe* and, based on that story, we created an article and produced three radio spots and a TV commercial. It was a dramatic demonstration that within twenty-four hours we could produce quality work. We got the job by doing it on the last day!

## BREAD & CIRCUS

Many new businesses today start with a mission beyond making money, and there was a very strong mission that forged the beginnings of Bread & Circus: make it easy to buy healthy foods, foods that are grown organically and not processed with chemicals or other foreign substances that are possibly harmful to one's health. Bread & Circus first opened in Brookline, Massachusetts in 1972, the brainchild of a young idealistic couple. Two years later they headed for California and sold the store to Anthony Harnett, an expatriate from Ireland by way of Holland, England, and Scotland.

Harnett's passion for the store evolved from his own experience of going on a macrobiotic diet in the 1970s and finding that the food he consumed actually made a difference in the way he felt. No one can deny that Harnett was extremely creative in his former eating habits. At a young age, he decided that if meat gives you strength (as it purportedly did according to the common wisdom of the time) and honey was a source of energy from its high sugar content, then, he reasoned, he should eat a pound of meat and a pound of honey each day to get the ultimate in energy and strength! Apparently, this combination did not work it's wisdom on his body, so he began reading about nutrition and came across an article on macrobiotics. He tried it and felt much better. In 1972, he opened a macrobiotic food store in Dublin, which he sold after two and a half years. He then moved to Boston, worked for Erehwon, one the first macrobiotic stores in the area, and watched its popularity mushroom. With a $30,000 loan, he bought the Bread & Circus store in Brookline. It became so successful that seven additional stores quickly followed in the greater Boston area within the next 10 years. The company was grossing over $70,000,000 dollars annually when Harnett sold it in 1994. Today, the Bread & Circus chain grosses over $800,000,000.

Was it intuition that led Harnett to be one of the first in the area on the upward curve of a trend? Is seeing future trends the same as intuition, or is it simply analyzing what exists today and then inferring what will be tomorrow? And how can you be certain, using only inference, what tomorrow will bring, knowing how quickly life changes and how random events can turn the best laid plans into unexpected catastrophes? Using inference alone will not tell you that the outcome is certain enough to bet your life's savings. To take that risk, it would seem, would require either a high risk-taking personality, or the sureness that comes from an intuitive leap that simply feels right.

The food at Bread & Circus is more expensive than at the chain supermarkets. How did Harnett know that customers would pay a premium for organic foods? "It's a matter of life-style," he said:

> I knew that if people knew how important it was, they would pay a premium. It was a gut feeling. If your gut contradicts the numbers, then the numbers are wrong. If you believe numbers over gut, you will make the wrong decision. If you intuit something, look for the numbers to back you up.

After selling the Bread & Circus chain, Harnett opened an herbal apothecary and juice bar, a first in its concept in the Boston area. It is doing extraordinarily well in Cambridge, with plans underway to expand to other cities. Whatever made him think that people would be flocking to his store for herbal remedies with strange sounding names like horsetail, eyebright, feverfew, and bilberry? His answer:

> It used to be that if you had something wrong and went to conventional western-trained physicians and they could not help you, you turned to the alternative medicine cabinets seeking a last-ditch cure, despite the fact that there was at the time little scientifically documented evidence that they would work. Today, people try the herbal remedies first before going to their doctors. Their desire is to cure their problems and avoid doctors if at all possible. They now see the use of *conventional medicine* as a last resort.

Harnett's world is that of nature and healing, going back to organic, natural beginnings to produce the food and medicine for health. Herbal remedies reflect this value, being kinder and gentler to the system than many prescription drugs. This philosophical mind set spills over to his view of how to treat employees. He encourages his staff to be creative and intuitive. If they come up with an idea that he does not want to use, he might say, "That's an interesting idea, but I don't think it will work for the following reasons, but *please, keep coming up with ideas.*" Great ideas get rewards in the form of bonuses and profit sharing, based on store performance goals when targets are exceeded.

Not having a formal college education didn't stop Harnett from running a business with foresight and brilliance. But what kind of a man is he? According to the Predictive Index, he scored as an adventurer, with a dominant ego, and an introvert who is impatient but has a low need to blame. This would seem to be a close to perfect personality profile for any kind of manager of people as well as a creative entrepreneur. (For more information on the Predictive Index see Chapter 10.)

## SHEPARD CLOTHING

Professor Daniel Isenberg, writing in the *Harvard Business Review,* described the senior executives' day-to-day job as one of making:

> minute-by-minute tactical maneuvers when they tend to rely on several general thought processes such as using intuition; managing a network of interrelated problems; dealing with ambiguity, inconsistency, novelty, and surprise; and integrating action into the process of thinking (Isenberg, 1984).

This appears to be a fairly accurate description of what Paul Kussell does every day. Kussell is the president and CEO of Shepard Clothing, a clothing manufacturing company that makes private label men's suits and sport jackets in New Bedford, Massachusetts. His day-to-day activities are mostly involved with people issues, such as settling conflicts, authorizing decisions, and a variety of other details. According to Kussell, much of his work also includes future thinking: deducing what the trends will be in the next few years so that he can create styles that will sell. He says that most of his big decisions are made on gut feel because there simply is not enough data to give him any kind of a meaningful analysis of what those trends will be.

Kussell notices that the best ideas seem to come to him when he runs. Lunch time for this marathoner is run time, which, he believes, quiets down his brain and allows him to experience intuitive insights. When he returns from the run, the answers are usually there. Like Kussell, Pat Hambrick also runs from 45 minutes to an hour a day. "It clears my mind and lets ideas come to me. I have also had dreams that led to new ideas," she said.

But, for Kussel, "personnel issues are the hardest, and firing is the very hardest thing to do."

Another difficulty that is common in many manufacturing businesses is the conflict between marketing and manufacturing: the marketing people want to have broader lines to sell for lower prices, and the manufacturing people want fewer changes to the lines. Each department views the problem from its own perspective, which seems to rest on the assumption that "if you allow me to control things my way, I'll be much more productive for you and the company." These kinds of issues do not resolve easily in Kussell's mind, and they need to simmer until the answer appears. As a result, he does not make quick decisions: "I am not impulsive, but I think my intuition gets better as I get older, because I see it coming from my experience. When you accumulate enough experience, the gut feelings are more accurate."

Kussell sees his vice president of sales and marketing as more intuitive than most other employees, but contrary to most intuitive managers, he does not generally encourage intuition and creativity at the lower levels. He wants the designers to design, the sewers to sew, and the accountants to add up the numbers—or subtract them, if necessary. "I need the facts," he stresses, "and I don't encourage intuitive ideas when I am depending upon them for hard data." Perhaps this comment suggests that although Kussell has learned to trust his own intuition, it is difficult to trust it in those holding other positions. While he might appreciate their intuitive insights, he does not see it as part of their job description.

Although Kussell would encourage creativity among the rank and file, Shepard Clothing is a unionized operation with contract provisions that can work against creative ideas from the shop floor. Being a member of a union, an employee's seniority is paramount to maintaining status and job security. Thus, for example, if Kussell would like to move people around to let them explore different jobs to get a better perspective of the operation, it could be against union rules. Depending on what the contract provides, such a move could result in a possible loss of seniority by being more subject to layoff in another part of the plant.

However, unions are not the only organizations that may be responsible for discouraging new ideas. Jack Stack, CEO of Springfield Remanufacturing Corp., wanted to see how morale was at one of their subsidiaries, the Heavy-Duty Division, where the employees were surveyed anonymously via written questionnaires. "The responses floored many of our managers." Stack revealed. "People were asked to agree or disagree with the following statements":

> At work, your opinions count.
>
> Those of you who want to be a leader in this company have the opportunity to become one.
>
> In the past six months someone has talked to you about your personal development.

"In our survey of Heavy-Duty," writes Stack, "43 percent of the people disagreed with the first statement, 48 percent with the second, and 62 percent with the third" (Stack, 1997).

If the perception among employees is that their opinions do not count, that they do not feel they could advance in the company, and that no one in management talks to them about their personal development, the message is loud and clear: creative people are not wanted here. Springfield Remanufacturing is perhaps one of the better organizations to work for, because it is owned and run by employees and there are no unions. However, it appears that some managers have created a similar effect on employees, without requiring union dues.

When speaking about intuition, all the executives I interviewed had one thing in common: an acute awareness of their inner life and how it had an enormous impact on their work and everyday problem solving. Yet there were many executives whom I contacted who declined to be interviewed, some of whom admitted that they really did not relate to this subject matter. They readily confessed that their everyday lives were too busy with immediate problems requiring difficult decisions, and that they never gave intuition a passing thought. Perhaps if they were more aware of their intuitive insights they would be aware of having, or not having, an inner life—a time when the business of business is put in second place while peer and employee relationships take precedence.

To those executives, I would ask whether there is any similarity between the character Kevin Kline portrays in the movie *Fierce Creatures* and themselves. Kline's character is an exaggerated version of a present-day tycoon who is focused only on amassing wealth and compelled by a ruthless drive to make more money than he could ever use in a lifetime. He is totally bereft of an inner life, quite unlike any of the entrepreneurs I interviewed. To illustrate the extent of this character's inability to understand that there are more meaningful aspects to life, the film uses a line drawn from an actual experience of Frank Pittman, a well-known family therapist who, in a session with a father and son, heard the son say to his father, "You messed up my childhood," and the father replied, "How could I, son, I wasn't even there."

When the absence of an inner life, as depicted in this film, seems so normal to an executive that he or she has no idea that it is missing, it may explain why intuition goes unrecognized as part of our inner life that conveys wisdom. Yet many managers regard intuition at best as being unreliable and, at worst, as non-existent. Our own intuition and its potential accuracy in guiding us should not be viewed as irrelevant or unavailable as we enter the next millennium. It is possibly the most important guide and compass that we will have! The question is, how do we recognize it? How can we learn to trust it? How do we get better at it? And, can we comprehend its value?

## TRAINING PROGRAMS TO REACH THE HIGHER SELF

In many organizations, managers are often thrust into their roles with little or no preparation. If they are given a quick overview of what is expected, often tossed off in passing with no warning of the pitfalls that may lie ahead, that is the sum total of the manager's formal training. Eventually, some of the luckier ones may be sent to professional seminars or given books to read. The most popular courses usually cover everything from time management to planning, coaching, mentoring, and so on. Yet few offer help in learning how to tap into your intuition, much less acknowledge that it can be a powerful, even critical success factor in business. There are some notable exceptions. In 1996, a course created and led by Dr. Laurie Nadel was offered by the American Management Association entitled, "Intuitive Leadership, Turning Gut Feelings into Competitive Advantage." In the three-day course, the participants acquired an in-depth understanding of the Myers Briggs Type Indicator. They then practiced several techniques, including some from neurolinguistic programming, or NLP, to engage their intuitive understanding. The course was an interesting beginning for learning how to tap into the unconscious mind to improve business practices. Dr. Nadel has developed another course, the "High Performance Thinking Program," also offered through the American Management Association. Nancy Rosanoff and Marcia Emery, whose work is described in Part Six, also offer intuition workshops for business and personal issues.

# Conclusion

Why do we need to develop our intuition? The short answer: Because we are overwhelmed with data that is often conflicting and at times too complex to sort out. Then how can we possibly make a rational decision? Chances are, under these circumstances, we can't. But, if we can trust our intuition, we may be able to make the wise decision, despite these formidable odds. The future depends on learning how to access this inner, often hidden, intelligence—*now*.

Jim Taylor and the co-authors of the *500 Year Delta* agree with this analysis. These futurists note that we are living in what appears to be an unpredictable and chaotic world, and sometimes the only way to make decisions and move forward is to use one's intuition. "Reason," they say, "is useful only when there is a predictable outcome. Because very little is predictable today it leaves us with intuitive decision-making as the last resort." Their prediction: "Intuition will be the most important intelligence we could cultivate to plan for the future."

Perhaps Vaclav Havel, the President of the Czech Republic, expressed this best when he spoke before the World Economic Forum and remarked that we are at the end of the modern era, "which has been dominated by the belief that the world—and Being as such—is a wholly knowable system governed by a finite number of universal laws that man grasps and rationally directs for his own benefit." The old paradigm represented "a cult of depersonalized objectivity," he said, but in the new era, "a politician [or an executive] must become a person again. He must trust not only an objective interpretation of reality but also his own soul" (Ray, 1993).

Because our world is changing quickly, seemingly minute-by-minute, with the chaos of the marketplace drifting into patterns not easily recognized, the complexity of our lives has increased to such an extent that it may require more training and abilities than we can assimilate quickly, as well as insight (a.k.a. intuition) to make sense of the newly evolving patterns. Where do we go from here?

Where we go may be determined by how we are led. Many highly profitable organizations are guided by intuitive consultants who will most likely be our connections to understanding and meeting the future. They come in two varieties. One is the conventionally unconventional consultant found in both internal and external roles, whose work and methods for enticing intuition will be described in Parts Four and Five. Then, in Part Six you can read about the definitely unconventional, yet quietly relied upon, consultant who secretly offers multinational corporations his or her intuitive or psychic insights.

# PART FOUR

# The Internal "Whiz Kid" Consultants

The management climate of the future will place an increasing premium on intuitive skills in the strategic-planning and decision-making process. . . . Devoting organizational time and resources today to develop intuitive brain skills will likely offer dramatic payoffs in the future in terms of increased productivity and better strategic planning and decision-making.

...Weston Agor

The dramatic payoffs that Weston Agor predicted in 1989 are happening now, with the help of some of the most brilliant and intuitive idea-generators, otherwise known as consultants. Every organization needs to predict the future, but reliable crystal balls are scarce. Every manufacturer wants to know what it should make next year and the year after that. Can we predict what will be hot in ten years, and if so, how do we get there? The answers to these questions are never easy, and today the stakes are so high that a bad decision, whether based on extensive data analysis or an intuitive feel, can do severe damage to the bottom line. For many people, intuition is seen as a form of guessing, simply a hunch that often cannot be proven, and for this reason some consider it as being so soft it borders on wishful thinking or naïveté.

On the other hand, many people who were interviewed conceded that market research can be unreliable: that the data will say "go" and the item flops, or the indicators suggest that there is no market for the product, that no one will buy it, but it sells anyway. As one market researcher put it, "if you torture the data long enough, it will confess." In the final analysis, there is nothing that can be predicted for certain except death and taxes, and lately we have come to regard death as being optional. Every industry analyst knows that the most valuable information is foresight, yet they cannot reach a reliable read on the future without tapping into their intuition. Most businesses want to be the leader in the next wave. For them, the crucial questions are, "What's the wave going to be? Will we be able to get on our surfboards in time to catch it? And who can help us survive in these shark infested waters?"

Innovation today is not a luxury, it is a necessity. Jack Welch, Chairman of General Electric Corporation, said, "If the rate of change inside an organization is less than the rate of change outside, the end is in sight." And the value of a new idea, said John Martin, former CEO of Taco Bell, "could be worth $500 to $700 million to his company in the first year!" Some of the people charged with jumpstarting ideas for innovative new products are the internal and external consultants whose work may be behind the scenes. They have no public persona, yet their work in bringing new products and services to life is the soul of innovation that changes our world.

# 14

# *Future Thinkers in the Mega-Corporations*

Mapping the future is now a priority in many organizations. Long-range strategic planning is a tool that attempts to predict which new products or services will evolve in response to future trends. What kind of personality type is best suited to plot the course for business in the future? According to the Myers Briggs, it would be the intuitive, because one aspect of an intuitive personality is his or her natural inclination to look toward the future, as opposed to his opposite type, the sensor, who tends to scroll backwards to the past, seeking the wisdom of the past to predict the future.

This preference for the intuitive's natural disposition to look to the future is seen in Japan, where businesses plan twenty-five to fifty years ahead and are less pressured to show a profit each quarter. Not so coincidentally, according to research on personality types, 75 percent of the Japanese are intuitive, in contrast to only 25 percent of Americans. This is evidence that there is no right or wrong way to think, necessarily, but the attitude toward what is "correct" thinking is learned within a cultural belief system. We know from this comparison of the two cultures that an individual's penchant toward intuitive thinking cannot be explained as a peculiar blip in his DNA. Rather, it is an ability found in most people but not particularly encouraged in the American culture.

There is some research that says by the age of 40, most adults are only 2 percent as creative as they were at age 5. The reason that has been suggested is that our schools squelch intuition and creativity. The explanation for this phenomenon had been attributed to the stress placed on left brain learning in our schools. However, as we have noted earlier, the Japanese school system is far more rigorous than ours, and in the judgment of many in that society, it is seen as backward leaning in their rigid adherence to a very strict curriculum and grading system. Now, if 75 percent of Japanese believe their intuition helps them to find solutions and 75 percent of Americans do not believe intuition is reliable or even exists, then 75 percent of Americans are, to some extent, handicapped by this belief.

We, in this country, are led to believe that nearly everything we need to know can be researched and quantified, that if we do our homework and collect enough data, a reliable answer will be there for us. Conversely, the Japanese seem to understand that one cannot know enough, that the information is never complete, and that while data is indispensable, in the final analysis it is only one's intuition, one's gut instinct, that can make the difficult decisions.

## IBUKA AND THE WALKMAN

One example of the Japanese reliance on intuition was evident in the development of the Sony Walkman. When the company was considering the Walkman—a tiny tape recorder that would not record, but just play—there was no history to help them. In 1978, a small group of Sony engineers had tried to redesign a small conventional portable tape recorder so that it produced stereophonic sounds. They failed. Instead, they produced a small stereophonic tape recorder, but one that could not record.

Masoru Ibuka, founder and the late honorary Chairman of Sony, thought the sound the machine made was interesting and linked the "failed" product with an entirely unrelated project where an engineer was working to develop lightweight portable headphones. This was an intuitive leap, or a moment of blissful connection-making. Ibuka suggested that the engineers work together to develop a playback machine with headphones, but without recorder functions. He directly challenged the conventional assumption that a playback machine had to have a speaker and a recorder. Nothing like this had been done before, so no one knew whether anyone would buy it.

Conventional wisdom warned that it did not make sense to manufacture a tape player without a recording feature as well because everyone expected a tape recorder to have this dual function. Intuition carried Mr. Ibuka beyond the facts. His gut instinct told him that a tiny portable tape player would fill a gap of which the consumer was presently unaware. Sony went ahead with the Walkman and marketed it as a "new concept in entertainment. People could now listen to stereo sound while jogging, on the beach, or in the shopping mall, without disturbing others."

To sell this new concept, an unconventional marketing approach was also risked. Free samples were sent to celebrities in music and show business, and the Walkman press release came out on cassette rather than on paper. On the day of the product release, Sony bused the press to Yoyogi Park in Tokyo, where a throng of teenagers, all of them listening to free Walkmans and shimmying to the beat, roller-skated circles around the press. As the world knows, it became one of Sony's greatest successes. No one could have predicted from that early "failed" product how popular the Walkman would become.

## CHASING STICKERS

It may be useful to point out here that intuition is not the absence of rational thinking, but something outside of logic. For example, when Swiss engineer George de Mestral went for a walk in the woods and came back with sticky burrs all over his pants, he first wondered what it was about these burrs that made them stick. He put them under a microscope and saw how each tiny blade had a curved end to it. Those of us who grew up in the country may have been covered by burrs quite often, but to make the connection between a burr sticking to clothing and constructing a closure from this principle took an uncommon intuitive leap. De Mestral had the scientist's curiosity to try and figure out how burrs have such stick-to-it-iveness. He also had the inventor's penchant for taking creative leaps into connection-making when he foresaw that plastic "burrs" could be useful in making closures for garments, now known as Velcro®. Or, perhaps, he was simply spurred by the burr because he hated to sew buttons and his zippers always got stuck. If the latter were true, it would be another case of necessity being the mother of invention.

Once de Mestral's intuitive flash came and went, it required painstaking logic and research to manufacture and market the product. Velcro has since become a generic word, such as Kleenex, which people use interchangeably with the word "tissue." We now say "It sticks like velcro," not "It sticks like a burr."

Although large organizations may have the financial resources to investigate promising new product ideas by constructing prototypes and conducting extensive projects for market research, the statistics show that their hit rate is only 10 to 20 percent successful in producing a winning packaged item. In contrast, many entrepreneurs beginning new companies, such as Tender Loving Things and HandsOnToys (see Chapter 12), must rely only on their intuition and creativity with little to no market research. Without resources for market research, they begin with an idea for a product, manufacture it, and present it to the public. Many became enormously successful. Debbie Fields of Mrs. Fields Cookies is a case in point. She decided to begin a business because she loved baking cookies. Her professional advisors said, "A cookie store is a bad idea. Besides, the market research reports say America likes crispy cookies, not the soft and chewy kind that you make." Her intuition told her to open a cookie store anyway. Within a few years, there were over 600 stores selling her baked delicacies.

Yet with every entrepreneurial success there are likely to be three times as many failures. When that happens, it may result in a personal tragedy where people may lose their life savings, even their homes, and acquire debt as a steady companion. If a large corporation stumbles, however, the consequences may go well beyond losses in market share and profits; it can cause the disappearance of thousands of jobs, as we have seen recently with both IBM and Digital Equipment Corporation. Because of this tremendous need to be careful where they step—or in the case of these two giants, where they *don't* step—large corporations have become far more cautious and seek the ministrations of a variety of consultants in marketing and strategic planning in order to tap as many minds and gather as much data as possible.

The next chapter will look at how some of the leading internal consultants bring their intuitive insight to the needs of the corporation. Many of them, it would seem, strive to bring about in their client the ability that the short story writer O. Henry used to impress his teachers. He was able to do mathematical calculations with his right hand while his left hand sketched drawings, thus, working his left and right brain simultaneously. The consultants use their considerable talents to elicit the creativity within their clients using a variety of similar techniques. Sometimes they temporarily "numb" the left brain to allow the right brain permission to leap into future-thinking fantasies. Although each consultant has a different strategy for stimulating off-the-wall thinking, they all have one thing in common: a reliance on their own intuition to understand the client and the client's needs, whether the client is completely aware of them or not. When the consultant arrives on the scene, it is usually with a fierce dedication to finding the best solution for the company.

# 15

# The Internal Advisors

## BIG G PACKAGING

Dave Ross is Manager of Packaging Design at Big G Packaging, a division of General Mills in Minneapolis. His job is to figure out how to package cereal to drive sales. "Our group brings ideas to fruition, we make them happen," he says. When Ross wants to get his team to break out of the box, one of the things they do is go on a Thinking Expedition with Rolf Smith. They take three to four days off in order to experience a seminar that is patterned after a mountain expedition. During this simulation, the group experiences the following seven levels of change:

1.  Understand what you do well and concentrate on that.

2.  Eliminate doing what isn't necessary.

3.  Take another look at what you believe cannot be done.

4.  Know how to execute ideas and create a method for implementing ideas.

5.  Generate ideas using a variety of creative problem-solving techniques.

6.    Experience divergence, a "what if" exercise to brainstorm a variety of ideas.

7.    Create convergence by pulling together a team of people to work on bringing the idea to fruition.

As you can see, the first four steps are based in logical thinking, the key words being "understand," "eliminate," "look at your beliefs," "know how," and so forth. It would appear that the purpose of this method is to get emotional feelings out of the way at the beginning and to go for the nub of the problem, insofar as logic will take it. The next three steps are meant to elicit the intuitive response: to "generate ideas," "experience 'what if' scenarios," then pull it all together with an intuitive flash called convergence.

As Ross explained:

> There are usually about twenty-four people involved at the beginning of an expedition, then a smaller group is reassembled who had passion for the idea and an interest in following it through. Personal commitment is a big driver to success here . . . if no one is passionate about it, the idea goes nowhere. Expertise in an area is not enough, you also need to be bulldog persistent. It generally takes thirty to forty-five days to boil several ideas down to get them distilled into something that works. Then we form a core team with eight or nine volunteers led by an idea champion, someone who is passionate in carrying out the idea with others who will execute it. The team is self-selected from those who initially had an intuitive "wow" response when they first heard it. With their enthusiasm, plus the rigorous analysis the engineers put the ideas through, our percentage of getting the idea to market is close to 100 percent.
>
> To get a product to market requires a combination of technical expertise, an intuitive feeling that it will be successful, and most important, a passion that will drive the idea like a tank through enemy minefields—those people who do not see how it could work, why it would sell, and why it would be profitable. They are, it would appear, the nonintuitives who live and work among us.

Considering that the facilitator is responsible for spurring a spontaneous intuitive reaction, it would seem that he or she has a very important and difficult job, because most people—75 percent of Americans, as noted earlier—do not score as intuitive on the Myers Briggs and other similar test instruments. Thus, asking a facilitator to bring out an intuitive response with a group of people who may look upon idea-generating as tantamount to learning to speak a foreign language, is a daunting task.

When asked what qualities make a good facilitator, Ross replied:

> The best facilitator not only generates ideas but also leads the group to an action plan. She must be fluid, observe and tune in to everyone in the group and have an element of charisma, because she has to deal with basically nervous business people who are distrustful of any new process they have never before experienced. She also needs a good sense of humor to drive the energy of the group. Unfortunately, there may be some people we call bazookas, people who criticize and shoot down ideas. We ask everyone to suspend judgment by reminding them that Einstein once said that if the idea doesn't seem absurd, then there's no hope for it.
>
> When we generate lists of ideas, our method is focused on what's going to work. Some people who are very intuitive go immediately from step A to E in one leap, while others find this too fast and need to have the steps in between, B, C, and D, explained in detail. This requires skill on the part of the facilitator, so that the less intuitive people will catch on quickly to what is going on.
>
> It is important for the facilitator to remove herself from the content and be aloof to the idea. Rather, her role is to be a catalyst for innovative thinking. In a nutshell, you need to have a desire to serve, nurture, be intuitive, and have fun.

It seems strange, yet comfortable and most welcome, to hear a businessman talk about nurturing others. Only a few years ago using the word "nurturing" would have sent men into corporate oblivion because it had a new-age, touchy-feely connotation. Today, the ability to nurture ideas, new products, and people is an expected role for both men and women. This serves as a verification of Faith Popcorn's prediction from the *Popcorn Report* that she dubbed, "Female Think," or the feminization of business. What was once considered a feminine trait, nurturing, is now a desirable ability for both men and women, not only in terms of leading ideation sessions, but also for managers who must use this skill to coach and mentor their staff.

## KIMBERLY CLARK

Julius Nagy, a Research Scientist at Kimberly Clark in Neenah, Wisconsin, works undercover in new product development. Although his project at the moment is top secret, his intuition is not. He knows that it is a very useful tool in the new product development process.

"For me," Nagy says, "intuition is the result of all your experiences in your life, personal and professional. As I get more experience, it's easier to make better decisions. Emotions have an effect on objectivity, and you are not always aware that your emotions are coming into play, which is why it is useful to have more heads involved in developing a product." He suggests that the best qualities for a facilitator are being sensitive to the different personality styles in the group, having the ability to get everyone involved, being a good listener, and being able to anticipate what the next question should be with intuitive skills.

Nagy has had experiences, however, with some consultants who were a turn-off. He divides them into two types: East coast and West coast:

> The East coast style seems to have a harder edge, wants the answers to snap out quickly based on experience and data, and there is less space and time for intuition to percolate. Some people can come up with ideas quickly, while others need more time. On the other hand, the West coast style is, 'Let's get more touchy feely, let it sit, simmer, digest, and get in tune with your intuition.' In the Midwest, we are more easy going, and some consultants with a rushed East coast style can really bomb here.

Nagy sees creative people as being able to get beyond the parameters of a situation. A new product idea is the result of a combination of getting a creative idea, and then taking the intuitive leap to understanding how to manufacture it easily. As Nagy said,

> If you want more creative ideas, you are better off asking the users of the product rather than experts or people familiar with the product. We look at consumers early on, and then later the more knowledgeable people come into the project to come up with creative ideas on how we are going to manufacture it. Although intuition is a factor in the final analysis, it would be perceived as a big negative here to say that you do anything intuitively.

This is an example of a cultural conditioning that offers little respect for the one quality without which no new products would ever have been developed. It was Einstein who once said that no advances in science ever came about without an intuitive insight first. Apparently, in this culture it's okay for scientists to be intuitive, but others are expected to be far more logical.

## BLACK & DECKER

Bryan DeBlois has been named in twenty patents and has received numerous design awards. He says his reliance on intuition is basic as Manager of New Business Development at Black & Decker, in Stamford, Connecticut. DeBlois invented the snake-light, a battery-powered flashlight mounted in a long, bendable tube that can be used to hook around anything, such as a body or machine part, to assist in enlightening spaces when one's two hands are otherwise occupied. He came up with the idea in 1989, when he was doing some work on his Victorian home. Then he proposed it to the Advanced Concept Development group at Black & Decker, which developed it in time for its debut at the National Hardware Show in August, 1994. It became an immediate success and, according to the press, stole the show!

How did the team turn the concept into reality? DeBlois replied,

> They defined the rules of the game early. Think high quality, high volume, and automation. Resist the temptation to design and market a "one-trick pony" and let the design support a derivative strategy. The team took on a lot of challenges. Things had to be done swiftly and, if need be, differently. The team took over ownership of the mission: to provide consumers with true hands-free task lighting.
>
> We believe in a prototype driven process. I can dream a good depiction, but if the prototypes are too crude and don't work well, the end user cannot really understand its purpose or use. We began with making a prototype that functioned with a good flexing and bending action. We then brought potential users into the problem and let them experience it. What happens is that when the new concept is better understood, the end user finds more uses for it than we had anticipated. This helps us find more reasons why people will buy this product and makes its proposal to the company that much stronger.
>
> Informed intuition is insight into consumer trends. Our mission is to create new products for household use. Beyond new products, however, I believe intuition also plays a role in whether a culture change will be successful in any organization. To change the way people interact with one another and keep the business moving is a monstrous expenditure of time and energy. And without intuition, it may become dead in the water. It is, as one visionary manager put it, "like trying to change a fan belt while the engine is running."

DeBlois believes that people who can empathize with consumers, define the right problem, and synthesize it with a multitude of other input will create a compelling solution. His emphasis is definitely on empathy, intuition, design, and reaching the consumer needs.

When the subject of intuition was raised he said:

> I believe all people have and use intuition to some degree. In the business world, these people are sometimes referred to as "visionaries." In the quest for an answer, direction, or image, the

visionaries will be called upon to generate the power of their intuitive skills and immerse their mind in a large pool of collected memory, experience, and information. It is from this intelligence that they form an idea and draw the passion to want to take action on it. [Yet,] I believe that business management has under-achieved in the area of recognizing how important a role intuitive judgment plays when trying to stimulate people to be agents of change.

## 3M COMPANY

Ron Kubinski has a most unusual job at the 3M Company in St. Paul, Minnesota. He is Manager for Advance Planning and is responsible for new product commercialization, from concept to delivery. In other words, his work is similar to writing science fiction.

Educated in engineering with a minor in psychology, Kubinski leads a comparatively minuscule department of five people—within the organization of 74,000 people—to generate new product ideas, among other tasks. One of their roles is to assist business units within 3M to generate new product ideas. They accomplish this by drawing up a plan to create ideas for products that will be marketable ten years in the future. Once they have that plan in mind, they backtrack to the present year with new product ideas that are possible with today's technology. They then predict which additional products will be added year by year that will build upon each year's new technological advances to achieve their tenth-year vision. This process is called Customer Inspired Innovation.

The process begins with the study of the links between present technology and the future, after which Kubinski's group projects the concepts out ten years ahead to see what could evolve. They may take one concept and generate several different possibilities for the future out of a single idea. The next step is to determine whether some concepts are more interesting than others. If one idea is compelling, it could stimulate several others. From here they proceed to backfill, with product enhancements that will lead to their tenth-year prophecy, although they fully understand that the end result may never materialize.

In their book, *Competing for the Future*, Hamel and Prahalad observe that "Far-sighted corporate leaders may not be any better prognosticators than more short-sighted managers, but they are almost certainly more curious" (Hamel and Prahalad, 1994). Kubinski is not only far-sighted but definitely curious.

In their future-predicting process, the Advance Planning group involves marketing and customer relations people in its brainstorming sessions. In these sessions they use a variety of techniques, such as DeBono's Lateral Thinking and others. "But at some point you have to bring the left brain into the equation," says Kubinski. "If you can't, you won't get anywhere; you'll be perceived as fluffy and not bottom-line oriented."

Kubinski looks for three qualities from team members:

1. They need a degree of naivete toward the business. Although they are brilliant technologists, they are not locked into the paradigm of the business we are researching.

2. They should be explorers who like to get out of the box, that is, beyond the corporate box, and be able to blue-sky ideas. We define how current products are used, put ourselves into the mind set of the end-user, and then think solution.

3. I look for creative people for the team, people who are easy to talk to and friendly, which says to me that they would be good team players. I also look for people who have a degree of excitement about them and who are highly creative and intuitive, as well as respectful of other people. Most have knowledge in either the technology or in customer interfacing, and some have it in both.

Kubinski says that his core team, which may number about fifteen people, includes stake holders (i.e., the division vice presidents) and those from one level below, including Group Vice Presidents. As he explains,

> Our core team goes all over and outside the company talking to academics, consultants, and end users. Then we get together and share all the information to determine where we have the most dimensions or factors that will offer products based on our moving from the future to present, not present to future. This has been a very successful system for coming up with excellent ideas.

In strategic planning, most people go from past to present to future, which leads to incremental thinking. Doing this in reverse, going from the future to the present, yields a different migration plan of opportunities and results in a vision that is often compelling and unique, but which, until now, has gone unrecognized. While Kubinski's organization is only three years old, its methodology has already dramatically improved the outlook for three business units that were having some difficulties. The Advance Planning Group came up with new products and new markets for these businesses, and thanks to Kubinski's idea-generating skills, they have experienced a welcome turn-around.

How does this method stack up against the professional future readers? Do they use companies that chart trends or predict the future? His reply was almost apologetic: "Really, no, because we are so far ahead of the future readers, we don't use them."

Kubinski defines intuition as:

> when the direction I am going in feels right. It's when I have insight and foresight and ideas all aligned together. It's when I have an idea for the future that bridges concepts by synthesizing ideas. Creative people have lots of ideas, but intuition comes from the inner self. You can get creativity from experiencing a process, but it's not necessary to be intuitive to be creative. Edison came

from his inner self to conceptualize a light bulb and Edward Land knew intuitively that he could develop film in the camera.

Intuition is another way of knowing, and when it isn't followed up, wrong judgments are often the result. One example: I have had the experience of being in a meeting where the group made a decision that didn't feel right. Although I felt it at the time, I didn't say anything, because I had no way to prove it. It was an intuitive knowing that something wasn't right. Sure enough, it didn't work out.

What percentage of their work is intuitive? In the final analysis Kubinski figures it is perhaps 30 to 40 percent that "comes directly from the gut."

What does this manager look for when he needs people to help him read the future?

Someone with a wealth of knowledge. Usually it is a person with a viewpoint. It's also someone who has self-confidence and is able to bring something to the table by being able to get out of the box. But that is still not enough. He or she also needs to have a passion for ideas and pushing them forward.

Passion seems to be an extremely important quality for getting anything accomplished in most organizations. It would be interesting to know whether those companies whose employees are not passionate about their work are also businesses whose performance in the marketplace is suffering.

This insight may offer us an interesting clue as to why the 3M Company has been so successful for so many years. Many of its people not only have that passion but are also encouraged to express their creative ideas. Kubinski says that the company is highly focused on stimulating innovative new ideas. Creativity is encouraged everywhere; for instance, everyone in the company is aware of the 15 percent rule, which means that they are encouraged to spend up to 15 percent of their time on any new product idea of their own choosing.

If the Kubinski group's success is the result of working backwards from ten years out, then let's all lunge forward with what is seemingly an impossible dream, and then dance backward into creative new ideas. They apparently begin the idea-generating process from a fantasy of what things could be like in ten years, perhaps not unlike the imaginings of science fiction writers like Jules Verne, who predicted many of the technological advances that we have today—over 100 years ago! Intuitive minds like to live in the future and imagine what could be. This tendency is somewhat different from the creative process, which makes connections to form something new, but the new may not necessarily be marketable, useful, or futuristic. For that, the creative mind needs to plug into intuitive insights.

# Conclusion

As you have read in the last two chapters, the internal consultants can perform extraordinary services for their employers with their intuition, research, logic, and enthusiasm. In the next chapter, you will see the secrets of how external consultants perform equally remarkable feats of magic with their clients to extract remarkable new products and services.

# PART FIVE

## Leading External Consultants in Ideation

> Intuition is one of the most powerful tools we have . . . to reinvent our personal and business growth . . . and the more you use intuition, the more confidence and trust you have in it.
>
> ...DARWIN CLARK, *Vice President, General Motors, Europe*

Internal company consultants have the luxury of being able to tap into a broad information data base because they have access to a large number of experts in a wide variety of disciplines within the organization. Without this support the external consultant must rely more on his or her own experience and intuitive wisdom, as well as a variety of creative methodologies, to assist in solving their clients' problems. From my interviews with outside consultants, they unanimously agree that they rely on their intuition to understand the problem, its solution, and their client's sometimes unarticulated focus. Having this intuitive mindset seems to be a key to the internal consultants' success in finding unique and highly profitable new product ideas for the companies they serve. External consultants may have an assortment of business backgrounds and frequently bring in experts from a wide variety of areas to tap into their collective intuitive wisdom.

While both men and women have similar approaches in their consulting practices, there are also some interesting differences. For that reason, this part of the book is divided into two chapters: the first is from the male point of view, the second, the female. Since popular culture commonly refers to "female intuition," it may be of interest to see whether there are any significant gender differences, either in the methods used or in the final results.

# 16

# The Intuitive Male Mystique

## BRYAN MATTIMORE

Bryan Mattimore is the author of *99% Inspiration* and principal of The Mattimore Group in Stamford, Connecticut. When he connects with his clients, he uses a variety of different strategies for eliciting brilliant ideas which evolve over a two-day period. Day 1 is for pure ideation; Day 2 is when the best ideas from Day 1 are developed with testable concepts. Mattimore says,

> When we do an ideation session, we get between 100 and 200 new ideas that we record. From these ideas, first individually and then as a group, we decide on the top 15 to 20 ideas for further development in Day 2. It really speeds up the new product development process. After two days of work, you have 15 or 20 concepts that can be tested in focus groups almost immediately. We then put them up on a board and let everyone pick their favorites.

One of the techniques he uses is called Picture Prompts™, a collection of interesting pictures designed to stimulate ideas. Generally, he uses this technique at the end of the day because, as he says, "focusing on how a picture relates to the problem is tapping into the intuitive language of our subconscious minds, which is usually more available in the late afternoon."

According to studies in brain physiology, the brain can more easily go into a sleep- or trance-like state sometime around 4 P.M., the time most people feel their energy and attention waning. If they are working in an office, they may reach for an injection of caffeine. The reason for this mental down time is that the brain is going through a switching process in its circadian rhythm, from daytime alertness to evening quiet. It is during this in-between period that we are most likely to get intuitive insights, because it is a time when the left brain is quiescent, allowing the right brain to become more available for visual stimulation and insights. Thus, using pictures at this time activates the right brain, which "sees" in pictures, grasps meaning, and has a better feel for what makes a good idea. It also tends to trigger answers people may intuitively already know.

Many of us may awaken slowly in the morning for similar reasons, because we are in that same blurry state when the break between sleep and consciousness occurs. While some people manage to wake up fully alert and raring to go, others need to jar their wits into some version of animation with a strong jolt of java. Again, it is our brains that are functioning in the switching mode. This may be another reason many of us wake up in the morning with clearer insights to a problem than we had the night before, because it is this switching time, or being in a theta or alpha brain state, that seems to allow intuitive insights to occur. Einstein, too, wondered why he got his best ideas while shaving. Chances are that he shaved before his morning coffee, which allowed the creative ideas to emerge from this just waking intelligence.

Mattimore explained how the Picture Prompt™ has been useful with an example of his work with clients at Alpine Lace Cheese:

> The task was to find new ways to promote its low-fat cheese. Someone saw a picture of a fruit basket and got the idea of holding fruit/cheese parties in the supermarket as part of the promotion. It became a successful way to get their cheese displayed in the produce department in the grocery store. The idea came from a Picture Prompt™ exercise that took less than an hour to facilitate!

One of the most powerful techniques that he uses for coming up with new ideas is called "kill the sacred cow," or "question the obvious," because the obvious is not as obvious as it appears. You may see something in front of you that you are certain you know or understand, but when you analyze it, it may be something entirely different.

Mattimore tells the story of how this method was used with a direct marketing organization. It had developed a number of mail order books and, in case the customer did not want to keep them, promised easy return. However, they also purposely packaged the books to make them difficult to return by having the package fall apart when it was opened. The "sacred cow" here was that "returns are bad," and if we can reduce the number of returns by making the return to shipper box fall apart when you open it (making it a hassle to repackage the book) fewer customers would take the trouble to return it and that would mean we would make more profit. Mattimore challenged this sacred cow with the question, "What if we made the books easy to return?" He suggested that more people would order the books if they really were easy to return.

To slay this "sacred cow," the company improved the package design and added a return-to-sender mailing label, making it even easier to return the books—and at no cost—so that ordering them became much more enticing. As a result, once customers learned that it would be easy to return unwanted books at no expense, they were more likely to order them in the first place. Although the changes did in fact increase the number of returns, they also dramatically increased the number of orders. The net effect of destroying this sacred cow was a substantial increase in sales and profitability.

For the customer, making it easier to decide whether he or she wants the product or not without feeling pushed into it, makes it far more likely that a purchase will occur. In this case, it is empathizing with the customer, but the process of empathizing is also intuitive. The intuitive aspect is found in ignoring a business practice that guaranteed sales by making orders difficult to return, and knowing that to make returns easier would increase orders. This is a case where empathy for the customers, combined with intuitive knowing, worked. The good old golden rule became a golden means for increasing profits. Other clients, such as AT&T, Kraft, and Unilever, have experienced this technique.

Although Mattimore prepares a detailed facilitation plan for each session he runs, he considers the plan only a map to guide him in the possible direction he might lead the group. "Frankly, I don't know which technique will work best with a particular group. I've done sessions where we've only used 10 to 20 percent of the techniques I had planned." Believing that *intuition is critical* to his work, he lets his intuition and experience guide him as to which technique to use during the actual session and which ideas to develop with the group. For example, he tells of a single technique that was used with Clairol that was almost entirely intuitive.

> During the session itself, my intuition told me we needed to try a radically different exercise than the one I had planned if we were going to get a true, breakthrough concept. At the break I came up with an idea to have participants imagine and role-play one day in the life of a hair. From that exercise alone we got two seminal ideas for new hair products!
>
> When I facilitate I go into an altered state. It usually starts when I begin writing. Somehow I have the ability to write

down ideas, watch body cues, know which ideas to pursue to develop into workable concepts, and ask idea stimulating questions . . . all simultaneously. It's a hyperaware, very intuitive state.

When Mattimore describes the qualities of a good facilitator, they seem remarkably like his own. He feels one should be:

> self-effacing, intuitive, and flexible; have a sense of humor, a business background, and be able to recognize a big idea. If you don't have that experience and intuition, you could miss the seed of a good idea and not encourage the group to nurture that seed into a full-bloomed, exciting concept.

The techniques Mattimore uses are actually geared to elicit the latent intuition in his session participants. When he does word games, or shows pictures, or advances the destruction of the sacred cow, none of these activities can be accomplished successfully with only left brain analysis. For example, how can you look at a series of pictures that have absolutely no relationship to your business and come up with an idea that leads to solving your problem by using your analytic left brain? It defies logic. When you get answers from this type of stimulus, you know that it was conceived by your intuitive brain, whether or not you're aware of its presence.

## ROBERT BEACHY

Robert Beachy has an entirely different approach to getting to the intuitive brain; he uses pipe cleaners! Beachy holds twenty-six patents in chemical, mechanical, and electrical engineering products, and he is also a principal at Axiom in Minneapolis. He likes hands-on activities in the idea-generating phase of a consulting session:

> People tend to think with their eyes, so I hand them pipe cleaners and molding materials and let them play with the pipe cleaners.

Working with the hands often brings ideas into the head. Intuition is definitely a part of what we do, and we find that the most creative people are intuitive as well.

There are nine consultants at Axiom, each with different sets of skills and with backgrounds ranging from human resources and engineering to finance. When they conduct group ideation sessions, one to four of the people on staff participate, which may include anyone from marketing managers to the CEO of any given company. Beachy notes that preparation is the most important part of his work, which includes defining the clients needs and targeting their customers. He feels that people who have broad business backgrounds from having worked in different areas over the years have a broader perspective; working with these people often leads to more intuitive ideas.

What is intuition? Beachy says, "It's making connections; creativity is also defined as making connections, but intuition is knowing that those connections are very likely to work."

## MICHAEL SCHRAGE

Michael Schrage is another hands-on consultant who believes that making prototypes is the way to creative new ideas. A research associate at the Sloan School at MIT and the Media Lab, Schrage also consults on innovation issues. His clients have included Hewlett Packard, Proctor & Gamble (where he worked on Pampers, among other products), and McKinsey & Co. Schrage spurs new product development by building prototypes as a way to understand which new product would be the most successful. He believes that you don't buy ideas, you buy things, and that you can only decide quickly and clearly on a new product if it is modeled on a prototype. If people do not like the prototype, you can quickly learn what it is about the nature of the product or the market segment that did not connect. When there is a slip between gut feel and data, it becomes a dialectic that forces the product developer to become more explicit. This creates a healthy tension, in his view, and calls for more rigor in proving the point. As for intuition, he says, "Yes, trust your gut. It should be a driver, but then let reason be the guide."

It is interesting that Schrage sets up a distinction between intuition and reason. He says that intuition is not necessarily "reasonable," so one must be able to separate the two and know when to switch gears. He cautions, "let reason be your guide." The problem, however, is we never know what is truly reasonable. When the telephone was invented, a Western Union internal memo in 1876 stated, "This 'telephone' has too many shortcomings to be seriously considered as a means of communication. The device is inherently of no value to us." At that time, the statement was most likely regarded by the general public as reasonable, considering its source. Likewise, in 1945, Vanevar Bush, President of the Carnegie Institution, told President Truman, "The atomic bomb will never go off, and I speak as an expert on explosives." That comment, too, was offered by someone with a distinguished background who was also considered reasonable. And how can we forget the "foresight" expressed by another expert, Marechal Ferdinand Foch, Professor of Strategy at the Ecole Superieure de Guerre, who said just prior to World War I, "Airplanes are interesting toys but of no military value."

None of these statements were correct, or intuitive; in fact, they were just the opposite. They reflected a lack of imagination as to what could be, which required making connections that were not available at the time. For example, a telephone is useless without wiring being available in the home, and at that time there was no wiring. It would have required an intuitive or creative leap to ask oneself, "what if wiring were possible, would a telephone be useful then?" George Bernard Shaw once said, "The reasonable man adapts himself to the world. The unreasonable man persists in trying to adapt the world to him. Therefore, all progress depends on the unreasonable man [or woman]." If the word "unreasonable" suggests being stubborn, as in holding onto a conviction that stemmed from intuitive knowing rather than following a conventional thought process, then perhaps he was right. The short-sighted statements from the aforementioned "experts" were reasonable. It took the "unreasonable" intuitives to grasp the future.

## BOB GILL

Bob Gill has another way to get to the intuitive understanding of a problem. He believes that the customers who use products in nontraditional ways are the trendsetters, or lead users, and watching them will reveal the broadest clues as to what is needed in the future. Bob is a partner in Product Development Partners, Inc. in Newton, Massachusetts, a company that focuses on new product development.

How does he generate new product ideas with his clients? "First," he said, "we scan the environment to understand it, looking at the space for opportunities and the space they are trying to explore. We try to understand past, present, and future trends and map them out." This is followed by identifying a customer's unarticulated needs and observing customer patterns in their work processes. For example, watching a mother changing a diaper with a pin in her mouth suggested a suboptimum work process. Disposable diapers with Velcro-like fasteners addressed this issue. It is this type of observation that leads to new ideas by generating alternative capabilities for a technology that is already in place. In another example, the observation of melted items left on top of kitchen appliances led to the development of insulated toaster ovens. This was also a solution to address a frequently occurring problem.

What are the tools of Gill's trade? When he is in search of new applications for current products, he begins the process with a review of strategic documents. Then he generates a fact book capturing socioeconomic trends and places maps on the wall with a time line showing when key innovations occurred in the development of a particular product, such as a camera. This clarifies the product's past and present history and suggests the future capabilities of the product by taking note of its technological capabilities as well as additional technologies that might be available.

In poster sessions, in which information is posted on the wall, the group shares ideas and evaluates them against preliminary market research and unmet customer needs by asking three questions:

1.   Do customers want it?

2.   Can we make it?

3.   Can we make money with it?

Then they develop a business plan. Decision-makers put all the pieces of information on the table and make a rational decision based on facts and data. Start-ups often develop new products with no research, often using only intuition; once the company matures, it will eventually have to get more information to move it forward. "Initially," he says, "it's a lot of intuition with a start-up, but the days of intuition in the boardroom have been replaced with enormous research."

What criteria does Gill have for a facilitator? His reply:

> A good facilitator needs to be able to listen to be objective, needs to know about team dynamics and how to work towards compromise and consensus, needs to be structured and keep the team on track. But perhaps most importantly, [he or she] needs to be able to listen to each proposal and reframe it in such a way as to get the group to buy into it.

What else does an ideation generator need? "It helps to be intuitive," he replies. "I am more intuitive now than I was earlier. Intuition gives you clues as to where to pursue opportunities, and I trust it more now as I get older. Perhaps life experience helps." As Jonas Salk said, "Intuition tells you where to look next to get the answer."

## MARK SEBELL

Mark Sebell, President and Founder of Creative Realities, in Boston, helps clients and corporations to innovate new products, services, and business development by facilitating ideation and implementation sessions. He says that his gut reactions always come in handy. In his consulting method, the groups usually take one to two days to brainstorm using a variety of techniques, such as Synectics excursions, analogies, and role-playing. Then they sort and refine the ideas and evaluate them against specific criteria. There are several stages for each consulting intervention, and each session is based on the needs of the individual client.

"When you facilitate breakthrough innovation that works," Sebell says, "intuition always kicks in. To tell the client what they need after listening to what they want definitely requires intuition on the part of the consultant."

He continues with a case in point:

> A few years ago, when we worked with Walt Disney World, they wanted to come up with an idea for a new theme restaurant to be built in the Disney/MGM theme park. We got the finalized concept for this restaurant in only a day and a half.
> The group began with an excursion that asked them to think back to their favorite TV shows from the 1950s. *Happy Days* was selected as something that may have some possibilities, but the technical details involved in pursuing that option discouraged further thinking along that line. Another fond remembrance that came out of the group was science fiction movies, and they thought of how this might work, but again, technical difficulties began to emerge as barriers. Then someone combined the two ideas! The concept of a restaurant that looked like the Arnold's Diner from *Happy Days* emerged, where customers sat in their

cars and waiters roller skated the orders out to the parking lot while showing science fiction movies.

When they put these two ideas together on the second day, they had constructed the full-blown concept of creating the Sci-Fi Restaurant, where the restaurant encloses about 100 "cars" facing giant movies screens, like drive-ins. The diners sit inside the cars at tables and give their orders to wait staff who roller skate to the cars, take the orders, and then return with the food, still on wheels. Meanwhile, on giant screens in front of them, the patrons can watch humorous science fiction movies such as the *Tomato That Ate Chicago*, while they devour their stuffed tomato or Chicago pizzas. And, like the drive-ins of yesteryear, each "car" is equipped with a squawk-box that carries the sound for the movie, with the volume adjustable by the customer. The entire process, from first bite of an idea during the excursion to the final completed concept took one and one half days! It was brought to Michael Eisner one week later. Since the opening, the restaurant has won many awards for its creativity.

Creative Realities has twelve full-time and six part-time consultants on staff, frequently using two to four people to lead its client groups. Sebell says that the best facilitators have a sense of "performing" and are to some extent theatrical and charismatic. This is absolutely essential if they are working with a room full of reluctant corporate people who are afraid of pursuing newness at every level, from top to bottom. "We like to have multifunctional people involved who have a strong desire to serve as a consultant to the company's business development. Patience is also more than a virtue, for this job it's a necessity." Another requirement for the job: "You've got to be big on humor and a good coach."

It is interesting that Sebell stresses humor. In a study commissioned by Bell Labs some years ago, a researcher wanted to know what personality characteristics creative people held in common. After interviewing a number of inventors, scientists, and others who had made significant contributions to their field, they were able to came up with only two common personality traits: they kept messy work places and had well-developed senses of humor.

## RICHARD FEDER

Richard Feder also looks first for the intuitive response with his clients; logic comes later. Feder is a principal with the Marketing Group in Stamford, Connecticut, and he works with clients such as McDonalds, Kraft, and AMEX, who seek his services to solve a marketing problem or to find ways to enhance customer satisfaction. He reviews the research on the usage of the product, noting what the customers like as well as what ticks them off, and separates what is important from what is unimportant for the customer. "At this point," he says, "we go fishing."

Feder's ideation process uses verbal, visual, and kinesthetic exercises and physical activities such as playing with things, like blocks, nuts, bolts, pennies, or anything that can spur creativity. Sometimes, he says,

> instead of creativity, these "toys" tap into aggression or inspire extreme exertion, but creativity usually occurs after awhile, with a combination of logic and intuition. Generally, when we tap into the nonverbal senses, there will be an interactive quality that results in more breakthrough ideas, as well as a greater proportion of nonusable, fanciful ideas. We have learned that verbal stimulus elicits about 20 percent of ideas that are feasible. When we use nonverbal stimuli, only 3 to 4 percent of ideas may be feasible, but they are much more likely to be unique!

Anarchis in 600 BC said, "Play so that you may be serious." In Feder's experience, the more successful people are those who can play and take their intuition seriously.

## CHRISTOPHER MILLER

Of all the external consultants I interviewed, Christopher Miller, Ph.D., has what appears to be one of the most structured organizations that gets people to be unstructured in their thinking. He is a founding partner of Innovation Focus®, in Lancaster, Pennsylvania, and has twelve employees who lead seminars in concept creation and new product strategies. At each session the number of facilitators varies, usually from three to six, depending on the needs of the client. Each facilitator is assigned a role, such as the following:

- The Process Facilitator takes care of the Process, to make sure it goes smoothly.
- The Producer takes care of logistics and details, such as knowing where to make copies or where the circuit breakers are located. It is his or her job to prepare for virtually any unforeseen problem.
- The Visual Facilitator draws rapid imagery on flip charts as the session proceeds, so that the client can see the idea in a sketch that gives shape to a concept of what is seen in the mind's eye.
- The Creativity Facilitator's task is to think up novel exercises to bring out ideas from the group.
- The Customer, a special friend, is someone who can participate with the group as a customer and offer comments about the product or service. Often, noncompetitive new product development professionals who are not customers can take this role as well.
- The Technographer types and sorts notes based on key words, takes notes on what's going on during the session, and pulls out specific clues and distributes them to the group. In addition, if there will be work with children, they get a child specialist to help facilitate.

The bottom line: don't facilitate alone.

The teams that Innovation Focus puts together are a good mix of personality types. Each one includes an intuitive who will pump everyone up with her excitement and keep people stimulated with new ideas, and her opposite type, someone like a sensor who may move more slowly, but will add other facets to the discussion. As Miller says,

> We never start a project if we can't bring it to resolution. At times, creativity is not needed, we simply reformulate an old idea and get it to work better. We have found that when we work with a team having a diversity of backgrounds and ways of perceiving the world, it lends added strength. It also makes the process more challenging. Different thinking styles prefer different processes.

In Miller's view, the best facilitator acts as if he were a great butler acting in the service of others, one who knows how to serve; someone who can step up and step back with impeccable timing. The intuitive facilitator must anticipate others' needs before they make them known, like Radar O'Reilly in M\*A\*S\*H. Miller is also aware that when he has a sensor in the client group, he must take more time to talk out the idea.

While verbal skills are important for facilitators, Innovation Focus also requires that their group leaders write legibly, quickly, and backwards on the flipcharts, all the while focusing on the audience. Miller recalls how he got part of his training in writing backwards by teaching in a tough Cleveland school, where he always had to have his back covered, even when writing on the blackboard.

When I asked Miller if he sees a difference in the intuitive skills of people at the top of an organization from those on lower levels, he said,

> I have found that people in the highest positions tend to be very intuitive and flexible and they deserve to be on top. They can be detail-oriented, yet quick to grasp ideas. I rarely have encountered a senior manager who was not a creative, intuitive, and thoughtful person.

This matches the experience of Ned Herrmann, who gave his HBDI to hundreds of executives and noticed that many of them had similar patterns; that is, they scored about evenly in all four brain quadrants. This means that they were equally comfortable tapping on their thinking, sensing, intuiting, or feeling functions.

Miller, however, sees intuition as informed intelligence.

> Do not mistake spontaneity for intuition. After thirty years experience facilitating creative ideas, I can feel people think. I tend to aggressively withhold judgment and give them a long time to let their intuition percolate. It is said that Estée Lauder could smell a scent and know instantly how many bottles of perfume it would sell. And she was always correct.

## BOB JOHNSTON

Because delving into the intuitive part of our brain may be uncomfortable for some people, Bob Johnston, a principal at IdeaScope, a bicoastal consulting organization, begins his ideation sessions by trying to make everyone comfortable. He assures them that what they will be doing is quite unlike the way they spend 90 to 95 percent of their time. He explains,

> I have people introduce themselves by stating three things about their personal lives, two that are true and one that is false. Most people can pick out which is false, although it is rare to have an entire group get a perfect score. However, with one group of fifteen people, fifteen actually got it right. This began their introduction to intuitive knowing.

IdeaScope employs twenty consultants with offices in Cambridge, Massachusetts and San Francisco. Their client work includes strategic innovation, identifying how systems within a company impact the bottom line, looking at new business opportunities, defining the marketplace, and gaining specific industry foresight. "We serve a client's needs, whether articulated or unarticulated," says Johnston. This is a theme that is repeated frequently by many consultants. It suggests that many clients may be unclear about what their needs are, or may not articulate them well. Whatever the situation, many consultants feel that their job is to get beyond a stated need to the crux of the problem. The confusion between the actual need versus the presenting problem with a client company is comparable to what the physician experiences with many patients.

Some physicians, such as Dr. Bernard Lown in his book *The Art of Healing*, suggest that many patients come in with a self-diagnosis that has little to do with the real problem. For example, he tells about a man who came to see him complaining that he had heart palpitations and felt as though his heart was weak. After speaking with the patient about his home life, it was revealed that he was being kept prisoner in his home and was being abused by an adult child, which turned out to be the real problem. Despite his "imprisonment," his heart was healthy, but he was "sick at heart." Psychologists often see family dynamics very differently from the way family members do, also, and the role of the enabler is one that can come as a shock to many clients. Perhaps the lesson here is that most of us do not see our own situations as clearly as another person who is not emotionally involved with our problems. To seek the opinion of an "outsider," someone who is not tied emotionally or financially to our lives or business, frequently offers an invaluable insight into our problems that brings significant improvement.

Johnston illustrates the creative results they get by tapping into the clients' intuition when he tells the story of one intervention they did some years ago with the Hewlett Packard Company in San Diego. Lewis Platt, the president, had relocated the large printer division to Barcelona and in the process left the people in San Diego without work. They were told that they had to create their own jobs. IdeaScope consultants were brought in and began by asking the group to describe probable scenarios for the future, that is, future trends. Someone noticed the beginning of a trend that was just a blip at the time, that more and more people would be working out of a home office. The employees felt that the market for home office machines would skyrocket in the next five years (which it has) and agreed that they could fill that future need by creating a new product called the Office Jet, a home office machine that copies, prints, and faxes, retailing for about $750. When it was first introduced, in April 1995, *Business Week Magazine* recognized it as the product of the year.

"In my experience," Johnston says, "people at the top levels of management of most companies are intuitive, and they are permitted to be more intuitive than those on the lower rungs because they must often make important decisions without the benefit of strong data to support them." One example is Bob Galvin at Motorola; his intuition told him that wireless communication would be a gigantic opportunity for the future, although he had no strong data to support this. Still, he had to fight long and hard to get Motorola's board to agree: as a result it moved the company into an entirely new industry. This is one reason why it is not enough for only one person at the top to be intuitive. Had the board members been tuned into the same intuitive wave length, Motorola would have gotten there sooner and avoided a difficult fight.

During my survey, several executives told me that while they may be intuitive, their lower-level employees are not encouraged to be intuitive. Johnston confirmed that this attitude was common in his work as well; although senior executives relied a great deal on their own intuition, they did not encourage its use at the lower levels.

One method Johnston uses to elicit the groups intuition takes about one and a half days to find the resolution. After spending the first day using a variety of ideation techniques, the group is told to go home and sleep on the problem and come back the next morning with an answer to a fictitious but related problem. They are told not to do any work on this new problem before they go to sleep, not until they wake up the next morning. Before they went home for the night, they were given "newspaper" articles that warned of EPA laws scheduled to take effect within three years that would ban the use of the plastic materials that their company currently used. (These were actually doctored

articles made to look like the real thing.) This did the job of sufficiently scaring the group to come up with new ideas for materials. The next morning, each person came in with a business
proposal based on the information they had been given. When
everyone's ideas were shared, they were able to produce a new
product concept and a strategy to fulfill future needs.

This technique successfully tapped into the group's dreaming mind, a great initiator of intuitive leaps. The reason: when
the conscious mind that "knows" what will work and what
won't is turned off, it allows the subconscious mind to pull
together various strands of knowledge and imagination so that
in the morning, although there may be no memory of dreams,
the problem will seem much clearer. The use of logic alone can
sometimes deter or delay the creative process during waking
hours, but during sleep, without left brain interference, anything can happen!

The typical presenting problem for many organizations,
Johnston says,

> is an inability to grow their business at the rate that they think it
> should be growing, and they agonize over why they aren't more
> innovative. For some businesses, an incremental innovation is a
> breakthrough, yet others look for real breakthrough ideas. Our
> business has become international, and we spend time in Mos-
> cow, Beijing, Singapore, Munich, Asia, and Europe. The move
> now is to innovate on a global scale.

When Johnston was asked what are the qualities needed
for a good facilitator, his answer sounded very much like those
of his competitors:

> He should be able to understand and master the dynamics of the
> facilitation process to foster higher levels of creativity. He also
> needs to be a great listener, empathetic and sensitive to client
> needs, able to identify insights and unarticulated ideas and have
> a presence. He needs to be credible, capable of working well
> with others, and intelligent. Having expertise in different areas

is helpful. In our firm, we have people with backgrounds in research and development, chemical engineering, financial services, cultural anthropology, and an expert in creative problem solving.

## ROBERT HANIG

Robert Hanig, a principal at Innovation Associates, includes exercises in intuition with each course his firm offers. Innovation Associates is a consulting organization that was begun by Peter Senge, Robert Fritz, and Charlie Kiefer in the 1980s, incorporating the philosophy of Senge's Learning Organization and the work of the other two founders. They are now owned by the Arthur D. Little Company in Cambridge, Massachusetts. Its clients are major corporations around the world, such as BP Oil and the United States government organization, NASA.

What is remarkable about their approach is that cultivating intuition is an integral part of their training. During a three-day Learning Organization seminar, for example, where the subjects covered ranged from systems thinking to how to think critically, there is an intuitive exercise given at the end of each day. Critical thinking is defined as being aware of a tendency to jump to conclusions based on specific events, and then to regard these conclusions as facts. The course objective is to learn how to distinguish correct from incorrect conclusion jumping.

Hanig begins the intuitive part of the learning experience by suggesting that the seminar participants engage in a willing suspension of their disbelief. The reason: if we avoid that which is uncomfortable or strange, we will never learn anything new. Most people feel a great deal of anxiety with any new experience, whether it is going skiing for the first time, or taking a plane trip, or experimenting with a new way of thinking. He understands that for many people the idea of learning anything new pushes the safety net of what feels comfortable too far away.

One exercise Hanig describes is where people are partnered with someone whom they do not know and are asked to go through a "tour" of the other person's home without any coaching. He reports that some people will come up with such accurate details as, "I saw a newly refinished desk in the upstairs bedroom and on it was a green shaded lamp." His unscientific estimate of how many people get "hits" on this kind of intuition is about 70 percent.

Although about 20 percent of the group at the beginning may be uncomfortable with the intuition exercises, by the end of the training session this number is usually reduced to about 5 percent. Why? Possibly because participants have come to learn that intuition works—and that it can be a very powerful part of their world. Hanig observes no difference between senior managers and senior executives in their acceptance or use of intuition. However, he finds that women more readily accept the existence of intuition than men. He also observes that European and Asian people are more open to intuition, which is in line with the data from the published studies referred to in Chapter 11. If there are any differences between men's and women's intuition, it may be in the way that it is received. In the next chapter, women tell their stories. Is their intuition different or is it merely a variation on a theme?

# 17

# The Intuitive Female Mystique

There are many women who head firms that specialize in creative problem solving. Most are either solo practitioners or affiliated with small groups. The following people are a few who are making impressive contributions to the field.

## SHIRA WHITE

Shira White, President of S. P. White, Inc. in New York, finds that "for most people, intuition is not trusted. And so, rather than fighting that, we try to lead people to a path that illuminates and supports their intuitive feelings. Still, some things can never be known as fact: that in itself can be illuminating." S. P. White Inc. is a six-member consulting firm focused on new product development and innovation management.

White tells how she used her gut feelings with one of her clients, a major food products company that was looking to market a new product. To verify their initial marketing strategy, the company assumed that buyers would purchase this product because of the perceived value of its extended shelf life. But when White expressed her feeling that this assumption ought to be questioned, a research project was begun to get the opinions of both industry experts and potential customers. From the interviews, White learned that people were afraid to buy a product with a long shelf life because they feared that it would be filled with undesirable chemicals. Instead, they preferred a food that promised more nutrition, a value the manufacturer had not previously seen as an important factor to induce people to buy the product. White's intuition kept the client company from introducing a product that would have bombed, saving it from a financial disaster.

According to White, the best qualities for a facilitator are curiosity, empathy, creativity, tenacity, clarity, humor, warmth, and a multifaceted intelligence. It would appear that she has many of these qualities, most notably in the diversity of her interests. In addition to having held creative and development positions at advertising agencies such as Ogilvy Mather and Saatchi Grey, she is also an accomplished painter with a large body of work in both corporate and private collections throughout the United States. And, she has founded a not-for-profit organization called Hope Harvest that distributes food surplus to those in need.

## DEBORAH MCCONCHIE

What kind of issues inspire people to call Deborah McConchie, of Bottom Line Consulting in Newton, Massachusetts? Deborah is a management consultant specializing in marketing. Her clients may have problems such as how to improve their sales, how to move from existing customers to new ones, or how to reposition themselves in the marketplace. Sometimes they seek out McConchie's services when they need to manage change with a new product. As she describes it,

> The clients usually appreciate my ability to unearth the real problem within a short time. When a problem is presented to me, I see very quickly that the issue as it is defined by the client may not be the actual problem. How I get to the underlying root is mostly intuitive, and I do it quickly and accurately within a short time. Even when I don't know anything about an industry, my intuition is useful. I do the research following my initial observations, and it usually validates my intuitive understanding.

A case in point. An assignment at Digital Equipment Corp. (DEC) presented McConchie with the problem of how to reverse declining sales of the company's technical training business, particularly from those who had been significant buyers in the past. The problem is how to change the content and marketing of the Technical Training Services. She explained her approach as follows:

> I looked at the way they were positioning the training package and it immediately made no sense to me. I knew the problem was centered on how they were packaging this service, as well as other unmet customer needs. It was a quick intuitive insight that got me to the heart of the problem. Then, I went to their clients to find out what issues about the training program were important to them, as, for example, how they were purchased and delivered. I discovered what the needs of the client were and whether they were being satisfied or not, and I was able to offer specific suggestions on how to vastly improve both the types of services offered and the ways in which they could be purchased.

McConchie eliminated all of DEC's existing programs, which were only contributing about 18 percent of the total revenue of the Education & Training Division. She replaced them with a single comprehensive program that, within four months, accounted for over 50 percent of the Division's total revenue.

When asked how she would define intuition, McConchie replied,

> For me, intuition is when you get a feeling, a sense of knowing what the problem is without knowing a lot of information. I can get the answer faster because I don't need to go on data. Sometimes I sense that the person is the issue and not the product or the marketing approach. In that case it calls for a very different kind of consulting.
>
> Creativity in business is being able to look at a problem differently and come up with a different solution. Seeing the problem in a different light is creative but not necessarily effective. When it is effective, it is usually intuitive as well. It's also true that some people have great luck and great instincts, or perhaps they have great instincts and just plain luck!

Do clients trust her instantaneous intuitive analysis? "It depends on the relationship with the client. If they brought me in and believe I will help them by offering a perspective that they did not have before, they will; others who are less familiar with the way I work will wait for the proof."

## LYNN SCHWEIKART

Lynn Schweikart, of LKS Creative Counsel Associates in Boston, Massachusetts, creates advertising on a freelance basis. "The creative process begins," she says, "with a good deal of product research." Then she tries to get into the mind of the consumer, taking on a character as an actor does before she plays the part, until she gets some fragments of thoughts about the product down on paper. Then, she gets away from it by doing something physical that doesn't require a lot of thought, such as gardening, playing the piano, or kneading bread. At times, what she finds most effective is taking a nap, when ideas spring up out of a dream. "I put ideas down on paper and look for what sparks a connection to find the thread that becomes the ad."

What keeps good ideas from blossoming into great ads? In Schweikart's view, it is "corporate politics, jockeying for position and power, and the need to be safe." Her answer supports the conventional wisdom that what is already known is perceived as safer, yet relying on safety often becomes more deadly to innovation than risking the unknown.

## NANCY GUST

Nancy Gust, President of Stage One in Medford, Massachusetts, uses considerable intuitive skills in her work as a market research consultant to test new products, being involved both during and after several stages of evaluation. The evaluation process begins by asking a lot of questions such as: What's out there already? Are people happy with it? Is there an established need? Which needs are most hot, most widespread? "We do qualitative research and quantitative surveys and occasionally test with prototypes in focus groups," she explained.

When does Gust know that her intuition is kicking in? She says that she gets a real gut reaction, that her body actually gets excited and ideas resonate with a visceral response. When she speaks, it is usually in analogies or metaphors, which is often the language of intuition. She relates how her intuition came into play in figuring out how to resolve a problem in connection with the introduction of a new Polaroid camera.

Polaroid wanted to know if the instruction booklet that came with this new camera would be clear enough for the average person to understand. The problem: how could she create a focus group to reveal this information without exposing the group to the research objectives? Her first reaction was, "they want me to run a focus group with each person reading the instruction booklet and then telling me whether it was clear? I didn't think that would give them the answers they were looking for," Gust said. "I felt that the focus group needed to know what kind of information was necessary in the directions, and this could only be ascertained by using the cameras."

Then Gust hit upon a clever idea. She decided to use about two dozen people individually in their homes as her focus group. She invited a pantomimist to come to each home and act out various roles while the subjects were asked to take her picture with the camera. By combining a picture-taking opportunity with the antics of a lighthearted romp into fantasy by a white-faced actor, she was able to take the pressure off the people in the focus group to do well in their picture-taking task. Also, since they were able to take pictures in the privacy of their own homes, there was no competition with others as to their skills in using the camera or in understanding how to operate it. As a result, she accessed information from these "photographers" and received many suggestions on how to modify the camera to make it more user friendly, although, this finding had not been a goal of the study. The result was that the camera should be constructed to be more intuitive, so that only a glance will reveal how it was to be used. Now, the instruction booklet had become nearly irrelevant; the camera would say it all.

Gust's experience turned out to be a case where the company was trying to solve the wrong problem. Although, the presenting issue was, "How do we write better directions for camera use"? The answer revealed another question, which was, "How do we design a camera that needs little to no directions?"

# Conclusion

Each of these external consultants finds that reliance on his or her own intuition is absolutely essential. Whether intuition is used in spotting a trend or a new product, or in being able to elicit ideas from a reluctant group of executives, it is an indispensable element for success. How large a part it plays in achieving their goals probably varies, depending on the consultant, the client, and the situation.

An interesting observation made by several consultants was that very often the best ideas came from beginners, that is, people who were not knowledgeable in that area. It would seem that this "beginners mind" relies on intuition more than logic, since they do not have any technical expertise upon which to draw in these areas. Therefore, they do not come into the project knowing what is or is not possible.

While this is an interesting theory and often mentioned in Zen teachings, Professor Ellen Langer at Harvard University tested the theory. She and Itiel Dror conducted three experiments to test whether prior knowledge affected creative performance. Earlier research had established that certain kinds of previously learned information can restrict creativity. In Langer and Dror's experiments, undergraduate participants, divided into two groups, were asked to build a bridge over an imaginary river. They were given small custom-made blocks and told that the height of the bridge would determine the size of the boats that could use the river; thus, the higher the bridge, the better.

One group of students was shown examples of how the blocks could be used in a different building task. The other group was given no instruction nor prior exposure to the blocks, nor were they told how to use them. Ninety-two percent of the group that were shown how to use the blocks used them in formations identical to the ones that they had been shown, whereas, only 8 percent of the other group that were not shown how to use the blocks used these same formations. The group that was taught how to use the blocks came up with two solutions; the second group came up with ten! These results were replicated in two other experiments. Their hypothesis was that the group shown examples would have difficulty forgetting those examples, and this was confirmed.

Hamel and Prahalad also write on this theme. They suggest that "when it comes to creating the future, one wide-eyed innocent may be worth ten sophisticated scenario planners." They give as examples the unpredictable successes of the Polaroid camera and Swatch watches from ideas that were not only contrary to conventional wisdom but regarded as naïve; to think that film could be developed in a camera or relatively inexpensive Swiss watches with creative faces would find such a tremendous market was considered, by the experts, absurd.

In Part Six, you will meet another variety of consultant. They work mostly one-on-one, sometimes in groups. Often they have had very little background in business, yet they have been known to deliver extraordinary information, insight, and even strategic direction to their corporate clients. Some are known as intuitives, others are called psychics.

# PART SIX

## *Intuitive and Psychic Practitioners*

> The intellect has little to do on the road to discovery. There comes a leap in consciousness, call it intuition or what you will, and the solution comes to you and you don't know how or why.
>
> ...ALBERT EINSTEIN

Some professional intuitors refer to themselves as intuition consultants, others are known as psychics. Their names are not well-known to the general public, although they are quite well-known among a select group of like-minded individuals. They represent a growing number of people who consult with organizations for the specific task of engaging their own or their client's intuition to solve a wide variety of problems, whether related to team building, new product development, marketing strategies, or executive selection.

Most intuitive practitioners work with their clients on a one-on-one basis or in small groups. Their techniques focus on the three major receptors for intuition: images and symbols, feelings and emotions, and physical sensations. They use a variety of methods to access the solution while in a relaxed or meditative state and their accomplishments are often nothing less than astonishingly accurate.

What is the difference between an intuitive and a psychic consultant? It is often a very fine, almost imperceptible line. Both appear to get accurate, yet apparently unknowable information out of thin air. While the intuitive consultant may use some interactive methods, such as visualization techniques, the psychics generally do not. Instead, they appear to go into a slightly altered state of mind in which they turn on their receptors to receive information: they are mediums who deliver messages.

Those who consult as psychics seem to be gifted in something like clairvoyance, and for these individuals the rewards are both spiritual and monetary. Corporations pay them at the rate of a top-level consultant to tap into their precognizant powers. Most psychics say that they first became aware of this ability some time during their childhood. Some describe their early years as ones in which they grew up in a dysfunctional family and experienced a frequent need to escape into another world.

In *Your Sixth Sense*, Belleruth Naparstek gives a composite view of a "typical" psychic. She would be in her mid-forties, have an advanced degree in one of the mental health professions, and would say that she was born with her psychic ability. Other traits that she may have include a tendency toward bilateral dominance, that is, being able to use both right and left hands fairly well; some talent or experience in the arts, often in more than one, such as music, dance, theater, poetry, art, or design; a tendency to being either a little dyslexic or else an exceptional student, sometimes both. She would also spend a lot of time in nature and have a tendency to experience a temporary endocrine system dysfunction from time to time, that is, an over- or under-functioning thyroid gland or set of adrenals. She might be a night owl and sleep very little or with frequent interruptions, and have an above-average chance of having sighted a UFO or encountering an extraterrestrial.

However, Naparstek is quick to point out that many psychics whom she interviewed had none of these characteristics, and some are even male rather than female. All of this is to say that if you do not have any of these characteristics, you, like many others, may still be able to develop psychic abilities.

If we look at the work of the physicist David Bohm, we can see that there is psychic potential for all of us. Naparstek explains Bohm's theory as follows:

> His system reconciles relativity theory and quantum theory and is becoming more and more widely accepted and developed the world over. It describes how we are, at the most basic levels, unrestricted nonlocal beings, in spite of our current primitive concrete ideas about space and distance. It tells us that time can be only something that happens in the present and how, in spite of our artificial constructs of past and future, we are really beings who live in a lot of parallel, concurrent nows . . .
>
> Bohm's central thesis is that the world and everything in it is a vast ocean of energy. What we perceive as separate parts— you, me, the chair, the dog, the trees, the air we breathe—are all part of a seamless whole (the holomovement) that is pulsing with life and intelligence. He calls this ocean of living energy the implicate order because it cannot be seen (or measured, except mathematically), only inferred . . . We and everything around us are made up of this energy, which in a subtle but very real sense, is conscious and alive. . . . The energy of the implicate order is pure movement. It is vibration, loaded with potential for manifesting itself in an infinite array of forms. . . . Our visible, palpable three-dimensional world is derived from the multidimensional reality. . . . Everything in our world consists of this teeming, vibrating system of conscious energy, all around, between and through everything.

It is the psychic and intuitive who have learned how to tune into these pulsing vibrations of energy, and if this theory is correct, it is available to all of us.

# The Intuitive Consultants

When you read the following brief descriptions of the wide ranging skills of the intuitive consultants, you will get a sense of the unusual accomplishments they achieve with their clients.

## LAURIE NADEL

Laurie Nadel, Ph.D., co-author of *Sixth Sense* and creator of the "High Performance Thinking Program," concentrates on the very tangible aspects of her clients lives. She helps them to be better at their work, whether it is a business issue, such as strategic planning, or a personal challenge, such as overcoming a fear of cold calling. She is a seminar leader for the American Management Association and her clients range from managers to executives, some employed in Fortune 500 companies. Their questions range from, "How do I get more sales?" to "How can I change my thinking to be more effective?" to "How do I tune into my inner resources?" In the course of her work, Nadel helps her clients understand the images generated by the right brain in response to specific problems and opportunities. She uses many techniques, some of which come from a self-actualization system called neurolinguistic programming (NLP), a personal growth technology developed over twenty years ago that combines neuropsychology (brain research) with linguistics. Many of the NLP techniques are designed to assist in accessing the intuitive or subconscious mind.

An example of how she works is demonstrated by the client who asked, "Why do I not like cold calling?" She will then ask in return, "Why do you think you don't like cold calling?" If the response is "I don't know," she then would follow that with questions such as, "If you did know the answer to that question, what would your answer be?" This is a form of indirect hypnotic language that speaks to the intuitive part of the brain and goes directly to the unconscious mind. Its function is to bypass the left side of the brain that tends to censor experience and proceed directly to the right side of the brain that understands the feelings involved in the problem.

For example, a stockbroker client said, "I feel like I have a big black cloud of anxiety hovering over me." The method she used to help him get over his anxiety is similar to a progressive desensitization approach where one gets closer and closer to the hated image in order to accept it without undue anxiety. She urged him to talk to the cloud, whereupon the cloud told him that he did not like to make cold calls. Next, she told him to picture the person on the other end of the telephone being bigger than himself and then put that person on his imaginary screen. She then asks him to describe what he is thinking as he looks at the person on the screen. He says, "The person is unfriendly." Now she asks if he can push the movie screen further away, making the image of the person smaller in size to neutralize his fear response. Gradually, after reducing his fear, he began to feel more confident in making the calls and gained control over his anxiety. After only one session with Nadel, he went back to the office with his fear overcome and ultimately received a promotion based on his increased effectiveness in cold calling.

When she works with developing teams for specific areas, such as teaching a technical group how to interface with customers, Nadel begins with the Myers Briggs Type Indicator (MBTI), which was discussed in Chapter 10. On the first day, each person learns the personality composition of the team. During the second day, there is self-assessment and role playing of one's opposite personality types. Each team member learns how other personality types like to be rewarded, and how to use their own intuition to read people better by observing behavioral cues. For example, they learn that sensor types are more comfortable with details, but the more intuitive types tend to use a "fly by the seat of the pants" modus operandi, having little to no patience for details. Once they learn how the various behavior patterns are played out, they are able to understand others better, as well as themselves, and know who is more or less likely to be intuitive.

Nadel's clients include people who work in banks, auditors, and vice presidents. They, too, want to become better able to trust their intuition by learning how to detect patterns in behavior so that they better understand where the other person is coming from. Once understood, it makes their interactions far more productive.

She defines intuition as being able to "see" relationships—making them consciously visible, "Intuition permits the right brain to see patterns in bits of information that are invisible to the left brain." For her, intuition is unconscious and spontaneous; creativity, on the other hand, is sometimes conscious, although it can be spontaneously intuitive as well.

When she was asked whether intuition is always right, she replied,

> If you are sure of your personal signals, whether it's butterflies in your stomach, or having the conviction that you know it, then it is right for that moment. When you learn to trust your interpretation of these signals, it will become more available to you. As we get older and more experienced, we can become more skilled at using our intuition.

## JOHN PEHRSON

John Pehrson, with Sue Mehrtens, author of *Intuitive Imagery: A Resource at Work,* has experienced many unusual ways of knowing in his life. He is an organizational development consultant who had worked for twenty years at the DuPont Corporation as a manager in one of its polymer producing plants. One of his responsibilities was to encourage employees to become more creative by offering courses that stimulated creative thinking. In his work as a consultant, he incorporates intuitive imaging processes whenever possible.

Working with salespeople in one assignment, he taught them how to use their intuition to screen raw, unqualified sales leads before calling on the company. With their insights gained from Pehrson's methodology, they were able to deduce which companies would be more likely to be buyers and which would offer the least opportunity to make a sale. When the probability of the company purchasing the product was regarded as at least 60 percent, the salespeople would make the first telephone call. This assessment proved to be correct about 80 percent of the time. When there was only a 40 percent probability that the targeted customers would buy, the salespeople declined to approach them, ascertaining from their intuitive imaging that it would most likely be a waste of time. The obvious question is, how would they know if the potential customer in the 40 percent range would not buy, if they were never approached? The answer is that the group unanimously "knew" through a "blind" intuitive technique (that will be described later) that approaching those companies would be a waste of time.

For a group of top-level DuPont executives who had important questions for which there was little or no data available, Pehrson constructed a creative session to reach their intuition by using a collage of computer-generated images on video set to music. He asked the group members to write down their thoughts as they watched the video. Then he suggested that they ask a question they wanted answered and to link it to these video-inspired thoughts. In ninety minutes, the group confirmed what it had suspected as problems existing in the company, and this helped them to develop new insights into important issues. Using this technique in 1990 in relation to larger economic issues, the DuPont group surmised that the economy would take a dive the following year. This insight prepared them for the recession that occurred one year later, and for the layoffs that soon followed.

What is Pehrson's success rate in getting people to experience deeper insights? He says it is upwards of 75 percent. However, some of those 25 percent for whom this practice was not successful included people who felt that the methods they experienced for getting information were contrary to their fundamental religious beliefs; they became angry and walked out—despite their own on-target insights.

This behavior became an interesting learning experience in the psychology of belief. If your own experience shakes your belief because you "know" it cannot happen, then you will discredit your own experience rather than your belief. For some people, there is too much anxiety involved in being asked to alter an opinion, because these deep-seated beliefs give stability to their lives. For some, to be wrong or mistaken in their fundamental beliefs is tantamount to admitting that for years "I have been living in naïveté or a lie." Their self-image cannot or will not accept this. It is as if they were saying, "I feel safer in trusting the words of the authority than my own experience. Therefore, my own experience must be mistaken because the authority that I believe in is correct; if not, why would I continue to believe?" This makes sense when one's sense of identity is closely tied to religious or other beliefs and it often becomes a convenient "authority" to disparage or reject the validity of intuitive or psychic insights. For others, their "religion" is the logic of what can be seen, heard, or verified. If they experience a glimpse of the "unknowable," this shakes their faith in the logic that holds one cannot know the future because it hasn't happened yet.

## NANCY ROSANOFF

Nancy Rosanoff is another consultant who uses intuition in her work. She is also the author of *The Intuition Workout*. Rosanoff works with individuals at all levels of the organization, with the main focus on upper management, innovation teams, new product development, and strategic planning teams. Some of her recent clients include McGraw Hill Broadcasting and Oscar Mayer.

In Rosanoff's experience, everyone is intuitive:

> The only difference I find is that the higher the level of the executive in a company, the chances are that more intuition is expressed; for the lower-level worker there seems to be less permission to use or acknowledge their intuition. However, I see a big cultural shift coming with people who are now in their 20s, 30s, and 40s, who, when they move into the top positions, should bring about a change in the general attitudes toward intuition. I remember hearing Peter Senge say, "Death is on our side," which was meant to suggest that eventually the people who hold the outdated values will be gone, allowing the younger people to follow and prevail.

Rosanoff believes that when you get intuitive insights into a problem it can be solved far more rapidly, especially in cases where logic alone seems ineffective. Some of her clients solved problems using their own intuition within a matter of hours. It is interesting to note that for many consultants who see part of their role as tapping into a client's intuition, they get results far more quickly than most others—from Bryan Mattimore who helps clients discover breakthrough new product ideas in one day, to Nancy Rosanoff who has penetrated through long-held barriers in as little as twenty minutes. Contrast this with other consultants who take several days, weeks, or even months to get "logical" answers that often prove to be inferior to those intuitively-generated.

Here is an example of Rosanoff's quick-result approach. She was asked to consult with Inset Systems Software, Inc. to solve a team-building problem. She was told at the outset that the software developers were finding it difficult to work together as a team. She began the process by asking each of them to describe the methods for designing a new software program. Each team member described the work as beginning with an intuitive insight and then completing the project using logical expertise. In twenty minutes they discovered that since they all worked the same way, the real issue was the management style of their supervisor, which worked against their functioning as a team. The crux of the problem was discovered almost immediately, and the rest of the morning was spent discussing how they could work as a team despite their manager's misguided interventions.

Another of Rosanoff's intuitive techniques is to have a group of participants imagine their problem as a seed that they plant in the ground. They are asked to watch the seed come up and observe the forces that play on the sprouting plant as it pushes up from the earth. This technique worked extraordinarily well with a problem at Boxtree Communications Company, an advertising agency that was having difficult in successfully pitching an ad to a new client. There were six people in the problem-solving group. Of the six, only four were aware of the problem involved with presenting their services to the client. The other two had no idea of the problem. When Rosanoff suggested that they "plant the problem seed and watch it grow" one of the two "outsiders" who had no inkling of the real issues, saw the plant sprout two medieval knights, complete with armor, astride horses and engaged in a jousting match. This, it turned out, indicated the root of the problem. It seemed that the client company consisted of two partners, each fighting for control of the firm. When it was realized that the problem lay in the potential client's partnership rather than in how the agency's skills were presented, Boxtree was better able to concentrate on an appropriate approach. This is also an example of "beginner's intuition."

Boxtree also asked Rosanoff to assist in deciding on an advertising promotion idea. The system she used to engage their intuition in this session was somewhat different. She had them write three different possible scenarios for an ad campaign on three note cards and then shuffle the cards. Then they were to take each card with the face down, look at the blank side of each card and "see" an imaginary graph on each one. The directions of the lines in the graph would indicate whether the idea on the reverse side of the card, of which they had no knowledge, was either good (line going up), bad (line going down), or not strong (line staying flat). When the group combined the visions of each member, it knew which proposal would be the most successful because each member of the group chose the one card where they had seen the line in the graph heading up. Further checking with several other techniques verified the initial results. By combining all the information, one of the options became a clear choice, and this became their successful ad campaign.

When Rosanoff was asked whether intuition improves with experience or as you get older, she replied,

> Not necessarily. Mathematicians are extremely intuitive when they come up with solutions, and they are usually over the hill in their mathematics careers by age twenty-five. Education and experience are a minor part of intuition. When we get older we tend to trust it more, and we validate it with experience because our experience tells us that it works.

Is intuition always correct? In Rosanoff's view, "It is more often [correct] in the short term, but tends to be more difficult in the long term. Intuition functions in a completely different way from analytic thinking. Analytically, there can be a right or wrong way. Intuitively there are many equally right ways to go." Apparently, when you focus on achieving a specific goal or set of goals, for that moment the appropriate action will emerge intuitively relative to the immediate resources and opportunities. "Once a plan of action has been decided upon, generally it is beneficial to stick with that plan," she says.

I posed a perplexing question to Rosanoff: If intuition is natural for everyone, what prevents so many of us from using it? Rosanoff answers this question by relating a story. She had delivered a speech to a group of business executives. Later, after her talk, six out of seven people who worked at the same company came up to her, one by one, and told her that their company was about to release a product that they knew would fail, but none of them had expressed this view at the decision-making meeting because they had no solid data to back them up. This was a gut feeling that six of the seven people shared, not with each other, but with Rosanoff alone. Why didn't they share this premonition among themselves? Because there is a strong pressure at work to back up what you say with data, and tremendous peer pressure; no one would say that it just didn't feel right (without documentation) and expect to have that statement fly. Their company lost over $1,000,000 because of this decision. It could have been avoided if the company's culture supported the expressing of gut feelings.

Rosanoff believes there are two basic difficulties with using or trusting intuition. The first has to do with the level of anxiety triggered by confusion and uncertainty. All of us experience anxiety, but to different degrees. People whose anxiety is easily aroused by ambiguity or lack of precision will protect themselves from any thinking that is not based on fact. Speculation, guessing, ambiguity, or hypothesizing can arouse instant discomfort, especially for sensor/judger types who are particularly uncomfortable with ambiguity. The fear of being wrong leads them to insist on a decision in many situations where a good outcome is not predictable on available data. Not so coincidentally, many of these people have risen close to the top because they have avoided mistakes by proceeding with logical analysis only and no risk taking.

They do what worked in the past. Being in the majority at the management level, they create a climate that tends to punish thinking that cannot be supported by facts, and they distrust the validity of intuitive insights. This tendency may be industry specific, however, since many industries today are clamoring for innovation and cannot permit the status quo to persist for lack of intuitive thinking.

The second difficulty in accepting and using intuition is rooted in emotional need. Intuition can be distorted or blocked entirely by emotions such as fear, anger, jealousy, and so on. For example, if someone is desperate to win at a horse race because she needs the money, that emotional charge may well block the ability to be in touch with the right brain image that can whisper the name of the potential winner. Likewise, the stakes in new product development are almost always high. Similarly, the emotional pressure to be right can easily obscure the signals of intuition.

Another problem is that we get too attached to results. Intuition focuses on the next step, and it is usually correct for the next moment. Perhaps the reason why so many people say that they trust their intuition more as they get older is because when we are younger we are often more caught up with fears and desires that can mask intuitive insights. "Sometimes," Rosanoff says, "when you experience failure it is telling you that there is another reason to pay attention to your intuition. It may be telling you that you need to learn something." The "something" could be to begin to do what you believe is right, and sometimes this can clash with what others expect of you.

## MARCIA EMERY

Marcia Emery is an intuition consultant and the author of *The Intuition Workbook* and the Nightingale Conant audio cassette series, *Intuition: How to Use Your Gut Instinct for Greater Personal Power*. Emery has many methods that she uses to help clients tap into their intuition. One, called the "Mind Shift," helps clients shift their awareness away from the logical mind to receive insights from the intuitive mind. Her groups learn how to meditate and breathe so that they can lower their brain waves from the Beta to the Alpha level, while encouraging logic and intuition to flow together. She defines intuition as a clear knowing that goes beyond the logical and the rational: intuition is not emotional and the emotional is not intuitive. "You know it is intuitive when you get a feeling of contentment in your body," Emery says. "I feel completely balanced when it's intuitive. If my body is restless and fidgety, then it is out of balance and I know that it is emotion, not intuition."

One emotional block to our intuition, she adds, is wishful thinking, sometimes defined as hoping that what appeals to us emotionally will be the correct choice. For example, some people make hiring decisions by offering the job to someone who is extremely good looking but unqualified. To rationalize this choice, they say they know "intuitively" that this person will learn quickly and master the job. If that happens and the new hire works out well, they say they knew it intuitively. If the person does not perform to expectations, then they may blame their intuition for being faulty; in either case the decision was not necessarily intuitive, but based upon emotional or sexual desire.

Another emotional block to accessing your intuition is believing a negative self-fulfilling prophecy. For example, being told as a child that you would never amount to much in life often produces underachievers. If a good job offer came along, you may feel that you would fail at it and refuse to take it. When one relies on this kind of thinking, it leaves intuition unavailable to inform you of how to make the best choices. However, there are exceptions to the downward spiral that listening to a self-fulfilling prophecy can create. Larry Ellison is one of them. When he was ten years old, and many times thereafter, he was told by his father that he never would amount to anything. Fortunately, he did not buy into that. Today, at the age of 52, he is America's second richest software tycoon, next to Bill Gates, and worth about $8 billion as a 22 percent owner of the software giant Oracle Corporation.

Other emotional blocks to intuition are fear, anxiety, fatigue, and depression. Whenever these are present, intuition may be absent. Emery also cites projection as another culprit that interferes with intuition. For example, if you need a vacation yet insist that your friend really needs it and should take it, you have projected your own desire to escape onto him; this is not intuition, it is projection.

During Emery's twelve years of experience teaching courses in intuition at Aquinas College in Michigan, she found that many of her students used the methods learned in her course to solve some of their problems at work. In *The Intuition Workbook*, she relates the story of one student:

> Kim finds herself in a dilemma over a pricing problem that has had her stumped for several weeks. All the pricing methods and procedures are so different that she is unable to develop a record layout and supporting file structure to handle all the variations. Kim states her problem as follows: "How do I handle the pricing problem for the manufacturing project I am designing for a client?" She begins by affirming that her intuitive mind has the answer and will help her find the right solutions . . . In the process she gets the image of a baby bottle. Using a method similar to mindmapping, she began associating to the baby bottle and thinks of such things as, baby, milk, formula, food, etc.
>
> Formula is the word symbol that seems to fit her pricing problems. She had not thought of using the pricing formulas to drive the file structure . . . Formulas, the arithmetic kind, not the baby food variety, can be used to handle all the different pricing relationships. The records can all be the same format, while the formulas could be used to handle the variability.
>
> Kim described her results: "I can't express how important this formula discovery is. I have spent so much time trying to figure this problem out. I only wish I had used the intuitive problem-solving process earlier. I have laid out the necessary structure for the project and our data base administrator has approved the layout. He even questioned me on how I was able to come up with such a creative idea!"

## CHERYL GILMAN

"I use intuition in getting to know clients, listening at a certain level," says Cheryl Gilman, a career consultant and author in the Boston area. She describes this process as follows:

> When my clients come to ask about a career, I will ask questions to get them to tune into their own intuition, such as, "What's missing in your life?" It usually has to do with having more meaningful time, seeing more beauty, deepening relationships. I ask them to discover what it is that they really love. What do they love doing? Creativity is an act of love, trusting ourselves, making it safe. Sometimes it's seen as eccentric, but we often stifle our creativity with old tapes running through our heads, or the need to be liked, or feeling we must follow parent's expectations.

Gilman tells of one client, a burnt-out therapist looking for another career. She asked her, "what do you love?" The therapist replied, "I love color. It makes me happy. I also love shopping and I found some beautiful rugs in Arizona." Thinking about putting together her love for color, shopping, and rugs, she decided to become a rug merchant. She took courses in business while continuing to work as a therapist and began planning for what would in time feed her soul. Two years later she had created SouthWest Weavers, a thriving rug business in the Boston area.

Gilman advises that another way to use your intuition in finding a career is to go to a magazine rack and see what jumps out at you:

> See what articles you are attracted to and watch yourself as an impartial observer. When you come up with an idea, tell someone about it so that it will crystallize in your mind. The problem with using gut only, it's a sixth sense, and we are afraid to rely on it because most of us aren't trained to use intuition. You check, double-check, what you think; go with the gut; and then verify what is good for you.

The answer then will appear.

Another exercise she gives clients comes from Julia Cameron's, *The Artist Within*.

> Write three pages first thing in the morning, every morning with your coffee. Keep writing about anything that pops into your head no matter how mundane, i.e., "I must remember to pick up at the cleaners," or, "I am still feeling angry over that argument I had last night with B.," or, "I must remember to call Paul and thank him for that tip". . . until you get to at least three pages, keeping your hand constantly moving. Then, put it away, not to be read for at least three weeks. When you finally read it, you will get an eye opener! You will see thoughts and ideas that you may not have been aware of that were distilled during sleep and recorded in the morning before they were lost forever.

It is interesting to note that, like Bob Johnston of IdeaScope, Gilman makes use of the unconscious mind's wisdom during sleep to reveal thoughts and ideas the following morning.

## MARY ANN CLUGGISH

Mary Ann Cluggish is an independent consultant in sales training to high-tech and service organizations. By the first meeting with a client, Cluggish says she knows at least 50 percent of the time whether he will ultimately buy her services. When she gets these insights she is correct nearly 100 percent of the time. She also feels that she is far more intuitive now than she was at a younger age—or perhaps she has learned to trust it more.

In addition to training salespeople, Cluggish has also been able to forecast revenues for a company with an accuracy of 90 percent or better. She attributes this skill to a combination of experience and intuition, which creates a synergy that allows for greater insights. For example, she may predict an event by looking at specific facts and seeing their probable effect, although she does not attribute this skill to having extraordinary insight. It may be that her intuitive mind sees a particular pattern that suggests an action to follow. However, when her client does not understand why she makes specific predictions, she believes that they do not see the same patterns, are not clearly recognizing the causes of the problem, or do not believe, granting the cause, that what she predicts will occur. Enter Cluggish, who informs them that, "If this occurs, this will follow." This "insight" is sometimes acknowledged but at other times resisted until the reality of the "what follows" actually comes to pass.

This is not unlike the method investor extraordinaire George Soros uses. As William Shawcross wrote in *Time* in 1997,

> Soros' Quantum Fund makes money by anticipating economic shifts around the world. In 1992 Soros thought the British pound would lose value because of political and economic pressures. [Here Soros is seeing a pattern of causes to a future event.] He borrowed billions of British pounds and converted them to German marks. One week later the pound collapsed. Soros repaid the loan with interest and pocketed the difference. His profit: $1 billion.

While Soros's style may be seen more as that of a gutsy gambler than an intuitive, especially since he has lost huge amounts of money in similar ventures, it would appear that there is more than mere logic associated with most of his moves. If his balance sheet shows far more gains than losses, even considering the many millions of dollars he donates to other countries around the world—exceeding in some cases the contributions made to them by the United States—there must be something else, like intuitive knowing, that has been a mostly accurate guide for his wildly successful investments.

Cluggish said that her intuitive insights became more apparent to her about five years ago, when she was one of a group of six high-pressured career women renting a home for the winter in Truro, Massachusetts on Cape Cod. In the winter the Cape is cold, windy, and deserted, with few people and fewer distractions. In the solitude of walking on windy sand dunes or listening to the ocean's slapping waves, she began to listen to herself. Watching the ocean's spectacular moodiness, she could at last hear her inner voice, and so was born an appreciation of her own intuition. For some people, getting away from everyday responsibilities and experiencing a period of solitude brings a greater depth to understanding the wisdom of the intuitive mind. Like the plains Indians who went out into the desert for several days on a vision quest, Cluggish also found an inner knowing through solitude.

## GIGI VAN DECKTER

When some of the world's largest corporations want to know how to construct a deal in a practical and productive way, what investments to make or which candidates to place in key positions, or when they want an executive coach to help them balance their personal and private lives, they call Gigi Van Deckter, an organizational consultant based in New York. They call her to Japan, Italy, Germany, and France as well as a number of cities in the United States.

A Silicon Valley chip maker, for example, was looking for a strategic partner. The company had two choices: either allow a large company to buy them out or align themselves with a smaller manufacturer to expand their marketing base. Using her intuition by acting on the signals she received, Van Deckter advised them to make a deal with the smaller company, despite the fact that if the larger company had bought them out, the client would have realized a significant profit. But the chip making company acted on her advice and ultimately became far more successful than it could have predicted, even though the move went against a formulaic business model.

Van Deckter has also advised companies on the future vision of the company and where to find capital. Again, her method is to allow the wisdom to flow into her. Her areas of expertise are not industry specific. She has also successfully filled a unique niche in being able to answer staffing questions by advising companies not only which job candidates would work out best in their organization, but also informs them of which type of manager would work best with the new hires.

## BARBARA SCHULTZ

Barbara Schultz is an organization consultant in California who draws her methodology from an intuitive model that she calls "The Corporate Body." Her objective is to balance the tangible aspects of her clients' experience with the intangible, more intuitive parts of their lives. She relates how a hospital administrator noticed that although his organization appeared to be doing well in terms of efficiency and profit, through Schultz's model he became aware of the fact that the organization was lagging well behind in creating an environment where the less tangible elements of community, heartfelt caring, and, oddly enough, healing, could advance. Once he was able to see these intangible factors, he was able to address the specific problem areas and make the necessary changes to improve the caring quality of the organization.

The methods described above represent a small sample of intuitive approaches toward problem solving, where the client's own intuition is tapped to find a unique solution. In the following chapter you will read about the psychic consultants who use their own abilities, rather than the client's, to offer solutions.

# 19

# *The Psychic Consultants*

Intelligence highly awakened is intuition, which is the only true
guide in life.

...KRISHNAMURTI

Exploring and developing our own intuition may be enough
for most of us, but what happens when you rev it up one more
notch, or maybe several notches into warp speed? This may be
the process that leads to becoming psychic. What is the difference between intuitive and psychic knowledge? One difference
is that intuitives appear to get their knowledge either from a
sudden insight or with the use of insight-generating tools such
as cards, pendulums, and so forth. They are also able to see
larger patterns forming and intuitively know what will happen
in the future as a result of these patterns.

Psychics, on the other hand, seem to be able to read auras,
that electrical field around us that is invisible until you learn how
to see it. They see pictures of your past, present, and future in
these auras. Or, they may have spirit guides who whisper the
information into their consciousness. Whatever the system, they

appear to be tuned into another source of knowledge that is actually different from the intuitive's, yet may deliver similar insights.

While "psychics" are held in some disrepute because they are often identified with fortune tellers, palm readers, and the psychic hotlines advertised on television, the truth is that a number of people seem to be gifted with this skill, some from early childhood. Many psychics say that we are all born with this ability, but some are more "tuned in" than others. For example, we all have the ability to throw a ball or play a musical instrument, but some are better at it than others—and the difference is not simply one of practice. The talented athlete is born with the talent and with practice can become outstanding. So, too, the psychic. One psychic healer revealed that when she was about six or seven years old she noticed the auras around some of her relatives as they sat around the dining room table. She would then ask her mother why Auntie Anne was orange and Uncle Ed was purple. Her mother was baffled by these questions. A similar story is told by psychic Sonia Choquette; she describes how her mother, at age 12, was able to survive Nazi death camps by listening to a voice that told her what to do every time danger approached. If you have a reading from a reputable psychic whom you have never met before, you will be surprised at the specific, very personal information that he or she can reveal about you.

For example, I had a reading with psychic Lloyd Sheldon Johnson. He told me a number of things about myself, including the following, which were all true: that I needed to repair a floor in my house; that I would be going on a business trip soon; and that I was the type of person who was always working on two or more projects at once. He also pointed out that I was concerned with my hands and asked if I was using a computer. I did have a painful hand at the time, and its cause stemmed from an excess number of hours at the keyboard.

What I have learned, however, is that each psychic operates on a different wave length. My consultation with Margo Schultz, a psychic who counsels executives in the Boston area, revealed none of the things that Johnson did, but told me what would be happening in my professional life and where I would be traveling. She also noted a physical problem and offered a remedy, although this problem did not concern the hand. While Johnson seemed to be reading my thoughts and giving them back to me, Margo Schultz read my future, which was completely unknown to me. Although one of her predictions has already occurred, I will have to wait about a year to see whether the other predictions will also come true.

It appears that each psychic follows a different pathway to penetrate into a mysterious world of past, present, and future. Each of their insights may be partially or mostly correct, and each psychic focuses on a different theme. Some say that they have guides or angels that assist in their visioning; others say that they simply see images that reveal past lives or the future. Whatever their system, the talented psychics are generally 80 to 90 percent accurate, and many corporations find their services indispensable.

## BARBARA COURTNEY

The psychic consultant Barbara Courtney, otherwise known as the Seer of Silicon Valley, offers her services to individuals as well as corporations and is listed as a business consultant in the book *100 Top Psychics in America*, by Paulette Cooper and Paul Noble. She has clients in Europe, Japan, and the United States who call her frequently to get insights on crucial decisions affecting their businesses, or to get a read on the future of their net sales, or to receive advice on personal or family problems. Dr. Gabriela Hilberg, a psychotherapist in San Francisco, refers many of her clients to Courtney to identify the source of their problems prior to entering into therapy. Courtney has also been one of the invited speakers at the Commonwealth Club of San Francisco, an organization that invites world leaders to address its ranks. A few years ago, she and the chief economist at the Bank of America spoke to this group to predict future economic trends. The economist based his forecast on extensive research. Courtney based hers on what felt right to her. A year later it was observed that both she and the economist were 80 percent accurate in their predictions.

Courtney works with organizations such as Apple, Hewlett Packard, and IBM, and includes among her clients their CEOs, executives, programmers, financial analysts, and attorneys. However, because of the general feeling of cynicism about psychics in this country, the companies who hire her do not always tell their employees that she is a psychic. "They call me their 'vision consultant,'" she says.

Two years ago, in an interview with the *San Francisco Examiner*, Courtney predicted, among other things, the collapse of the TCI-Bell Atlantic merger, the Apple Computer-Sun Microsystems acquisition flap, and Microsoft's wrangle with the Justice Department in 1995. She was uncannily accurate in her predictions of the above events, but she was also wrong about predicting an IBM-Apple partnership. Still, her 80 percent batting average compares favorably to the accuracy rates of professional analysts.

Her record notwithstanding, Courtney says, "I would not want anyone to make any life and death decisions based on what I say." Yet what she has said has prevented many people from unwittingly failing. One such experience involved a company that had invented a new product and was seeking venture capital to proceed to the next leg of product introduction. Courtney told them that their invention still had some kinks to be worked out, and she advised the company to concentrate on this first. This advice was not what they wanted to hear, so they approached other people who knew the business, but got the same message Courtney had given them. Only then were they persuaded to pull back and redirect their energy toward perfecting the product. "I didn't know anything about their business" Courtney said, "and I certainly was not qualified to talk about the technical problems, but I felt a snag, and that's what I told them. It prevented them from possibly taking a very big loss by going out on a limb that was unsteady."

Courtney became aware of her psychic abilities when she was in her 20s, when she received an extraordinary insight while mowing the lawn. At the time, the experience was not only bizarre but frightening. As she walked back and forth mowing the lawn, she says, "I suddenly I saw this scene in my head—almost like I was remembering something. I saw my aunt's husband in a hospital bed and the doctors telling my aunt that he might not make it. But I knew at the same time that he would."

She was so moved by this image that she had to call her aunt with whom she hadn't spoken in three months. When she related this vision that she had just experienced, there was a silence at the other end of the telephone; for a moment it seemed to go dead. Her aunt then recovered and said that she had just finished speaking with a doctor from the hospital; he told her that her husband was suffering from an internal hemorrhage and that she had better get there quickly because his survival was in doubt. Courtney assured her aunt that he would survive after being hospitalized for ten days. As she predicted, on the tenth day her uncle came home.

Where does this kind of ability come from? Inquiring researchers wanted to know. Courtney was invited to a lab at a hospital in San Jose, California, where they measured her brain waves to see if the patterns were different from those who do not have this unusually high level of intuitive or psychic ability. Courtney's description of the experience:

> They wired me like for outer space. They put me in this pitch-black room closed off by thick metal doors. It was terrifying at first. They had lights that flashed inside the room, and they monitored my brain wave patterns. In the end, they did see some differences in the brain patterns of sensitive people like me, but they ran out of money to pursue it further.

It would be fascinating to learn more about the brain waves of people who have this psychic ability. It is hoped that research will be funded in the future to explore these abilities further.

# LYNN ROBINSON

Lynn Robinson is an East coast intuitive reader who also consults with business issues. She works in the Boston area with people at all levels of the organization. Ninety percent of Lynn's clients are women; one of the reasons they seek her advice is to gain support as they struggle with corporate politics. These women are high achievers who may be hitting the glass ceiling and often do not have a support system of people they can trust, so Lynn becomes their ally and confidant. Since she is psychic, she has an inside understanding of the personality problems within the corporation that are problematic for her clients.

What kinds of questions do they ask? Usually, they are of an interpersonal nature. For example, an executive who is battling against the glass ceiling may want to know who in the organization can be trusted, and who may be working against her interests. Robinson will ask for the first names of those people whom the client is concerned about. Then she will give a personality sketch of each one, including their potential relationship to her client and their level of trustworthiness in the politics of corporate life. She has several people who call her every two weeks to keep abreast of what is going on at work.

One of Robinson's clients is a top real estate broker who works with multimillion dollar properties. She calls Robinson to better understand her clients needs so that she can save time for herself and the clients by showing them exactly what they want.

Robinson believes her talent is related to the theory of the collective unconscious that was first espoused by Jung and later by Edgar Cayce, a psychic who could not only diagnose illnesses but was able to come up with cures as well. Both Jung and Cayce believed that there is a pool of knowledge in the universe that all of us can know, and that it is simply a matter of learning how to penetrate its invisible barriers. Robinson achieves this by closing her eyes and becoming aware of pictures she is receiving. She then talks about what the pictures may suggest as general themes in her client's life. She asks the clients what questions he or she may have, because that is often helpful in focusing her thoughts. However, sometimes she gets pictures that reveal things that the client was not asking about. "The type of things that I predict are related to personalities or trends," Robinson says. "For example, I can predict what the trend will be in the toy industry and how to create a sales strategy to appeal to a specific market segment."

Robinson's feelings about intuition appear to be born in a very spiritual place. She believes that we must trust in a higher power to guide us. She also feels that we all have "buttons" we press inside of us: some that tell us we believe in ourselves, and others that tell us we do not. When we experience challenges or problems in life, they are sent to us because we are meant to learn from them. She calls these challenges "reset buttons." As she puts it, "We're here, in part, to develop wisdom, love, forgiveness, and compassion. We can use these reset buttons to help us bring forth these qualities. One way of doing this is to trust in the higher power of our intuition."

Many people, however, confuse fear and emotion with intuition, which now raises the question, how can we differentiate intuition from our fears and emotional feelings? For example, suppose that I have a fear of flying and I am about to embark on a trip. Suddenly I get an "intuitive" flash and see planes going down, or I dream about planes crashing. How can I know whether these images are an intuitive insight warning me that the plane I'll be on will crash, or whether these images are of my fear of flying being released as I panic before the trip? The answer, says Robinson, is to use the same technique that was advised in that old joke, in which a man is stopped by a tourist in New York and is asked, "How do I get to Carnegie Hall?" and he replies, "Practice, practice, practice." With practice, and testing out our "intuitive" thoughts, we will learn how to differentiate feelings of fear and panic from an actual precognitive experience.

Women, in general, seem to be more open to accepting psychic insights than men. Robinson suggests that one reason for this is that men, generally, are more defensive against what appears to be irrational. Since most have never experienced anything even remotely like this, they are unwilling to concede this ability in others. Also, we must consider that our culture places a very strong emphasis on knowledge that can be gleaned from the left brain talent for analysis and logic, with this their only source of "reliable" information. Whatever comes from the right brain is viewed as mysterious and capricious. This is not true in other cultures, such as that of the Japanese, who are very much aware of their intuitive insights and some of their largest corporations have used psychic consultants for years.

## WINTER ROBINSON

Winter Robinson (no relation to Lynn Robinson) is based in Maine and is another psychic who consults with many business organizations. Her area of expertise appears to be with people issues within the organization. For example, she can tell you who may be trusted and who to watch. This talent was demonstrated a few years ago when she was called in at Marquest Financial in Minneapolis. Ed Graca, the president, who had started the business a few years earlier, was experiencing problems in cash flow and bookkeeping that he was unable to solve. He brought Robinson into the office on a Saturday afternoon when no one was working and told her of his dilemma. She walked through the office, felt the energy in the building, pointed to two empty desks, and advised Graca to keep his eye on the people who sit there. He did. He soon learned that they were not being as honest as he had hoped, and both were let go. Since then the business has gotten back on track.

Another assignment involved working with the developers of a $1 billion mall. The question was, should they rebuild and enhance the present mall, which was not doing well, or sell it and build a new one in a different area. Robinson looked at the people involved and, through her psychic ability, learned that one of the partners was dipping into unauthorized funds.

The other partners investigated this assertion and found it to be true. They decided to sell the mall to straighten out the financial difficulties.

Robinson also advises on hiring decisions. She is given the name of someone the company is considering hiring and predicts what will happen if that individual is placed in a particular position. For example, she will "see" that Mr. X is a very creative person and that if he is put into a position requiring a lot of detailed work, he will be ineffective. Like other psychic consultants, her work takes her to places all over the country as well as to Switzerland, Hawaii, and Japan. Robinson has also used her psychic abilities in helping individuals to heal themselves, and she teaches doctors and others in the medical professions how to use their own abilities for diagnosing their patients' medical problems.

## SONIA CHOQUETTE

Sonia Choquette, author of *Your Heart's Desire*, is a psychic who works out of Chicago and consults with both individuals and organizations. In one of the cases she recounted, a client who had started a business had become very successful, but now the business was expanding to the point where he felt it was too much for him. He came to her with this dilemma: should he sell the business for a profit or let his brother run it. Choquette "saw" that her client's brother was incompetent, that the business was important for the family, and that the best solution might be to hire a CEO to run the company. She suggested finding someone who had about ten years of experience and would be anxious to learn and grow with the company. The owner then revealed that yes, he knew his brother would be incompetent because he suffered from manic depression and could not be depended upon on a day-to-day basis. He took her advice and hired a CEO. The company is doing well, and the owner is happily putting in less and less time at the office.

Choquette believes that her skill lies in "seeing" the real problem rather than accepting the client's presenting diagnosis. "The client's view is often superficial," she says, "being too literal and not insightful." Rather than taking the superficial analysis as being the cause of the problem, her psychic or intuitive ability allows her to penetrate to another level and get to the crux of the problem.

Another useful skill is Choquette's ability to predict the ups and downs of the stock market, an uncommon ability she shares with several other psychics. She maintains complete control of her investments and her stockbroker informs her that her picks outperform the Dow Jones average.

# 20

# *The Power of the Press*

Despite the many psychological profile tests that have been devised for choosing the right candidate to fill a particular job, and the many interviewing methods created to discern a candidate's actual abilities, many companies are still making costly mistakes in hiring personnel from CEOs on down. The one-year reign of Michael Ovitz at the Walt Disney Company ended when he agreed to leave with a $90 million parachute. Such cushioning for his fall may not hurt that organization very much, but what about smaller companies such as Ben & Jerry's Homemade, which has hired its second president in two years? Think what would have happened if they had had the advice of an intuitive or psychic consultant; it could have prevented a lot of wasted time and money. In the space of a few hours a psychic could tell them who would be best for their organization and perhaps bring them closer to getting the right person. However, because public opinion, which is largely influenced by the press, would discredit companies if it were known that they hired psychics for help, it is doubtful that we will see much public acknowledgment for using their skills.

Operating any business well requires having as much information and intelligence as possible, and most enterprises avail themselves of all they can possibly get. From elaborate accounting departments, sales reports, market information, and data bases, there is a hunger for information to make decisions more reliable. It would seem sensible, then, to systematically collect as much intuitive information as possible. As a company's managers became experienced in evaluating this input, it could give them a valuable edge in personnel selection and promotion. It might also add greatly to their ability to foresee future developments and prepare for them.

At present, there is a very real fear among many executives that if they take advantage of this unusual source of information they will be perceived as irresponsible or, even worse, be described as having gone off the "deep end." For this reason, we might ask psychics to divine a positioning for their services that would make them more universally acceptable to the conservative world of business.

Remember how the press ridiculed Hillary Clinton when she sought to deepen her own intuitive insights by imagining what her role model, Eleanor Roosevelt, would have done were she the First Lady in the 1990s? What the press did not understand is that this is a very common exercise that many ideation consultants use when trying to come up with new advertising strategies or new product ideas, and it is a far less bizarre experience than some of the techniques other intuitive consultants use. Even so, it was completely misunderstood by journalists, who seem to be looking for whatever reasons they can find to discredit anyone in public life, even for something as innocuous as trying to stimulate one's imagination to better understand an important social role. One reason for journalistic error might be that they need a story to sell newspapers; if anything done by a public person seems slightly unusual, building it up to something that sounds weird to the average person would certainly snare their reader's voyeuristic attention. The validity of the creative technique, its advantages or disadvantages, are apparently irrelevant to the reporter; their mission is to create interesting stories.

## REMOTE VIEWING

Because of this fear of the press, there was very little publicity about how the Central Intelligence Agency investigated remote viewing (psychic ability). During the 1970s and 1980s, an investigation into remote viewing was conducted at the Stanford Research Institute in Palo Alto, California, supported by the CIA for the purpose of acquiring information about Soviet activities thousands of miles away during the Cold War. This research was funded by the government for over twenty years. Jim Schnabel, in his book *Remote Viewers*, tells the story of how psychics worked with the Pentagon, the CIA, and other U.S. Intelligence agencies. The thinking was that the Russians were using psychics to gain intelligence and that we would be left behind if we did not use these skills as well.

During this period, one psychic was able to pinpoint the coordinates for where a missing plane was located. Another knew whether a world leader was ill or not by going into an out-of-body experience and "visiting" the leader. The researchers learned that each psychic had a specialty at which he or she excelled: some were good at finding people, while others could find missing hardware, such as planes and tanks. One method they used was to hand a psychic a sealed envelope with the problem written inside, but unknown to the psychic. He was then instructed to look at the envelope and give the coordinates of what he "saw." Without knowing what was in the envelope, the psychic could tell them what was missing, such as an airplane or tank, and where it could be found. Their accuracy was so phenomenal in leading to advances of intelligence during the cold war that President Jimmy Carter actually made reference to one psychic in one of his speeches: "She went into a trance. And while she was in a trance, she gave some latitude and longitude figures. We focused our satellite cameras on that point and the plane was there" (Schnabel, 1997).

As one physicist who has participated in several of the government's psychic research programs said,

> We are playing catch-up with the Soviets in the field of psychic spying, which is politely called remote viewing. In fact, the U.S. government is so concerned about the psychic gap that any time our officials believe that they are close to information that gives them an edge, they publicly discredit that research.

At a hearing of the House Subcommittee on Intelligence Evaluation and Oversight in 1981, Congressman Charles Rose reported that the results of certain remote viewing experiments at Stanford Research Institute had been confirmed by aerial photography. He said that there is no way it could have been faked and called remote viewing a "hell of a cheap radar system."

# Conclusion

It seems that the overwhelming number of intuitives and psychics in this country are women, although there are a few gifted men who also have this skill. Some scientists now think that they may have the answer to why women seem to be more intuitive than men. The *Wall Street Journal* reported a study of Dr. David Skuse and his colleagues who tested the social skills of eighty women with Turners' syndrome, a disease in which women are born with one X chromosome. Normally, women have two X chromosomes—one from their mother and one from their father—while men have only a single X from their mothers. Researchers found that when the Turner's patients got their X chromosome from their mothers only, they were like men in that they had poorer social skills than women with a paternal X. They were also more like men in that they were less adept in situations that called for some self-restraint. Instead, they were apt to say the first thing on their mind, were more lacking in their awareness of others' feelings, and were oblivious to the effect of their behavior on other family members, also like many men. Skuse and his colleagues theorize that the gene that regulates social skills is only active on the X chromosome from the father.

Another theory is that there is a genetic basis for female intuition, which the researchers have defined as the ability to read social situations that are not obvious to men. Dr. Skuse said, "Women are born with that facility and men have to learn it" (Langreth, 1997). Many male psychologists would agree with this. Psychologist Len Solomon, a Professor at Boston University, thinks that many female psychologists intuitively know the source of their client's problems, whereas men have to figure it out based on what they have learned.

Intuition has been variously described as "intellect without fear" and as a "state of knowing beyond logic and experience."

Belleruth Naparstek, author of *Your Sixth Sense,* said in a keynote address at a recent symposium, "We forget that we are surrounded and connected to an invisible sea of intelligent, living energy that pulses its information into us and receives pulsing information back from us in a continuous instantaneous loop." Perhaps it is those executives who are the most successful who recognize that they are, indeed, in this loop. When Jonas Salk said, "Evolution favors the survival of the wisest," he may have intended that the wisest are those people who see things that the rest of us cannot.

In Part Seven we will look at how intuition can be a major factor in addressing problems of diversity in the workplace. While consciousness raising has been shown to be helpful in eliciting empathy from others, it still does not address the core issues: who can you trust, and how do you relate to "other" people who not like you. Developing intuition may be a useful skill in overcoming this problem.

# PART SEVEN

## *Using Intuition in Diversity Training*

> We are far more deeply related with others than we know. This deep intimacy is not something we create but rather something revealed when the mind is still, open, and free.
>
> ...GEORGE BOWMAN

When we hear the word "diversity" used in an organizational context, it seems to be a code word meaning "minorities do not get along well with nonminorities in this organization." And when we get the call to bring Diversity Training into the workplace, it generally means, "We want someone to fix it." If this is truly what is expected, then those well-meaning consultants or employees who would genuinely want to find a solution are put into a very difficult position. Part of the problem is the complexity of the subject, which involves psychological needs, rampant narcissism, cultural conditioning, and a widespread need to establish a social pecking order. Few of these issues could be adequately addressed within the confines of a typical seminar. Beyond that, the very individuals for whom this would be most appropriate are also the most biased. They will resent, if not utterly discredit, anyone who attempts to relieve them of their deeply entrenched negative opinions.

# 21

# *Why Diversity Training Has Failed*

Bias and prejudice toward members of a minority group, whether it is based on race, ethnicity, age, or gender, are not going to be easily remodeled. Aside from the complexity of its roots and the cultural rewards that encourage the maintaining of bias, whether consciously aware of it or not, not many who hold a stereotyped opinion want to change it, much less hear about changing it. The diversity practitioner, therefore, is predisposed to failure. If she skips over the complexity of the problem and narrows the focus to only raising consciousness and, she hopes, empathy, it becomes an educational process at best. If she does attack the deeper issues, not many are willing to confront them, and it becomes a no-win game with emotions often fiercely bent toward destroying any shred of logic that may be in the way.

Sometimes, however, actions may speak louder than words. The action that took place in the following story was probably successful in eradicating the irrational roots of prejudice that were held by one Thai immigrant. Quynh Pham needed some money a few years ago to fly his mother from a refugee camp in Thailand, where she had been living, to the United States. He approached several banks for loans, but since he had little collateral, the Arizona banks turned him down. So he turned to the Jewish Free Loan Society in Phoenix. They cut him a check for $2000, interest free.

As the 1997 *Wall Street Journal* story goes on to say,

> Such generosity was a revelation for Mr. Pham, a Catholic. He had never met a Jew before coming to the U.S. from Vietnam in 1984. Mr. Pham says he had been told that Jews were "mean and stingy," yet he found just the opposite to be true. "Nobody else gave me a loan," he said.

Mr. Pham's bias was picked up from the neighborhood streets, which is not unlike how many of us learn about the "other" that we do not know. Although he had a very positive experience, the question is, will this change his opinion about Jews?

According to psychologist Daniel Goleman, it may be unlikely. He suggests that because people tend to remember more instances that support their idea of the stereotype than those that do not, they discount experiences that deny it. So, if one were to meet a charming and generous Scotsman, he would be regarded as an aberration from the norm, which we "know" to be tight and the opposite of lavish in spending habits. In our minds, we allow no room for variations from the stereotype, because we would then have to give up everything that we are sure we "know" about the other. Admitting to ourselves that we actually know very little, then, may be quite uncomfortable. Whether Mr. Pham will fall into that category or not is hard to say. He most likely has had no interaction with Jews at all, so there is no personal experience to back up the stereotype that he acquired. In fact, his ability to secure the loan, interest free, was just the opposite of the stereotype. In this case, there is a good chance that this exposure will reshape his attitude.

On the other hand, it is difficult to download a bias that was learned at an early age, when a child, for instance, was unable to question stereotypical opinions with logic. When the information is learned when we are young, no distinction is made between the stereotypes (the tales told to the child) and the reality that every person is actually an individual.

Another reason a stereotype often seems to be locked away in us forever and not subject to logic is because we may have had an emotionally charged experience that has been stored in the lower part of our brain from infancy. If, for example, a young child is bitten by a dog, that memory will always be there, and the fear of dogs may never disappear, even though the adult realizes that it is not logical or reasonable, all of which may cause anxious feelings every time a dog approaches. It is difficult to let go of these emotional memories buried so deep in our psyche since childhood. This same type of memory process may be responsible for keeping knowingly irrational views of the "other" alive in our consciousness.

If this is the case, then how can any diversity program overcome such a barrier? The short answer is, they can't and they don't. However, perhaps the most difficult issue is that we live in a racist society where the culture tells us what and how to think about everyone. Richard Brodie, author of *Virus of the Mind*, would say that this is one of many types of viruses or opinions that we are infected with by our culture. "Once created, a virus of the mind gains a life independent of its creator and evolves quickly to infect as many people as possible." This is another way of suggesting that we are all subject, to one degree or another, to "group think," that is, taking in opinions of the culture at large without necessarily being aware of it. And, of course, the antidote to this virus would be to think for ourselves, if at all possible.

## DO YOU KNOW WHERE YOUR BIAS LIVES?

The fact that many of us are unaware of our own bias was made painfully clear to me when I was in New York City a few years ago attending a gift show at the Jacob Javits Center. I am sure that the leading characters in this drama were entirely unaware of the gut-wrenching effect their seemingly innocent banter provoked in me. Several buses were lined up outside the Javits Center to take visitors from the show to various locations, and I boarded one that was to take us to Penn Station. As we filed onto the bus the genial African-American driver would ask each of us our destination to be sure we had the right bus. Whenever anyone said Penn Station, he would playfully inform the passenger that he had no idea how to get there. It made for a light feeling of camaraderie and amusement among the bus passengers until the joking suddenly escalated to another level. When one person heard the driver say he didn't know how to get there, she said in the same kidding voice, "If you don't get us there we'll lynch you." Then another passenger, apparently not to be outdone with such "cleverness," shot back, "Yes, we'll string you up."

At this point, my cheeks were burning. I could not believe that anyone could think of themselves as being light-hearted and kidding while using words that detonated such bombs of shameless sadism. Numbed by their hostility and, what was worse, their seeming lack of awareness of how devastating their remarks were, I felt powerless to say or do anything. The bus became silent as the shock waves overcame the other passengers. The bus driver stepped out of the bus and onto the curb and waited for the rest of the passengers outside, where it must have seemed much easier to breathe. I admired his courage and his cool, and wondered, did he have to face comments like this everyday simply because he was Black? Or, were these people aberrant freaks, not the day-in day-out characters in the bus driver's life? I wanted to ask him, but I couldn't speak. We arrived at Penn station in good time. He knew the way.

In the situation above, the bias appeared to be unconscious. Sometimes, however, the reason for bias is simply that because we do not know any members of a particular ethnic group, we mistrust any individual member because we do not know what to expect. Whatever the "other" is that you do not know, whether homosexual, White, Afro-American, Asian, male, female, etc., the same assumptions apply; the virus spread by parents, teachers, clergy, friends, and the movies affects your opinion of those you do not know.

There is another source of knowledge about others that may be even more difficult to deal with. Brandeis Professor Leslie Zebrowitz has researched how we perceive faces from a cross-cultural perspective. She found that if you have a baby face, whether male or female, you are perceived as naïve, not shrewd, more submissive, and are generally recommended for jobs that require less competence. This is true whether you are 60 years old or younger, whether you are Korean, Black, or White (Zebrowitz, 1997).

The cross-cultural study also suggested that people with low eyebrows were considered dominant, strong, and shrewd. A face with symmetrical features was perceived as attractive, and competence was related to faces that looked mature. This appears to be true no matter what one's race or culture.

We know that these physical characteristics tell us nothing about what is going on in a person's head, yet it has been suggested that these assumptions are inherent in our genes and not necessarily obtained through the media and movies. We usually see a redneck type portrayed in film by a large man with a huge neck and a baby face. Are casting directors choosing these types because that is the image they want to project, or is the image already in the public's consciousness and they are simply reflecting their "reality?" According to the researchers, the latter is the case.

Maybe so. I doubt if any casting director would choose a slightly built man with a very mature looking face for this role; he doesn't fit the popular image. In fact, men who have what is called "baby" faces generally have a more difficult time being respected as mature than do men with more mature faces. Stereotypes, then, are buried deep in multicultural consciousness often based on appearance alone. And, they are just as often plain wrong. In fact, the most likable type, the researchers say, is an average face and body. People with very overweight bodies are usually last hired and first fired—unless they perform at an outstanding level, such as the formerly heavy Oprah Winfrey. Employers claim that the reason they tend not to hire the grossly overweight is because of the medical liability involved; this may be true, yet most overweight people are painfully aware of a cultural bias against them. We rarely see a bank teller, a service person who deals with the public, a movie star, or a television personality who is grossly overweight, with perhaps a few exceptions here and there. Many models look as though they are starving anorexics or on drugs, a look that the media would have us believe is "in," although the trend in advertising now seems to be going back to a slim, but healthy look. Yet, chances are that those who reflect the gaunt image would have a better opportunity for landing almost any type of job than those who are overweight or who have asymmetrical faces.

If the outward appearance throw us off, what would happen if a diversity training program asked us to get to know the "other," the one who is different, not like us, whoever we may be, Afro-American, White, Asian, homosexual, female, male, young, old, thin, fat, whatever. Some would welcome it, while others would resent having to give up their stereotypical knowledge of the "other." There is an advantage to holding onto the bias: it means that there will always be someone else to blame, someone else to use as a common butt for ethnic jokes, which can create bonding among friends.

Most diversity courses will not address these topics because such issues are too touchy. After all, who would want to be told that he is using a member of the "other" group as a scapegoat? Who would enjoy hearing that he lacks self-esteem and so disparages someone else to raise his own sense of self-worth? Or, that it is comforting to have someone who is "safe" to put down? To talk openly about these issues would raise everyone's defenses, which in turn would likely result in more animosity than good will.

This is one reason why the intention of many diversity training courses is to raise consciousness, not hackles, and by so doing elicit empathetic feelings and changed attitudes. The theory is excellent, but several studies on whether such training has actually had the expected beneficial effect indicated that it has failed not only in improving attitudes, but also helped to fuel a White male backlash.

In *The Diversity Machine* (1997), Frederick Lynch suggests that most diversity programs have failed or backfired by creating a White male backlash, and that more than half of all employees resent having to attend the diversity seminars in their organizations. He writes:

> Short workshops offer a measure of protection against lawsuits and adverse government regulatory action by showing "good-faith efforts" toward overcoming discrimination, but more elaborate diversity management programs have not yet proved their bottom-line value . . . there is little systematic proof that the programs reduce intergroup tensions and increase productivity or creativity.

Lynch also quotes Bob Filipczak in *Training Magazine*, who said that "as a training topic, 'diversity' has spread like wildfire in the 1990s . . . a 40 percent increase since 1992." But Lynch also warned,

> It is also one of the most controversial training topics to gain a serious foothold in the corporate world. . . . Diversity is, to put it bluntly, a snake pit. And it keeps getting deeper all the time as more and more issues fall under its umbrella.

Lynch also quotes Shari Caudron:

> Ineffective training can raise the expectations of women and minorities, increase the fear and resistance among white males and harm an organization's diversity efforts. Thus, the rapid spread of diversity has remained somewhat formal and superficial.

More heated emotions are aroused, it would appear, by the presence of diversity training programs, and the consensus is that they have accomplished little in reducing tensions or increasing productivity. I submit that the reason diversity programs have failed is because they are too superficial, yet to confront the underlying causes of the problem would be too threatening. Either way, the current state of training does not and would not succeed in changing attitudes. It may be that there is one possible solution to this difficult problem: let's try intuition.

How could intuition be helpful in solving problems of diversity? The first step would be to put aside, if only momentarily, the emotionally learned biases of our childhood and youth. Then we could be open to our intuition to help us solve many problems in day-to-day life in the workplace. These issues are concerned with knowing whether the "other" is trustworthy, competent, and reliable; that is really the bottom line. We want to know who we can trust, irrespective of the stereotype. We want to be able to count on an individual's competency and reliability, no matter the gender, age, or the color of the skin. For business purposes, these are the basic questions that can make or break a working relationship.

Stereotypes, in the long run, are irrelevant and worse— they are misleading when it comes to knowing others. True, each of us may have some behavior that can be stereotyped, but few human beings would fit well into any media-driven or gossip-designed mold. Relying on the stereotype also leads to misinformation about members of the "other" group. There may be a correlation between those who rely on stereotype to understand others and those who are not original thinkers in other walks of life. If we permit ourselves to hear only one song with its one refrain playing over and over in our brain, we will become a nation of Johnny one-notes: boring and devoid of any ideas. If we are open to those myriad vibrations of the human personality that could enter our consciousness, we would be far more capable of creating our own original scores and become the most innovative thinkers.

If we do away with the stereotype, then the bottom line becomes, how do I know whether I can trust this person to be competent and reliable, and how do I relate to this person? The answer is, use your intuition. It doesn't matter whether a person is Caucasian, African-American, Asian, or other, your intuition can reveal the individual's essential character. If we can replace bias and prejudice with intuiting the values and competencies of the other person, then stereotypes and irrational prejudices should become irrelevant to our relationships.

## WHAT'S YOUR B.Q. (BIAS QUOTIENT)?

The following is a list of questions to determine the level of bias you now hold and how open you would be to allowing intuition to influence your relationships with the other.

> Do you feel that you are completely unbiased, that you hold no preconceived ideas about anyone based only on ethnic identity, gender, age, or color of skin? Would you say that you have grown up untouched by culturally-formed stereotypes? If your answer is yes to these questions, on a scale of 0 to 10, you rate a 0.

> Do you recognize that you have a slight bias, that the impact of culture has colored your feelings towards members of certain other groups, but that you hold no hostility toward them? Are people distinguished in your mind by either the color of their skin or their ethnic background? For example, might you refer to someone as that "Italian fella," even though his family has been in this country for four generations? If his surname is Italian, is that his distinguishing characteristic for you? If your answer to any of the above is "yes," give yourself a 1.

Do you admit to using a person's race, gender, age, or color of skin as an excuse to cast blame whenever anything goes wrong, as in, "Once they let these people in here, nothing goes right"? If you answer "yes" to this question, give yourself a 2.

Do you honestly feel that you don't much like people of certain other groups, but you know it would not be politically correct to raise the issue. A "yes" answer to this question rates a 3.

Do you feel angry much of the time, and vent freely and as often as possible and convenient to let your anger out at the "other?" You know it is fairly certain that this person cannot or will not retaliate. A "yes" to these questions rates a 4.

Are you actually a virulent racist? You would just as soon see all of "them" deported or at least removed from the workplace? A "yes" to these questions rates a 10.

Do you agree with W.C. Fields who said, "I am free of all prejudice. I hate everyone equally"? A "yes" here rates a double 0.

If you rate 1-4 on this scale, or know others who do, then you would benefit from a course in using intuition to relate to others. Those who rate 0 are too rare to be noticed, and those rating 10 or 00 are, hopefully, not only in a tiny minority but probably beyond anyone's reach.

# 22

# *Why Intuition in Diversity Training?*

If learning how to tap into our intuition were a focus in diversity training, in addition to consciousness raising, we could avoid the discomfort of discussing stereotypes, fears, emotions, and so on. For instance, what if a White man is taught how to use his intuition to find a place for himself where he is not competing with someone who is a minority for his position? Then the presence of the Hispanic or Asian or other minority would be irrelevant to him. Also, if we learned how to intuit the motives of others, we would know whom to befriend and whom to avoid. This is not to say that the underlying causes of prejudice are not important, but for our purposes, they are regarded as irrelevant.

It may also be helpful to avoid discussing root causes for bias and simply look at how it affects what happens in the workplace when minorities feel under attack. One method for getting a handle on this problem is offered in a film and workshop produced by Goodmeasure, Inc.

## A TALE OF O

Rosabeth Moss Kanter and Barry Stein, founders of Goodmeasure, Inc., wrote and produced a film about what it feels like to be the "other" in the workplace, *The Tale of O*. The only "actors" in the film are the letters "X" and "O." The Xs are people who share the similarity of belonging to a group that does not generally include the O, the Other, who is different. When an O is added to the group, the O may be a person of color among Whites, or an older person among younger ones, or a woman surrounded by men. Kanter and Stein cleverly use the symbols of X and O so that no specific minority is mentioned, so that the dialogue could be applied to any minority. The film and training program explore typical reactions of how Xs think when Os are among them. One interesting observation of how the Xs behavior changes whenever an O enters the group is that Xs tend to band together more closely than when an O joins the group. Also, Xs often feel awkward in not knowing how to behave among Os, which then leads to remarks that makes the O feel uncomfortable, different, and not part of the group. The film explores how this behavior affects both the Xs and the O, and their work productivity.

Most of the dialogue spoken by the Xs has a familiar ring, such as "Let a few Os in and right away they want to take over," or "I know production's down and absenteeism is up, but it's all because we had to hire Os," or "Things are lousy now, but think how much better we could make them if we could just get rid of our O." These lines are sad yet oddly amusing, perhaps because most of us have heard them or similar utterances at one time or another. While exposing some very common perceptions, the film also reveals how attitudes affect the work climate and future ability to be promoted for the O.

Because the film's clear portrayal of the emotional repercussions of being an X or an O is quite explicit, directed discussions that follow should provide an even more heartfelt understanding and awareness for every viewer. Xs learn how and why their behavior affects Os, and both Xs and Os learn why they may react sometimes without realizing that they are reacting instead of simply acting. However, as good as this film is, it does not address the issue of how the individual can learn to drop his bias. Raising consciousness can reveal how insensitive remarks can be hurtful, and it can also expose the often unconscious need to point out the "otherness" of the O. However, when this unconscious bias is revealed, it often creates an effect like the legacy of Pandora's box. The issues raised become far more complex, and the emotions that had been buried within an apparent politically correct exterior begin to fill the air, like the odor of a skunk when it feels threatened. How do you get past these deeply felt emotions? One way is to use your capacity for intuitive empathy.

## THE POWER OF EMPATHY

Intuition is closely related to empathy. When we intuit a characteristic about a person, we are, in a sense, empathizing. Empathy is seeing ourselves in another's shoes, vicariously experiencing her feelings and thoughts; intuition tells us where to look for the shoes. Harvard Business School professor John Kao says that empathy and intuition are critical for a manager. And when intuition and empathy are combined in understanding people, it may begin a gentle erosion of the roots of prejudice.

Empathizing, however, is not easy and is something that must be consciously willed. Carl Rogers, in an essay intended to educate psychotherapists to become as effective as possible, recommended that they engage in an empathic experience with the client. He describes it as follows:

> I have found it of enormous value when I can *permit* myself to understand another person. The way in which I have worded this statement may seem strange to you. Is it necessary to *permit* oneself to understand another? I think that it is. Our first reaction to most of the statements which we hear from other people

is an immediate evaluation or judgment, rather than an understanding of it. When someone expresses some feeling or attitude
or belief, our tendency is, almost immediately, to feel "That's
right"; "That's stupid"; "That's abnormal"; "That's unreasonable"; "That's not nice." Very rarely do we permit ourselves to
understand precisely what the meaning of his statement is to
him. I believe this is because understanding is risky. If I let
myself really understand another person, I might be changed by
that understanding. And we all fear change. . . . it is not an easy
thing to permit oneself to understand an individual, to enter
thoroughly and completely and empathetically into his frame of
reference (Rogers, 1961).

Psychologist Laura Hart understood this well. She writes,

When I was listening in that way (empathic) and the clients
responded with the joy of understanding and of being understood, I felt loving and effective. I had always considered myself
nonspiritual, an atheist. Yet, as those good feelings swelled
inside me, I was confronted with the paradox of feeling
"blessed."

The most successful business people also know the value of
empathy. In order to manufacture and sell the best car, Soichiro
Honda needed to know what people wanted. He wanted to
empathize with car buyers. One way that he approached this, in
addition to market research, was to assign his young engineers
to work on cars that were meant to appeal to their own age
group. As these designers aged, they moved to designing cars to
appeal to the older buyer, and younger engineers were brought
in to stay in touch with their own generation's taste preferences.
As Gary Hamel and C. K. Prahalad have written, "Again and
again, Honda has worked hard to ensure that those charged
with product development possess deep insights and real empathy for the customers they are seeking to serve" (1996). If large
organizations can commit themselves to empathizing with customers to produce a better product, it follows that they could
also commit themselves to empathizing with the "other" in the

workplace, especially when they understand how irrational bias leads to the disintegration of morale.

Being skilled in empathic understanding is not easy. First you must intuit and then empathize with the pain experienced by a member of the "other" group. It requires careful listening and asking questions. It also requires an open mind and a willingness to put aside judgments. If you genuinely want to know people and you want people to know you, you must relate to them as individuals, not stereotypes. Try to catch yourself when you fall back on the stereotype to define the person. If you know one person from a group, don't assume that all people from that group think the same way. (It seemed strange to me during the O. J. Simpson trial that the media seemed to concentrate on seeking out the "Black" point of view as if it were universal to all African-Americans. Since O.J. was a celebrity and a sports figure, I wondered why none of the talk show hosts and commentators didn't go after the viewpoint of the "celebrity" and "celebrity sports person" as well.) Allowing the essence of the individual to filter through the screen of the stereotype, and putting aside what you think you know about the "other," will permit your intuition to suddenly kick in with more accurate information.

However, in the last analysis, perhaps Tom Peter's take on understanding the other is most relevant to why nothing changes in diversity training. He writes,

> I was born a male, white, Anglo-Saxon, Protestant. We are the ruling class . . . to this day. And there's not a damn thing I can do about that.
>
> Which means I have a problem: I JUST CAN'T UNDERSTAND.
>
> That is, as I listened [during a seminar] to these very powerful women talk about the degree to which they had been slighted, particularly if they happened to be Asian-American women or African-American women it dawned on me that for all my liberalness, I just didn't get it. I did not—and cannot—understand what it means to be systematically slighted and/or ignored.

There's an important message here. I can pretend to be very receptive to women's ideas. (I am . . . and I mean it) But, I'm not one of "them." I don't know (K-N-O-W) what it's like to be short-changed. Again and again.

The implication here is that because he cannot know what it is like to be short-changed, his empathy is unable to cross that boundary. He is saying, if I can't relate to anything like this in my own life, how can I empathize with you?

Peters' brutal honesty is probably a good reflection of a common feeling among many White males who hold a liberal viewpoint. Thus, the White employer will hire someone like himself, both male and Caucasian, because he, unconsciously or not, feels more comfortable with someone like himself. To ask this person to empathize with the "other" and intuit the potential value that person could add to his organization may be pointless; his own discomfort with someone unlike himself may take precedence over the possible advantages to the firm. It has in the past, which is why affirmative action laws were written and enforced. And if affirmative action is no longer required, then, as Peters says, "we are in power, we are the ruling class," and by inference this "we" has no reason to make themselves feel uncomfortable with hiring the "other," unless forced by laws or persuaded by reason that the "other" will be good for the organization.

# 23

# Using Intuition at Work

## A HIGH SOCIAL INTELLIGENCE

Some call it being sensitive to other people or being acutely aware of their feelings. Howard Gardner characterizes having an intuitive understanding of what the other person needs to feel comfortable in one's presence as having a high social intelligence. Many people can be quite intelligent and accomplished in intellectually demanding pursuits, but if their social skills are lacking, they are deemed to be low in social intelligence. To be able to intuit another's needs and respond with caring is a form of intelligence that can be coached and that would be especially useful in diversity training programs. Scores from standard IQ tests would give no indication of an individual's ability in this area, but there are several techniques that can be helpful in vastly improving this skill. The following is an example of how one could use an intuitive social skill at work.

## INTUITION AT THE SUPERMARKET

A checkout clerk in the supermarket drops a glass jar of tomato sauce and it splatters everywhere. Her supervisor's conventional approach might be to chastise her for dropping the jar. "Can't you be more careful," he says in an angry tone of voice. Is the manager's handling of this situation emotionally intelligent? Will it be effective in changing the clerk's behavior? Will it help increase her loyalty to the company? Does it inspire her to be a better employee or advance up the ladder of opportunity? The answer is no, no, no, and most definitely not.

Now suppose we try a different script, one that requires intuitive intelligence. Let's say that the manager intuitively senses that the clerk is under a lot of pressure to process the order as quickly as possible, and in her attempt to please the customer and boss with her speed, she fumbles. If this is the case, it would be helpful for the manager to advise her to take as long as necessary to process the order to reduce the chance of such accidents.

Or, the manager may intuit another cause. Perhaps the clerk is working two or more jobs to make ends meet and does not get enough sleep to keep her alert. If this is the case, he could suggest an alternative work schedule.

As you can see, blame and chastisement are counterproductive because they do not get at the root cause of the problem, nor do they solve it. If the employee feels punished by the harsh words, it usually leads to even more errors and becomes a self-fulfilling prophecy. For example, if I am told I am clumsy and irresponsible, then I become even more clumsy and apparently irresponsible, not willfully but perhaps, unconsciously. There is something in the brain that translates chastisement into fact, which then becomes prophecy: it says, "If this is who you say I am, then, that's who I am—a clumsy person who is bound to drop things." Her performance may improve temporarily, but in time it will worsen, because that self-image will be played out.

Blame creates anger and shame. Blame destroys the spirit while a gentle application of intuitive social intelligence can heal and help the manager to be a better motivator. Consider this choice: would you rather have an affect on your employees that is reminiscent of that historical beheader, King Henry the Eighth, or of that wonderful empowerer, the Wizard of Oz? Intuiting the other's needs and trying to fulfill them could make all the difference between creating marginal or top performing employees.

# 24

# *Intuition in the Hiring Process*

> Dialogue requires an intuition, even before words come out of your mouth, about the person you are speaking with. Without calling upon the world of intuition, the dialogue we do with ourselves is deaf—and the dialogue with others blind.
>
> ...KAMENETZ, 1997

It is said that people form impressions of strangers within the first 30 seconds. Job seekers are advised to dress to perfection and practice their handshake in anticipation of passing the 30-second muster. If it is true that we form our opinions so quickly, on what do we base them? Is part of it intuition? If the impression is positive, perhaps it reflects a natural leaning toward an attractive appearance and sensing a common social background. That is, if the person being interviewed is reasonably attractive, of the expected race, gender, age range, and social status, then, in the first 30 seconds, he will most likely succeed. But, if one of these variables is missing—the clothes are déclassé, or the race or gender is not one the interviewer can easily relate to, or the appearance is unattractive to the interviewer—then the candidate will have flunked that 30-second benchmark.

Assuming the person's initial impression is satisfactory, how will the interviewer judge whether this candidate is one to pursue or reject? One method that has been useful for many people is to use their intuition to know character and potential. If the interviewer can sense the cues that reveal this information, then she will quickly learn whether this candidate is right for the position, regardless of race, class, or even educational background. (Incidentally, a formal educational background or the lack of same often has little relevance to ability. Many inventors and entrepreneurs never went beyond the eighth grade, including Sochiro Honda. When Thomas Edison's school teacher sent a note home to his mother informing her that this boy could not learn anything, he became a fourth-grade drop out.) Pamela Gilberd, author of *The Eleven Commandments of Wildly Successful Women* advises her readers to "Listen to your intuition when hiring. Someone could have the best credentials, experience, skills, and recommendations, but if you don't feel comfortable for any reason, don't override your hunches."

When we think about the interviewing process, the factors for assessment are delineated in logical left brain analysis. For example, the candidate must be dressed properly so that we can judge whether he or she knows how to dress for business—although today, in certain industries, this reliance on appearance has changed to some extent. High-tech companies, for example, tend to recruit guided only by the résumé and a telephone interview. If the résumé states that the candidate has the required experience, and if he can answer questions on the telephone to verify the knowledge stated on the résumé, then chances are that the face-to-face-interview is only a formality. At this point, showing up with nose rings or purple hair may be counterproductive in terms of the proper dress code. However, she may be hired, as was our local pharmacist who sports a lip ring, which may indicate that the hiring pharmacist could look beyond the outward appearance to assess her competency and qualifications.

Let's suppose you are in the hiring process and have interviewed several well-dressed, well-qualified candidates. How do you choose the one who will work best in the firm? During the interview, you ask questions about accomplishments. You listen for something that tells you he knows what he is talking about. Only one of the candidates may have the precise type of experience you are looking for, having worked on exactly the same product. Given this work background, is he the best choice? Not necessarily. Other questions remain, such as how will he work with others, will he be a good team member, will he be creative in offering ideas, and will he be reliable in a crunch? In the final analysis, you cannot possibly know the answers to these questions, and you will need to rely on your intuition to make the best selection.

Steve Conroy, Vice President of Corporate Communications at Hill Holliday Connors Cosmopulos, Inc., a Boston based advertising firm, says all of his hires are based on his intuition. Each applicant had a good résumé, but with an interview, he knows with an uncanny insight who will work out well; he has been right ten out of ten hires. Jennifer Vanderwerf, a vice president at FoxTV in Portland, Maine, says all of her hires have been based on intuition, and in some cases, she has selected people with less remarkable résumés because she knew that these hires would excel. Her batting average is also excellent, with only one less-than-optimum choice over a ten-year career.

Several people who say they use their intuition in hiring will note that the selectee's strengths are similar to their own. For example, a lawyer told me that he wanted to hire a woman who seemed to be "a little too aggressive" because he was also aggressive and felt that was a good trait. For this lawyer, intuition was intuiting his own qualities in the other. Generally, this is the way many people are hired. If the person hiring perceives the candidate to be a younger version of himself, there is often a tendency to hire that person, which is why it has been so "natural" for men to hire men, Whites to hire Whites, and so on. Also, it is difficult for many people to hire someone who appears to be older than they are, because it could be very uncomfortable to supervise a person who may be near in age to one's parents.

Unfortunately, feeding our narcissism by hiring in our own image results in a loss of opportunity for the "other" as well as the loss of potential cross-pollination of ideas and experience, because of the lack of cultural diversity. Once hired, chances are that the mirror-image and his boss will get along well and reinforce each other's opinions and work objectives. That's the upside. The downside is that there is less diversity in thinking that can bring another way of looking at things to the table. One of the results of studies conducted by Ned Herrmann of Herrmann International was that when the gender and educational backgrounds of group members were mixed, their creative output was far greater than with homogenous groups of a single gender with similar backgrounds.

Group diversity is also an integral part of the process when facilitating ideation sessions to develop new products and market them for large corporations. A successful strategy in many industries has been to bring together groups of mixed gender and educational backgrounds with people from product development, marketing, engineering, and human resources, along with ideation experts, inventors, and customers. Most companies have found this method so successful that they would never go back to allowing engineers alone figure out what new products to develop, or let only the marketing people determine strategy for positioning the product.

This leaves us in an ambiguous state of affairs. If we know and agree that a diversity of racial, ethnic, gender, and educational backgrounds leads to increased creativity in the workplace, then why do we still find reasons not to hire the O, the minority? Gallos and Ramsey offer this explanation:

> . . . we all hold espoused beliefs about ourselves consistent with
> our governing values—values we have learned as important
> from family and experience, values we believe all "good" people
> hold. It's common human behavior.

In the context of teaching and learning about workplace diversity, this is troublesome. It is as if something deep within us is "programmed" to collude with our inability or refusal to explore not-so-pleasant beliefs about and reactions to people seen as different from ourselves. Even the best and most open of us carry biases, stereotypes, and unproductive expectations about others we've learned from our childhood, education, and life experiences in a complex society. We have to work hard to acknowledge the prejudices, intolerance, and unacknowledged assumptions we secretly wish we did not carry (Gallos and Ramsey, 1997).

However, Zen teachers tell us to come to a learning situation with a beginner's mind. That is, if we already "know" all about the other, then there is nothing more to learn and nothing can be learned. It is only when we look at this situation with a beginner's mind, as if we knew nothing, that we can learn. This point is illustrated by the student who approaches the Zen master to teach him wisdom. The master invites him to have a cup of tea and begins pouring the tea until it overflows the cup and begins to flood the table until the student tells him to stop, that he has overfilled the cup. The master then explains that when the mind is full of knowing, nothing more can enter it. But when we can empty our mind of what we think we know and become free of our biases and prejudices, we will have the beginner's mind that is open to acquiring wisdom.

# 25

# *Feeling Fear versus Knowing Intention*

$A$nother type of bias is rooted in stereotype-induced fear, and it is probably the most pervasive. For example, I have a friend who is compassionate and sympathetic to many causes. She donates money to every type of charity, volunteers to serve in soup kitchens, and offers her free time in the service of others. Yet if she is walking down the street and an African-American male is walking toward her, she will cross the street. When I asked her why, she said,

"Because I am afraid."

"Afraid of what?" I asked.

"Afraid I might be mugged, or worse."

"Why do you feel this way?"

"I grew up in New York and that was my experience."

Then I asked her, "Do you look at the person to see how he is dressed to give you any clues as to his intentions?"

"No."

"Do you look at the expression on his face or his body language to see whether he looks like he is about to be violent?"

"No."

"Then how do you know his intentions?"

"I don't. I'm just playing it safe."

"Do you cross the street when you see a group of white teenagers?"

"Sometimes."

What my friend does not realize is that fear is needlessly chasing her back and forth across the street. This is where her intuition could come to the rescue. Actually, we are using it all of the time whenever we look at others, whether we are aware of it or not. We take in their clothes and their facial expressions. We look at the way they walk and listen to the way they talk. It may be entirely unconscious, but many people do this every day when they walk down the street. If we did not do this, even on an unconscious level, we would not know whether the person walking toward us might be dangerous, no matter what the color of his or her skin. We know that neither the color of the skin nor the apparent gender of the person can give us a clue toward recognizing violent intentions. Yet we are continually taking in a multitude of clues, knowingly or not. Sometimes we know just by the sound of the voice and the manner of speech.

There was a story in the *Boston Globe* about two young men, 17 and 18 years old, in Franklin, New Jersey, who allegedly telephoned five pizza parlors before they found one that would deliver to the remote location requested. Their intention was to murder the delivery person. According to the newspaper account by the Associated Press, April 1997,

> "The owner of Tony's Pizza, 24 and his employee, 22, were ambushed and murdered. At one of the other pizza shops that received a call for delivery to the abandoned house, manager Tim Kiester said the caller had trouble answering routine questions. Kiester said he had had a 'gut feeling' and told his employee not to make the delivery.

Apparently, those people who answered the telephones in the four pizza parlors that refused to take the order must have picked up something suspicious about the caller by listening to his voice on the phone, and did not want to deliver to such an out-of-the-way spot. Their intuition or gut feelings were working correctly. Most unfortunately for Georgio Gallara, owner of Tony's Pizza, he did not pick up the caller's evil intent and unwittingly went to his death.

## CLUES TO KNOWING INTENTION

In our adolescence we are socialized to judge others by outward appearance, and we are required to wear clothing like everyone else's to be judged favorably. The costume proves that you are "cool," ergo accepted. When we get a bit older, we understand that outward appearances can be deceiving; to learn whether someone can be trusted, or to understand how another person thinks, feels, and may behave is much more complex. How, then, can we know another's intention?

One way is to watch ourselves as we watch a movie. We get a lot of practice in figuring out someone else's intention when we see a film such as a murder mystery. When it begins, you may try to guess who the murderer will be. You notice the way that man is looking at the woman, which leads you to suspect that he intends to kill her. The director will also have the camera focus on the actor's face, who wears an expression that we read as having murder in mind, if he is a good actor, another clue to intention. The camera may also focus on a gun or knife, and we know that it is likely to be the murder weapon. If we can know what a killer looks like by grasping his intention in the movies, then we should also be able to recognize people's intent in real life when we have to judge someone's character.

When we are right, we know it was our intuition. But what happens when we are wrong? It could be that we are unable to be as detached from the situation as we are in the movie theater. We don't have a director with a camera drawing our attention to facial expressions and weapons. We can see the celluloid murderer's intent because we know we are not going to be the victim and are watching as voyeurs or spectators, with a more dispassionate eye. The situation may be quite different when you are making a business deal, or are in a position of lending money. While some people may be hyperaware, others may have their vision clouded by other factors. How do you know if the other person will be honest and deal with you honorably? The answer is that you must be able to detach yourself from your own emotions, to get out of your own way in order to see and trust your intuition. The following are some common blinders that prevent us from seeing the intentions of another:

1. **High Emotional Involvement:** As a landlord, I need to rent out an apartment. There are not many people looking for an apartment at this time, and I take the first person who says he wants it without sensing whether he will pay his rent. My fear of not renting masks whatever intuition I may otherwise have had toward this man's character. If I could have let go of my anxiety about renting and allowed my intuition to tell me whether this person would make a good tenant, I could have avoided the debacle that ensued. Could it be that the pizza store owner who was murdered in New Jersey was really strapped for business, and that the anxiety of not making enough money prevented him from hearing the caller's intent? **The lesson:** Be aware of your anxiety and learn to put it aside to become aware of your impressions.

2. **Misplaced goodwill:** I am asked to loan money to a young relative, the son of people whom I know to be honorable. Although I do not know their son well, I lend him the money and trust that he will return it by taking comfort in that old saw, "an apple doesn't fall far from the tree." Unfortunately, this "apple" had scampered out of the orchard and left the country! The money was never returned. **The lesson:** Intuit the lendee's intention. He is an individual and cannot be relied upon to assume his family's values.

3.  **Reliance on superficial information.** References and outward appearance may take on a disproportionate value when hiring an employee. The underlying assumption here is that if others have something positive or negative to say about this person, then I should rely on their judgment. The reason is that the person giving the reference has had a direct relationship with the other person and knows more than I do. I may also infer that she is possibly a better judge of character and whatever she says I will trust.

    In reality, many people do not tell the truth, or if they do, it is a "biased" truth. Because of the fear of lawsuits, business references will invariably offer something either positive or noncommittal. On the other hand, if the referrer says something negative, it may or may not reflect the applicant's true character or competence but could be based on personal animosity. If positive, it could be based on a close friendship. Without knowing the person who gives the reference, it is almost impossible to know what to believe.

    If we cannot be certain of the reference, then there is no other recourse than to rely on our own intuition. Furthermore, if we can use our intuition to sense the motives of the person giving the reference, we may have a better handle on whether we are getting a true picture of the candidate. **The lesson:** If you do not know the person giving the reference, give more weight to your own intuition than someone else's opinion.

## LISTEN TO YOUR INTUITION TO KNOW INTENTION

Intention cannot be accurately known by taking in the clothing (unless it is prison garb, and even then you could be wrong) or the accessories—such as the hardware that decorates many noses, eyebrows, or lips these days—or the spiked and unconventional hair styles. Then how can you know another's intention? Through your intuition. You look at the person and your brain takes in everything—the face jewelry, the hooded jacket, the entire image the person is projecting or attempting to project. But then you look beyond the get-up to see or feel that person's intention. I know a youngster whose hair is spiked, often spray painted with an array of startling colors meant to project a "with it" or tough exterior. Underneath those frizzy spikes I see only a sweet, caring young man, whose loving nature destroys the grunge "art form" he has so carefully constructed. Perhaps others see only the veneer, not the intent, and cross the street when they see him coming.

When you listen to your intuition, you will grasp intention. You will know whether the other person intends to harm you, or if their kinky couture is simply meant to speed their assimilation into a subculture that respects and defines one another by outward appearance. Gary Zukav, a physicist, expresses this thought in terms of the multisensory personality, which he defines as having more than the five senses that give us information. There is a so-called sixth sense of intuition as well:

> As a personality becomes multisensory, its intuitions—its hunches and subtle feelings—become important to it . . . It comes to recognize intentions, and to respond to them rather than to the actions and the words that it encounters. It can recognize, for example, a warm heart beneath a harsh and angry manner, and a cold heart beneath polished and pleasing words.

# Conclusion

I have often wondered why trainers who give diversity seminars do not use intuitive approaches toward understanding the "other." Trainers can do a very good job of drawing out unconscious biases and beliefs that we are often unaware of until we listen to the point of view of a person from a minority group. They may also be good at stimulating empathic feelings. However, we know that this is only a small part of the story, because there are so many other issues contributing to the problem.

One of the concerns in the field of diversity, as diversity consultant Patricia Arredondo explains it, is that that there are no set criteria for the material that a diversity consultant would cover. Therefore, whatever the trainer wishes to use is subject to the trainer's approach to the problem. She writes,

> As the field of diversity management evolves, so too does the number of individuals who have become diversity consultants. There currently is no accrediting professional body to designate who can self-identify as a diversity consultant, making the issue of expertise and credibility dependent on word-of-mouth referral, impartial selection processes of an organization, name recognition or a combination of the above (Arredondo, 1996).

Consultants involved in diversity training, as in other types of training, can differ in their perspective, and there is no way to know how effective any individual will be in any given situation. Many of today's consultants may also favor the raising consciousness aspect and may not be qualified to integrate other issues into their programs, such as dealing with the emotional roots of racism. To be proficient with some of the more complex issues, such as raising self-esteem, developing empathy, overcoming irrational fears, and developing intuition, may require a background in psychology as well as knowing how to foster intuition in others. The current state of the art may or may not include any of these subjects, which may be one reason why so many diversity programs fail in bringing about meaningful change.

To heal the racial-, ethnic-, or gender-based tensions in the workplace, it is important to open the heart in empathic understanding. When we understand the pain of those who feel they are discriminated against, whether homosexual, female, Asian, or other, we are more likely to be aware of our own actions and voluntarily change them. It also helps to develop an intuitive social intelligence, so that we may acquire an inner way of knowing how to relate to others. This could go a long way toward diminishing the ugly blight of racism and sexism on the American landscape.

However, the difficulty in gaining these insights was well understood by Carl Jung who, one year before the first rocket was launched into outer space, said "It is easier to go to Mars or to the moon than it is to penetrate one's own being." Forty-odd years later, we have indeed landed on the moon, and on Mars, and his observation still holds true. Poet Sharona Ben Tov expressed the inevitability of aggression toward others when she wrote, "The world beaten into a sword has served obedient in every age." Throughout history, when a leader had the urge to destroy others, it was never difficult to find willing foot soldiers. Will the new millennium bring change? We can hope.

In Part Eight you will learn how dreams play the role of a seer who can predict and reveal your intuitive thoughts. Dreams can offer a clearer understanding of intellectual, emotional, and spiritual issues and solve problems with intuitive solutions. What follows is a glimpse into how dreams have profoundly affected the lives of several people.

# PART EIGHT
## *The Intuition of Dreams*

A dream does not conceal, it reveals.

...CARL JUNG

Dreams may be the single most powerful source for intuitive insights and creative problem solving, and they are available to anyone simply at the drop of an eyelid because we know far more than we think we know—failure at game shows notwithstanding. It is often the dreaming mind that permits this information to be released from its secret vault. If creativity is defined as making apparently unforeseen or unrelated connections that produce something new and unique, then being in the dream state is an excellent tool. Through dreams we can find solutions to problems by making connections to possibilities that were unknown to our conscious minds.

Generally, most people agree that they often get fresh insights into problems or new ideas when they are away from day-to-day work problems and engaged in something completely different, such as running, washing dishes, driving, mowing the lawn, and so on. The dream state is another way to "get out of the office," although sometimes the stress from the office follows you to bed and provokes high anxiety dreams where you suddenly fall, or you are speaking before an audience and you lose your notes, and so forth. But most dreams allow our minds to roam freely and make unexpected creative connections—or possibly delve into the future. They allow stored knowledge, of which we are unaware during waking time, to expose its deeper insights without the burden of having to make rational sense.

Dreams can be more than problem solvers. They can tell you when you are sick, how to heal your illness, or that there is nothing wrong with your body despite a doctor's concern. I experienced several dreams of this nature when a doctor informed me that I might have some problems in my uterus. That same night I asked my dreams to tell me if anything was wrong. I dreamt of an empty room with white walls and a bare wooden floor. The next morning, when I began thinking about this dream, I remembered that the only thing I saw was an empty room, that there was nothing there. I knew then that the doctor's fears were ungrounded, that there was "nothing there," although I had to wait three months to confirm this diagnosis with another test.

Dreams can also predict future events. It is well-documented that paranormal dreams not only occur, but that they can be eerily accurate as well. Many people have canceled airplane trips after having dreamt of a plane crash. Unfortunately, their precognitions have often proved correct. However, some people who have a fear of flying may also dream of airplane disasters; these dreams are expressions of their fears and not necessarily predictive. The problem is that we don't yet know how to get the unerring precognitive dream on demand.

If we define intuition as "knowing without knowing how we know," then much of intuition's wisdom must be located outside of our ability to know directly. How do we get intuitive insights? In many ways. Some come in a flash, others when we are prodded into making bizarre connections in creativity workshops, and still others when we are in a trance-like state, usually in the late afternoon, perhaps during a long quiet drive or walk. And others come from dreams.

# 26

# *Executives' Dreams*

Some executives have learned that dreams can be so valuable that they rarely leave their beds without first revisiting the night's visions for business guidance. In *Executive ESP*, Douglas Dean and John Mihalsky write about some of the experiences of Bill Sechrist, franchise owner of Budget Rent-a-Car. One night he dreamt that one of his employees had his hand in the cash register. Sechrist clearly saw a close-up of his cash register and realized that the dream could be telling him this employee might be trying to steal. The next day he launched an investigation and discovered solid evidence that the individual was indeed claiming an unauthorized partnership in the business, and with no indication that the employee believed in a 50/50 split. When the employee was confronted with the evidence, he decided to resign.

Sechrist's wife Elsie has also received business guidance from her dreams. One of her most important dreams involved the very basic decision of where to locate the next car rental franchise. In a dream, Elsie saw the city of Houston, Texas with a large V-shaped structure in the distance that she interpreted as meaning "Victory." In another dream about Houston, water appeared; this indicated to her that there would be industry in the city, which would draw a lot of people to Houston, and suggested that it might become a tourist and convention center. In yet another dream she saw a star, and she interpreted the star as representing a "star" city of the South, meaning the city would shine like a star for them. This was well before Houston had been chosen to be a center of United States space exploration. They decided to build a franchise there, having no solid reasons that would predict success except for these clues from their dreams. One year later NASA headquarters was built in Houston and it became known as "Space City." The Sechrists never could have predicted the success they found in Houston only one year later.

Another of Sechrist's dreams offered him an important lesson in managerial skills that many other business owners would be wise to learn:

> I remember one dream quite vividly. It was around Christmas, and my partner and I had planned the bonuses for our staff. That night I dreamed I was putting pennies into a slot machine and just getting back pennies. Then I began to put gold coins into the machine and suddenly I was winning jackpots. I felt the dream meant that if the bonuses were increased, our employees would respond by helping us even more. We raised the bonuses, and our employees were extremely enthusiastic. We had one of the best years ever in our business (Dean and Mihalsky, 1974).

It is interesting to observe that Bill Sechrist learned the value of giving large bonuses from a dream and knew it would be effective. While this may not be a universally sound business practice, in many cases it can help to build morale and loyalty. Other business owners may learn the value of giving monetary rewards from either experience or an inner conviction that says, "If I treat my employees with respect and appreciation, because I believe it is the right thing to do, they will reward me with their best efforts." Most of the time, this philosophy works well, but for some organizations it has been a long hard lesson, and many still do not operate by this principle.

Aaron Feuerstein, the owner of Malden Mills in Lawrence, Massachusetts, which manufactures Polarfleece®, understood this philosophy presumably without a dream but from an inner conviction. In 1995 his mill experienced a devastating fire that put 600 employees out of work. At that point he could have relocated his business to another state where the salaries are cheaper, or contracted production to the Far East at a rock-bottom labor cost.

Instead, at age 70, he was determined to rebuild his business and continued to pay the salaries and health insurance for his unemployed workers during the many months it took to get the plant fully operational again. In order to do so, he had to obtain loans from banks, putting himself into what some may say was unnecessary debt. The result was that when the factory began to hum again, the employees produced almost triple the output of yardage as they had prior to the fire.

Why did productivity go up so dramatically? The employees said they were so grateful that Mr. Feuerstein stood by them and supported them during the rebuilding that they wanted to work as hard as they could to repay him for his kindness. Perhaps we can conclude that some people do not need the nudge of wisdom dreams may give us. For them it comes from a stubborn conviction of how human beings must live in order to live with themselves and the community.

Caroline Myss relates the dream of another executive in her book *Anatomy of the Spirit*. She tells of meeting an executive named Eric while she was in Belgium. Eric told her that ten years earlier he and two partners had begun a business venture manufacturing cat food. One day the partners informed him that they wanted out of the business and offered him a choice in the settlement: he could either take the equivalent of $35,000 in cash or all of the stock in the company, which was worthless at the time. Stunned, he went home to think it over and when he walked through the door said to his wife, "There's something I need to talk to you about." She replied that she had to talk about something also, that she had met another man and wanted a divorce. In one day he was being "divorced" by three people.

That night Eric had a dream,

> He was driving a car across the Alps during a ferocious storm. He felt that the roads were terribly icy, forcing him to grab onto the steering wheel hard so that the car would not run off the road. At one point it seemed as if he nearly lost control of the car by heading off into the side of the mountain, but he stopped it just in time. Finally he made it across the top of the mountain, and once he reached the top the storm evaporated and the roads became dry and safe. He continued driving until he came to a small cottage where he saw a candle burning in the window and a warm meal had been placed on the rough-hewn table.

As Eric thought about the dream, it indicated to him that the business would run into a lot of problems (the storm) but with a great deal of effort (he was able to keep the car on the road) he could keep the business running and keep himself, as well, from (going off the road) failing at life and business. When he reached the top of the mountain the storm evaporated, which he interpreted to mean all would be well, the going would be safe, and he would be able to make a living because there was a meal waiting for him in the cottage. He was also aware of driving a Jaguar in the dream, and because the company made cat food, he decided to take his partners' offer of all the stock in the then worthless company. Shortly afterward, several opportunities to boost the company's revenues came to Eric, and although the early months of getting the business off the ground were difficult, as the dream predicted, it became one of the most successful companies in Belgium. He also remarried a woman he described as a "life's partner in every meaning of the word. I never anticipated anything that I am doing now—only God could have known this plan."

This dream was a guide for Eric. It told him the going would be rough but that if he followed the road he would eventually find calm and peace and success. He knew the candle in the dream was burning for him, that someone was guiding him, and that the warm meal was satisfaction and completion. He met a wonderful woman and became more successful than he ever could have imagined. He says, "Now, when I meet people whose lives are upside down, I tell them, 'God is behind you. There is nothing to worry about. I know that for a fact.'"

# *High Tech Solutions from Dreams*

## INVENTORS' DREAMS

Californian Dan Gold had a very unusual dream. He is a former executive of Price Pfister, the California-based maker of plumbing fixtures, and was an ace product developer in the 1980s and early 1990s. He uses his dreams quite often to get his best design and engineering solutions. This seems to be quite common for inventors. Whenever I speak before inventors' groups, I ask for a show of hands as to how many people use their dreams to invent new products. Typically, over 75 percent in the room raise their hands.

When Gold was faced with a design problem, he would often wake up in the middle of the night knowing that he had just received a valuable insight toward finding the right solution. But one dream turned out to be more than every day connection-making to fix a design or mechanical problem. Gold was no longer working for Price Pfister at the time, but was now inventing on his own, and he had an idea for a promising new gizmo that is still under wraps. The problem was that there was

**254**

one part he needed to complete it, which he had been unable to find anywhere. Then he had a dream: "I was out in the wheat fields some place. I ran into this guy. We were chitchatting about who-knows-what. His final words were 'What you're looking for is in Kansas.'"

Gold woke up and wrote it down, although he didn't give it too much thought. He was puzzled by its meaning. Then he wondered if it had anything to do with motors, because he was still searching for the part he needed for his new invention. He had never been to Kansas, but he did know one person there. He called and asked him if he would look in the Yellow Pages for a machine shop in Kansas City. There was only one listing. Gold called the company, requested a catalogue, and discovered that they had exactly what he was looking for! It was the right size, the right price, and American-made. Because the company does not do any advertising, the salesman wondered how Gold had heard of them. When he told his story of the dream, the salesman was reduced to a one-word response: "Wow!"

Another inventor who relied on his dreams and meditations to access solutions was the late Itzhak Bentov. Ben, as he was called by friends, did not have a formal education beyond his junior year in high school, because that was the year that Hitler invaded Czechoslovakia, yet his extraordinary creativity as an inventor was prized by several companies involved in developing medical instruments. On his own he learned what he needed to know about human physiology, physics, and metallurgy to invent these devices. His former wife, Marilyn Bentov, tells of a time when he was on his way to a meeting to learn more about his assignment to invent a specific type of catheter, about which he knew nothing at the time. As they drove along the highway toward Miami, he casually noted a sign on the road pointing to a building called a Serpentarium, a snake museum. Later, he attended the meeting where he was briefed on the function the catheter had to perform and then he returned to the hotel to think about solving this problem. In the middle of the night, he woke up out of a dream and said to Marilyn, "Let's go to the Serpentarium." The following day they entered the snake museum. There he studied the skulls of a variety of snakes to see how they delivered their venom. From this research, he developed the first catheter with the ability to inject a dye that would allow veins to be x-rayed.

Bentov also wrote *Stalking the Wild Pendulum,* a book that describes *chakras,* the energy centers in the body, and other spiritual experiences. In a conversation with me some years ago, he told me that he saw an angel during a meditation. He described it as a very large male with huge wings covered with feathers that seemed to be hinged. Was this a glimpse into another reality, or was this a figment of his imagination? Is it common for inventors and creative people to have these kinds of experiences that seem to border on the twilight zone? Were the artists of the middle ages who depicted angels with feathered wings imagining what angels looked like, or did they have visions as well? We know that many people have learned to see auras surrounding other people and that these auras resemble the halos painted on sainted figures in the artwork of the fourteenth and fifteenth centuries. Did the artists see auras as well, or is this merely coincidental? Perhaps there is a connection between seeing evidence of a spiritual world and being highly creative in this world.

Dreams have a long history of assisting in the creative process. There is the well-known story of Elias Howe who had built a sewing machine but could not figure out how to place the hole in the needle to get it to pick up the thread from the bobbin. Isaac Singer was also hard at work on the sewing machine and the race was on to see who could perfect it and get to the patent office first.

One night Howe had a dream in which he was surrounded by cannibals holding spears who were threatening to make a stew of him if he did not complete his work. As they marched around him with the stewpot bubbling in the background, he noticed a hole at the tip of the spears they were carrying. He woke up in fright, as one does from a nightmare, but then quickly remembered the hole in the tip of the spear. Suddenly he knew that if he placed the hole at the bottom of the needle, it would work. He beat Singer to perfecting the invention and received the first patent for the sewing machine. Later, he sold the patent to Singer, which is why we have Singer and not Howe sewing machines today.

Thomas Edison also knew the value of dreams—or perhaps short naps. He was said to have slept at his desk with weights in his hands. The idea was that when the weights slipped out of his hands they would awaken him and he would remember his dreams. Edison held over 1000 patents, and it is possible that many of his inventions stemmed from that trance-like state between waking and sleep, or from his dreams.

## RESEARCH AND DEVELOPMENT DREAMS

On a plane trip from North Carolina to Boston, I sat next to a physician who told me he was the head of the dermatology department at a University hospital and was engaged in several research projects. I asked him if his intuition led him where to look for clues in his research and he said, "Of course, all the time." Then I asked if dreams were ever involved in helping him solve a research problem, and he told me the following story.

For two years he had been trying to find a cure for the bite that certain poisonous spiders inflict on humans, but he had run into a stone wall. Then one night, when he seemed to be at a peak of frustration in his research, he dreamt of leprosy. As he thought about this dream the next morning, he decided that it was telling him to try the medication that works with leprosy and see whether it would also be effective with brown spider venom. He soon put it through laboratory testing procedures and human trials, and it worked! In his dream, he made the connection between leprosy and spider venom that he probably never would have made consciously, that they would both respond to the same cure.

Dr. Frederick Banting, who was working on finding the cause of diabetes, had a dream that told him to tie up a dog's pancreas and perform several tests to learn how and why diabetes exists. Then he had another dream that told him to use insulin in the treatment of diabetics. This insight from the dreams pointed the way, and with laboratory experimentation, Banting was able to understand and treat this illness.

Al Huang was a research engineer at Bell Labs when he had a series of dreams about something very different than the project on which he was working. He dreamt of armies carrying piles of data, and often they would collide with one another. But in a final dream, he saw armies marching into one another, but this time they do not collide. From this dream, Huang realized that laser beams were like the opposing armies and that they could pass through one another unchanged, rather than colliding, as in his previous dreams. This revelation, that laser beams did not have to collide, led him to invent the first viable optical computer, which, according to some experts, was the most important breakthrough in computers since the invention of the microchip.

Another dream that seems to fall into that category of dreams that come from the most mysterious places, was that of David B. Parkinson, another engineer at Bell Labs, as Ira Flatow writes in his book about inventors, *They All Laughed*:

> In 1939 [David B. Parkinson] was an engineer working on the strip recorder that records voltages on a sheet of paper. A small round device, called a potentiometer, controls a set of magnetic clutches that adjusts the pen. In the spring of 1939 everyone was concerned about the rapid drive of the German army through Holland, Belgium, and France. The newspapers were filled with bad news from the war fronts in Europe, and it especially distressed Parkinson. The combination of his own engineering problems with problems from the war appears to have been a catalyst for a most vivid and peculiar dream:
> "I found myself in a gun pit or revetment with an anti-aircraft gun crew. I don't know how I got there . . . I was just there. The men were Dutch or Belgian by the uniforms—the helmets were neither German, French, nor English. There was a gun there

. . . firing occasionally, and the impressive thing was that every shot brought down an airplane! After three or four shots one of the men in the crew smiled at me and beckoned me to come closer to the gun. When I drew near he pointed to the exposed end of the left trunnion. Mounted there was the control potentiometer of my level recorder! There was no mistaking it—it was the identical item."

The whole scene faded out. Parkinson awoke still retaining a remarkably clear picture of the details. He realized that if his potentiometer could control the high-speed gyrations of a rapidly moving pen with great accuracy, why couldn't a similar device do the same thing for an anti-aircraft gun?

The first production model, labeled M-9, appeared in the field in 1943 and changed the outcome of the so-called Second Battle of Britain. In one month, August 1944, 90 percent of German V-1 buzz bombs destined for London were shot down over the cliffs of Dover. In a single week, radar-guided 90-millimeter guns controlled by the M-9s shot down 89 of 91 buzz bombs launched from Antwerp (Flatow, 1990).

The timing of this dream is extraordinary, because the United States was over two years away from getting into the war when Parkinson's dream occurred. And the dream made the outrageous connection between a small, a one-to-two-inch gadget used to regulate a moving pen, and a huge antiaircraft gun. Because the research to develop the M-9 was begun in 1939, the Allies were able to get it to the battlefield during the 1940s to significantly turn the tide of the war. Was it hidden intelligence or creative genius, or are they one and the same?

Dreams have fascinated people for thousands of years, perhaps because they can be vivid eye openers to hidden emotion, predictive of future events, or incredible problem solvers. Many researchers agree that the stuff of everyday dreams are random thoughts, fragments of the day's happenings, and regurgitations of emotional or embarrassing experiences that somehow got retained in the unconscious mind only to spill out during dream time as a cathartic release. These are usually quickly forgotten, or not remembered at all. However, if they are remembered and recur frequently, the unconscious mind may be attempting to make the dreamer aware of a problem or a solution to a problem that is important to address, whether related to an emotional or business issue. For example, if you have been considering investing in either a potato chip plant or an ice rink, and you experience several dreams in which you are eating potato chips and it leads to a good feeling in the dream, the message may be to invest in the potato chip company, or at least investigate the possibilities. However, if you see yourself skating around the rink on thin ice while munching chips, try sorting it out with another dream the following night.

When dreams come spontaneously and are very vivid and memorable—so memorable, in fact, that they may haunt you for hours if not days—they are worth thinking about. It is as if something is saying to you, "Pay attention, you are missing something that you need to know!" If you can grasp their meaning, as you will see that Floyd Ragsdale did, they can be worth millions of dollars.

# 28

# *Dreams to Solve Mechanical Problems*

> Reports of numerous cases as well as the collection of instances
> by Chabaneix (1897) seem to put it beyond dispute that dreams
> can carry on the intellectual work of daytime and bring it to con-
> clusions which had not been reached during the day, and that
> they can resolve doubts and problems and be the source of new
> inspiration.
>
> ...SIGMUND FREUD

## FLOYD RAGSDALE'S DREAMS

Carrying on the intellectual work of the day in dreams is nothing
new for Floyd Ragsdale. He habitually coaxes his dreams to solve
mechanical problems on demand by becoming one with his
machines, to empathize with hunks of steel and undulating tubes.
With only a high school education, Ragsdale has become an engineer, and his ability to maintain the machines that constantly
break down appears to be far superior to that of the college
trained engineers. Floyd works at the DuPont manufacturing

plant that produces Kevlar fiber, where he oversees the fiber-making machines. Kevlar is the substance used in bullet-proofing vests and in radial tires, among other products. As useful as the fiber has become, the machines used in this manufacturing process have a way of breaking down at inopportune times and repairing them is seldom easy.

DuPont had hired seven college educated engineers to locate the problems with these machines whenever they broke down, among their other duties. Empathizing with the needs of a machine was an unlikely required course in engineering school, so when the professional engineers found themselves unable to fix the machines, their best recommendation to management was to purchase new ones at a cost of over $500,000 each.

Ragsdale, however, used another approach. One night after one of the machines broke down, he imagined that he was the machine and tried to figure out what was wrong with "himself." Later, in a dream, he saw a picture of tubes with flexible wires inside of them resembling the Slinky® toy. When he woke up and thought about the dream, Ragsdale realized that if these toys were placed inside the tubes, they could keep the tubes from collapsing and, thus, failing the entire mechanism. The next day he went to his boss and told him about the dream. The reply, as any unimaginative but usually reliable boss might utter, was "Forget it and get back to work."

That evening after his shift ended, Floyd and a friend decided to try the Slinky® solution. It worked. It worked so well, in fact, that it saved the company over $3 million in lost revenue from downtime, plus the cost of a new machine. (The score: Dreams = 1, Engineers = 0)

When asked whether dreams are important to him, Ragsdale's answer seems to come from a deep reverence for their mysterious powers to guide him. He feels that dreams have been bestowed upon him as a gift that has not only solved mechanical problems whenever they have occurred, but at times predicted some in advance! He appears to be tuned into that "universal mind" in such a way that his dreams function as the ultimate universal-mind web server. Ragsdale says,

> When I begin dreaming about a problem, it helps me to focus on it so that I can understand it more clearly. I make myself part of the problem to understand it better. It's like putting yourself in another person's shoes to understand him better.

He tries to create an empathic bond between man and machine to understand the problem as well as solve it. He describes this process in another dream as well:

> I [dreamt] that I was at work troubleshooting the filter on the machine, and that I was working next to a man who was sweating terribly and then he passed out. His heart stopped beating. Someone came along and looked at him and said "We've got to get a pacemaker to revive him."

Ragsdale wrote down "pacemaker" when he woke up, but did not know what it meant. The next morning he looked at the word "pacemaker" and asked himself, how could I associate the word with this equipment? It came in a flash. We needed a pacemaker to run this machine! Ragsdale went to an electrician and knew exactly what was needed to keep the filter going. It had to be something new and invented just for this purpose. It had to be a series of timers in a box that would time out at a certain pace so that the filter would operate continuously. The electrician got excited about this idea and produced the timer box within two weeks. It not only solved the immediate problem, but also prevented waste and saved hundreds of thousands of dollars for DuPont. (The score: Dreams = 2, Engineers = 0)

Ragsdale also has precognitive dreams that warn of coming events:

> One time I [dreamt] that I was at work and in a place near some double doors where boxes of supplies were stored. Suddenly a flood of rushing water ten feet high came behind me. It was

very scary, like a dam breaking. I rushed out as fast as I could to keep from drowning.

I did not understand this dream. The next day a dryer—we had a problem with moisture in a dryer—kept going up to the point where we couldn't produce a quality product, so we were forced to shut the area down. The engineers couldn't find what was wrong. So we set it up again, and moisture would still be high, until one day I tried to fix the problem and got all kinds of water rushing out of the dryer, just like in my dream. We had a stream of water rushing out the door and into the courtyard just like my dream . . . it was exactly the same thing.

However, we were still baffled and did not know what was causing this problem. I felt that there had to be a rupture that caused it. Friday night I stayed late to solve the problem. I was sitting at my desk thinking about the centrifuge that separates water from the product. I fell asleep thinking about the equipment and dreamed that I was the centrifuge. Then it hit me. There had to be a malfunction inside the centrifuge. I got a mechanic there to look at it, and sure enough, that was it. (The score: Dreams = 3, Engineers = 0)

Another dream:

"I was playing basketball with the kids and twisted my ankle and I was hopping off the court in pain." I woke up and wrote down "twisted ankle" and went back to sleep. The next morning I asked myself what does "twisted ankle" have to do with the process that I was working on. I looked at the schematic that was on my desk and noticed that the valve stem was twisted, so that when it was in a closed position it was actually in a feed position. The word "twisted" helped me resolve the problem by telling me what to look for. (The score: Dreams = 4, Engineers = 0)

Two years ago, Ragsdale's department had thirty-six employees. Today, there are only seven, and none of these are college trained engineers. With his uncanny ability to fix complex machines which Ragsdale learns from his dreams, who needs more people? He adds, "With the downsizing productivity has actually improved in my department, and my own efficiency has increased by 50 percent!" His enhanced efficiency can most likely be attributed to the fact that he does not have to wait around for the professional engineers to do their studies, write up reports, and make recommendations based on their studies. Ragsdale just goes to sleep and waits for the solution to be revealed in his dreams. Perhaps schools of engineering should offer a course in how to find solutions in dreams—with their guest lecturer, Floyd Ragsdale.

That suggestion is not as bizarre as it may seem. Stanford University actually had a course on dreams for their business students, and Florida International University offers their business students a course on intuition. Also, the Pacifica Institute in California confers an undergraduate degree in dreamwork, and the Swedish government recently agreed to fund dream studies as part of its national health plan! All of this interest in dreams may lead to new discoveries in how to tap into our dreaming mind for health and profit—as well as mechanical advice.

How can Ragsdale's dreams be explained? How can he "know" so much about the workings of the machines that mechanical engineers fail to see? Does his unconscious mind actually know the solution that his conscious mind does not perceive? Or, are they a gift from a another reality, the hidden intelligence that he has tapped?

## JOE KILLOUGH'S DREAM

A gift from another reality could be one explanation for a dream experienced by Joseph Killough, a group engineer at the Bose Corporation in Framingham, Massachusetts. I met Killough in Colorado Springs when he came to a "Solving Problems with Dreams" course that I delivered for the Product Developers and Management Association. He told me about a most remarkable dream, one that seemed to come from his unconscious mind as well as from some mysterious place that is not in everyday reality.

He was working on a new design for a sound system and was considering which of three different configurations to begin working on, any or all of which could have design errors caused by others who had previously worked on them. However, it would be impossible to know which design might contain the errors until work was begun on them. As he was struggling with trying to decide which design would most likely be the most free of bugs down the road, he had a dream that solved the problem:

> I was a young engineer approaching a job jar or in-basket holding several tasks which would tell me which was the next job that I had to do. If I took out a task and discovered it needed rework, I would be under pressure to complete the work on time due to the errors of someone upstream who worked on this before me. I tried to figure out which one I should work on, and I knew that if I picked it right I'm golden, which meant I'm saved. I selected one from the job jar and an angel appeared and stamped the design I chose with the word "TRUTH" written in gold letters across the face of it.
>
> I interpreted this to mean that there would be no errors in it from the previous work. It had the ring of truth. It was gold! So I chose the configuration that the dream suggested and the answer was exactly what I was looking for. The task was truly complete, accurate and sufficient for the next person to test.

When I asked him to describe the angel, Killough said, "The angel looked like a large white man, [with a] white face with features that reminded me of a Greek statue, and white wings. He was very large and had a strong presence." Killough's angel reminded me of the description that Itzhak Bentov had described when he told me of his seeing an angel some years earlier. In a recent poll, 75 percent of Americans said that they believe in angels. Perhaps this is a common phenomenon that many other experience as well.

## ARTHUR LAGACE'S DREAM

Another engineer, Arthur Lagace, formerly with Arthur D. Little, is now a consultant in chemical engineering in Newton, Massachusetts. One day, Lagace received a frantic telephone call from a client. The client's problem was that one of his very specialized machine had broken down, a machine that makes a metal-filled plastisol that would disperse a liquid form of PVC. The PVC product is used to make the metal aprons that protect patients from x-rays. Because the metal is heavy and the particles want to settle, the mixture must be constantly stirred. If the key component to manufacturing the plastisol—the stirring—does not work, then the whole plant would have to be shut down whereupon they could lose many of their customers. The client's dilemma: it would be too costly to repair the machine and if a new one were purchased it could take over three months before delivery, causing the whole plant to cease operations for 90 days.

When Lagace received the assignment, he thought about the problem and began thumbing through heavy machinery catalogues of equipment suppliers. He found nothing that he thought would work. "So, I went to sleep," he said. "In my dreams I saw a cement mixer. I realized when I woke up that a cement mixer could probably do the job. Also, they were immediately available for purchase, no waiting." Lagace quickly typed up a memo suggesting that perhaps it would work for this process and faxed it to the owner who instantly loved the idea! He actually purchased a mortar mixer and found that it worked even better than the machine that had broken down. Rather than going back to the original mechanism, he actually prefers to use the mortar mixer now.

# 29

# *Dream a New Product, Dream a New Career*

When the Product Development and Management Association with the Institute for International Research sponsored a seminar on Idea Generating Techniques for New Product Development, one of the techniques it offered was my workshop on dreams, which Lauren Berger, a product developer at Clairol, attended. Everyone came with a problem to be solved in their dreams, but the group decided early on to work on Berger's problem and it became the focus of the workshop. Berger's request was to coach her dreams to predict what would be the "in" product for hair care, or color, in the next five or ten years. She was also looking for a new product that Clairol could manufacture and bring to market in the next two years. And, for a product already in the works, she was also in search of a name.

During the workshop that preceded the dream Berger would have that night, we used a Synectics-type word association exercise that elicited as many new ideas as possible. What usually occurs either during or after this exercise is that there is a word or several words that we have heard that trigger other thoughts in our connection-making brain. These thoughts can occur whether awake or in dreams. For example, one word a participant offered was "mermaid." That night I dreamt of a mermaid who was combing her long blond hair, which was also streaked with a more intense reddish-blond color.

I told Berger about my dream at the next morning's session, but whether the image I had will be predictive of a popular hair color in the next five years or so only time will tell. I discovered during the first day's workshop that the group was extremely diverse. It included product developers involved with a wide variety of assignments, from developing medical instruments to engineering tools to advertising campaigns and new food products. With this interesting mix of people we generated a number of innovative ideas that several people took back to the home office for further consideration. Then the group stretched out on the floor and listened to a relaxation monologue that suggested they would dream about a solution to whatever problem they presented. That night Berger had a dream that she could not recall, but she awoke the next morning with the concept of a new product in her head, as well as a name for another product! As of this writing, Clairol's new product and the name for the other product is still top secret, but they will both be on the market soon. Between her dream and mine, Berger may have hit three home runs for her company.

## A BABY SAYS IT ALL

Dr. Arthur Bernard, of Sherman Oaks, California, had just received his doctorate in psychology and was searching for a way to begin a private practice. One day during a meditation, he heard a voice tell him to open a Dream Center. That night he dreamt that he went to a hospital to pick up a new baby. "It was a beautiful baby with blue eyes and I was like the mother and father," he said. In the morning, while thinking about this dream, Bernard understood that the "baby" symbolized his new career and that opening the Dream Center was the way to go.

Within six months his new center became very successful. He was able to practice his new skill in psychotherapy using the client's dreams as part of the healing process.

Riza Federman, an expert cook and nutritionist who loves working with food and creating new recipes, was looking for a career that would use her considerable talents. One night, at my suggestion, she asked her dreams to tell her how she could earn money with food. That night she dreamt that she had baked a chocolate kugel, a noodle-based casserole that is not traditionally made with chocolate. Most kugels are mixtures of noodles, eggs, cheeses, and sometimes fruit. The next day Federman decided to do what her dream suggested, make kugels. She began developing different flavors of kugel, from pumpkin to jalapeno to chocolate, from fat free to "fat full," and many variations in between. She placed one ad for her kugels in the *Boston Globe* newspaper and received over fifty orders. In two weeks she had attracted over 100 customers, some of whom wanted her to do low-fat cooking for their special diets. All of this from a dream about chocolate kugel!

Another dream that influenced a career came to Californian Michael Stromph, who dreamt that he was sitting in his office waiting for phone calls to answer questions about grammar. He wondered why more people were not calling and the telephone was not ringing. Then he suddenly got the idea that he should let the whole world know of his skill and that he would call his business the "Grammar Hotline." Stromph awakened from this short dream and was too excited to sleep for the rest of the night. He called newspapers, radio, and the media in general to let them know of his new enterprise, and, thus, was born his new business. After this auspicious beginning, he now receives over 1000 calls a week and answers all questions relating to grammar.

Mark Sheron, another Californian, had started a petroleum distribution business in Poland. After two years of hard work and few tangible results, he was beginning to question his decision. At this time of uncertainty he had the following dream:

> I am talking to a man about my new business. He asks me specif-
> ically how it works. As I begin describing the process in detail, he
> gasps, takes a few steps backwards and says, "My god, you are
> sitting on a gold mine!"

A short time after this dream, some very positive events occurred
that turned Sheron's business around and made it very profitable. At this time, the future looks more than extremely bright.

## A HOW-TO DREAM FOR SALARY NEGOTIATION

Gayle Delaney has taught a course on dreams at Stanford Business School and is the author of several books on the subject.
She tells how one dream led to an excellent result during a
highly charged salary negotiation related to a position with a
radio station.

The night before her meeting with a vice president of the
station, she had a dream that guided her in negotiating the salary she was to receive for hosting a three-hour daily radio show.
She says that she incubated this dream, which means that before
going to sleep she asked her dreams to give her a strategy for
working with the vice president to reach an equitable agreement
on her salary. This was to be her first experience in bargaining.
She had always been in private practice as a psychologist and
had never before worked for a company. Feeling that this lack of
experience put her at a distinct disadvantage, she was desperate
to get some help. That night, she had the following dream:

> I arrive in a foreign land, very different from my own. As I get out
> of the car, I sense a bit of medieval Japan where "bushido" or
> honor, loyalty, fierceness, and courage are the cultural values that
> count. I suddenly realize that everyone in this land will try to kill
> me (or anyone) upon first encounter. If I want to survive and
> thrive in this environment, I must be ready to kill anyone I meet
> and let each one know that. Only then will there be mutual
> respect between myself and others.

This dream was rather unnerving because the message she received was, "If I want to survive in this land I must be ready to kill!" This thought gave her a surge of what she described as "warrior-like fierceness." She knew that she had to fight, but she still was not sure how it would be done. As she sat in the office of the vice president, the feelings from her dream surfaced again. When the vice president offered her what she knew was a modest salary, Delaney directed the conversation to other issues. Each time this occurred he raised his offer. And with each subsequent proposal, she diverted the conversation until the vice president agreed to pay her more than two and one-half times what he had originally offered, which was the exact amount that an experienced radio host and friend had suggested would be a fair deal (Delaney, 1988).

If you cannot remember having such helpful dreams you may wonder why it is that some people receive the most wonderful and valuable information from their dreams while others barely remember them? We have no real answer to that except that some people seem to be more open to dreams. Many people who report experiencing vivid dreams are those involved in creative occupations, such as advertising, inventing, art, music, writing, and so on. Gunther Schuller, a world-renowned composer, says that he often experiences a dream where he hears the entire work and simply has to transcribe the music in the morning, making very few changes to the final score. The comedian, songwriter, and musician Steve Allen says he writes between forty and forty-five songs per month, but that his most successful piece, *This Must Be the Start of Something Big*, came from a dream. In David Ogilvy's autobiography *Ogilvy on Advertising*, he describes a dream in which a baker drives his horse-drawn wagon down a country road. After having the dream, Mr. Ogilvy wrote a now famous Pepperidge Farm bread commercial with just that script.

# 30

# *The Language of the Night*

"One reason you don't recognize intuition is that it speaks a different language," says Laura Day, author of *Practical Intuition*. Dreams, too, have a language of their own. They are another form of intuition, but they speak to us in symbols or vivid pictures that are often metaphors representing feelings or events. Or sometimes we hear someone speaking to us in the dream, and we may need help in understanding the meaning. If you never got the hang of interpreting metaphors in your high school or college literature classes, you may find the meaning of the symbols in your dreams impossibly obscure. But you can learn to interpret them to get valuable information—if you put aside your need to have concrete answers and allow their ambiguity to play upon your mind like gently massaging fingers relaxing your body.

## A WRITER'S DREAM

Gerald Jackson, in his book *Executive ESP*, interpreted the language of one dream in its most literal form. He relates the story of how a dream led him to publish his work. He had been trying to get a manuscript published for quite some time and kept running into brick walls. One night he asked his unconscious mind for help and received the following dream:

> I fell asleep with this request strongly in my mind and dreamed that I'd taken a plane to the island of St. Croix. I saw an Indian there, in feathers and full regalia, outside a fancy hotel. I passed him, went through the lobby and out to the hotel's pool, where I met a gray-haired man. He was the agent I was looking for.

When Jackson woke up, he had to decide whether to take this dream literally or not. Was he really supposed to pack up and fly to the Caribbean? For the next few days he pondered this question and then decided that he would follow the scenario the dream suggested. He went to a travel agent and asked to see a listing of the hotels in St. Croix. When his eyes lit on Club Commanche he knew that was where he wanted to be. On arriving in St. Croix, he checked in at the hotel and headed straight to the pool. Right there, standing at poolside, was the gray-haired man from his dream! He struck up a conversation with him and asked if he were a literary agent. "No," the man said, "Why do you ask?"

Jackson then told him about the dream and the man was fascinated. He told him that a neighbor in New York had just published a book and that he would send her a postcard suggesting that she get in touch with Jackson. A short time later this New York author happened to see Jackson being interviewed on television. With that, plus the postcard from St. Croix, she called her agent, who eventually became Jackson's agent, and the book was subsequently published (Jackson, 1984).

## DREAMS OUT OF THE TWILIGHT ZONE

Sometimes we experience a dream that comes from a dimension that can only be thought of as the "twilight zone." A case in point is a dream that graduate student Kari Danziger relates. One night she dreamt of assassinations. She saw both Lincoln and John F. Kennedy being shot to death, and these visions filled her night with terror and fear. The next morning she was very confused and frightened by her dreams of the night before, and she could not understand why these thoughts would invade her sleep. When she read the newspaper the next day, December 8, 1980, she learned that John Lennon had been murdered the night before.

Not long ago there was a newspaper story about a Boy Scout who was about to go on an overnight trip with his troop. He dreamt that the train he was to travel on would be in an accident, and he shared this dream with his parents before he left. Since train crashes were very unusual, his parents reassured him that he would be safe. The train crashed and he was badly injured. His dream defied logic, but life events, it seems, are not always logical.

Sometimes we get notified of impending accidents or death from our dreams; sometime we don't. In my own immediate family, several people who have died within my lifetime were forewarned, sometimes only days or weeks before, and in one case, a dream predicted a death one year in advance. A few weeks before Abraham Lincoln was assassinated, he dreamt that he saw a crowd of people in mourning. He asked a bystander what happened and was told, "The President is dead."

The night before I learned that the U.S.S.R. had dissolved into several different states, I had a dream of tiny people standing in each of the states of the Soviet Union in the Mapparium of the Christian Science Center in Boston. The Mapparium is a huge globe of the world that fills a room in one of the Church's buildings. I had not visited this place in well over twenty years. In the dream, I saw these little people holding hands across the continent, and their leader, who was taller, suddenly shouted, "Let go!" And all of the people dropped their hands and fell to the bottom of the Mapparium. This dream was also puzzling to me until I read the newspaper accounts of what had taken place in Russia.

## A DREAM EXPERIMENT

Henry Reed, editor of the dream magazine *Sundance* in Virginia Beach, Virginia, understands dreams both literally and figuratively. During the course of his experimental work with dreams, Reed noticed that in the dream groups he was running, when one person in the group mentioned a personal problem that she would like to solve, the other members of the group would subsequently dream about that person's problem. For example, in one experiment a woman said she could not decide what college she should transfer to nor what she should study. The group went to sleep that night hoping to solve her problem, but they woke up confused. Several said that they had had dreams about illicit sex, which didn't seem to have anything to do with the woman's dilemma. At this point the woman confessed that she was having an affair with a married man and realized that it was keeping her from making a decision about her schooling. Confronted with so many "witnesses," she decided to end the affair and move on in her life and career.

In our culture we are taught to look for facts. If, for example, I dream of a tree, then it should have a definite meaning, such as representing life. But if you tell me that it could mean that or it could mean many other things then I may be left confused. How can I possibly interpret my dream if you don't tell me precisely what it means? The answer is that if you begin to sense the implications of the dream rather than looking for concrete answers—as if the dream were a do-it-yourself manual in self understanding—you will get it. In the context of worrying about the solution to a spider bite, you will see that dreaming of leprosy may be, not necessarily is, the cure for the spider disease. When Bill Sechrist saw an employee's hand in the till in his dream, the picture he saw may have been an old-fashioned cash register and not like the computer-generated car rental type that is used today. Yet the message he got was to watch the employee. He did not take it literally until he investigated what was going on. He watched, he saw, and then he fired.

Dreams can be cultivated, requested, and experienced in ways that are difficult to anticipate. If you read this chapter with disbelief because you have never experienced such dreams, or you cannot remember your dreams, perhaps it is because you never learned how to access them. Once this skill is acquired, you will be astonished at the wisdom your dreams can bring.

A dream can be as mysterious and literal as suggesting that you hop a plane to St. Croix or as symbolic as one a friend shared with me. As an only child, she was having a difficult time catering to the special needs of her elderly parents as well as keeping hold of a fragile sense of self esteem, which she felt was impaired from childhood. One night, after a day of feeling particularly vulnerable, she had a dream in which she was carrying both of her parents in a bed. What did this bizarre picture mean? To understand the dream's meaning it helps to visualize doing what you did in the dream. Carrying two people in a bed would be pretty heavy lifting, indicating how burdensome her parents felt to her. Why a bed? Perhaps she had a subconscious feeling that her low self-esteem began in the marriage bed, at conception. Or, maybe she felt that they were being kept comfortable in bed, due to her hard work, yet somnolent or even asleep in the sense of not being aware of her difficult struggle to please them. The imagery is quite rich and offered much to think about in interpreting its meaning. She realized there was "heavy lifting" going on in her everyday life, but that it had been pushed to her unconscious mind because she felt guilty complaining about caring for her parents. A dream provides a place to allow the expression of these feelings.

Or take the dream of another friend who ran a furniture manufacturing business. Her best craftsman was behaving like a prima donna by not informing the customers of the changes he was making to their custom-made furniture, believing that his artistry gave him the right to make any change he wanted without consulting the client. In my friend's dream, she found herself smashing dining room tables. Was the dream expressing frustration with the artisan? Probably. But why a dining room table when he had been working on bookcases? Dining room tables hold food, sustenance. The dream could have been expressing her frustration with the business, her source of income and sustenance. Smashing tables in these circumstances led her to reconsider whether she wanted to continue employing this artisan or even remain in the business.

# 31

# *Interpreting Common Dreams*

Only the dreamer can provide the most accurate interpretation of a dream. However, the dreamer may be baffled by the imagery and need help from another person to sort out its possible meanings. Because each dream is intimately tied to the nuances of an individual's life, no dream dictionary can tell you precisely what any given dream indicates; they can give you a rough indication at best, but you must fill in the details. Or you may wish to ask for help from a psychologist who works with dreams to help you sort them out. Another approach is to use that of the Senoi Indians, where you tell the community or several friends about the dream and listen to each person's interpretation. Chances are that if you relate your dream to several people, at least one of them may have an interpretation that will resonate with you. Keep in mind that there is usually not one absolute and irrefutable meaning to any dream, which provides a wonderful opportunity to be creative in interpreting its wisdom.

However, the following are a few suggested meanings to some common dreams that are offered only as a rough guide.

The final accuracy of their meaning and how they apply to your life will depend on your own insight.

If you dream you are driving in a car and it crashes, it may be telling you that you are on the wrong course, or have made a wrong decision, and that you had better get out of it soon. If your secretary is driving the car, it may be telling you that she is running your business and not you. If someone else is driving the car, or no one is driving the car, and you are in the back seat, then you are not in control of your life at this moment, either someone else is or no one is. If you are driving and narrowly escape one dangerous spot after another, the dream may be sending the message that you are on a potentially self-destructive course. However, if the issue is personal, and your car is going down hill and the brakes don't seem to work, it may be telling you that your body is going down hill and that you need to rest or perhaps get a medical checkup.

Dreams of falling are quite common and indicate feelings of vulnerability. Dreams of flying are also common, and while the interpretations in all cases must be referenced to what is actually going on in your life, flying dreams often act as a release from feeling tied down or constricted in everyday life. For example, women who are at home caring for children and feel they cannot do something else that they may want to do often have flying dreams. People who have been forced to take over the family business instead of pursuing their own interests may also experience this kind of dream.

If you are a man and dream that you lose your pants, find someone else's and put them on, put your hand in the pocket, and find that your money is gone, this dream may be telling you that you are embarking on a course that will leave you with a lot less money than you had before. If you are a woman and dream that you are pushing your briefcase around a swimming pool, but it falls in and you are frantically trying to get help to get it out, your dream may be telling you that you need to take responsibility in a work situation and not wait for someone else to solve your problems. Also, the swimming pool may be symbolic of feeling that you are in something deep—as in "over your head"—and the briefcase may be symbolic of your livelihood. When you finally do fish it out by yourself, the dream is telling you that you can overcome your problems on your own; you can succeed; and you do not need to be rescued by someone else.

In another woman's swimming pool dream, she fell into the pool and her beach bag kept pushing her down deeper and deeper until her toes felt sand at the bottom. At this point, she pushed her way up from the bottom of the pool and was able to keep the "evil" bag from drowning her. The key to understanding this dream is to figure out why her beach bag had pushed her into the pool, and why her feet struck sand at the bottom. Her interpretation was that she had been addicted to sunbathing and was very much aware that too much sun could lead to cancer. The catalyst for this dream was an appointment she had the next day to see a dermatologist; this dream revealed her fear that she would find a melanoma, due to too much time spent lying in the sand.

Both of these swimming pool dreams express a feeling of crisis in their dreamer's lives: the first was a fear of not being able to make it in the work world; the second was literally a fear of death from an overdose of pleasure—lying in the sun. For each of these women, the dreams provided an important wake-up call.

## HOW TO INCUBATE YOUR DREAMS

You can begin to experience problem solving in your dreams whenever the need arises, whether it is a personal or business-related issue. The following method is suggested to resolve a business-related issue that you can share with at least two other people who are actively connected to the problem. In this example, the president, vice president of sales, and vice president of marketing met to solve a problem which was how do we find new ways to expand market share.

Step 1.  Brainstorm solutions to this problem with the group, setting as a goal the specific outcome desired. During the brainstorming period, write down any words that spark your interest, without being aware of why the words are of interest to you.

Step 2.  Go home and prepare for bed by reviewing the problem in your mind. Write down any thoughts that come to mind. Just before falling asleep, tell yourself that you will remember the dream in the morning.

Step 3.  Form a short one sentence question, such as "How do we expand our market?" Silently repeat this question over and over until you fall asleep.

Step 4.  If you wake up during a dream, or just after, write it down, or have a voice-activated tape recorder by the bed and record your dream.

Step 5.  Do not get out of bed in the morning until you have reviewed the last dream that you can remember. Write down as much of it as possible.

Step 6.  Look for clues as to how it revealed an answer to the question you had asked.

# Conclusion

In December 1997, a Massachusetts woman dreamt the winning numbers to a lottery ticket; she won $66 million. A Californian invented a profitable leaf blower from a dream. If you learn how to use your dreams to reveal your intuition, you may watch your IQ (*Intuition* Quotient) and/or financial status rise dramatically! But dreaming is only one tool that can bring intuitive insights into your life. In Part Nine, several other methods will be offered to stimulate your intuition in solving problems, whether it is developing new products, exploring new markets, or finding profitable new investments. As you will discover, these methods will work best when you are awake or even only semi-awake. And, if these methods do not give you the answers you seek, your dreams will always be there as an alternative source of wisdom. You will be able to wake up and delve into your unconscious mind, or sleep on it. Either way, you win!

# PART NINE

## *Igniting the Intuitive Spark*

The most creative people seem to be those with the easiest access to the unconscious.

...NANCY NAPIER

If the most creative people, as Napier says, are those who can access their unconscious minds easily, then the following exercises created by a number of intuitive consultants will help you tap into your own unconscious core of creativity.

"Few people are gifted 'innately' with supersensory perception," says Masatochi Yoshimura, President of Sanyo Chemical Industries, Ltd. He continues,

Yet even ordinary people can reach or get near to this level of ability through intensive training. With practice, one can develop the ability to see things correctly, predict how others will behave, and decode messages received nonverbally. This ability is a form of insight, prediction, telepathy, or precognition, all of which are products of an intricate working of the superconscious.

Not many of us are innately gifted in this area. Yet we are all capable of being intuitive, because this is how we were wired from birth—although some of us seem to be better wired than others. Most of us can get intuitive insights when we need them by learning how to quiet the constant muttering that goes on in the brain using meditation, yoga, creating specific images, or with physical activities such as walking, running, or swimming. All of these are found to be useful in luring the shy, faint sounds of your intuitive mind to speak up and guide you in your business and personal life.

However, there are other methods you may wish to use to regain that special intuitive ability we had as children. Practice will take some time and patience, but with conscious attention to unconscious processes, it will become more available to us when needed. Intuition is not unlike learning a language. If we had learned a foreign language in high school and then did not speak it for ten or twenty years, it would come back to us after some review, but with far less effort than learning a new language. While most of us have experienced the occasional intuitive insight, such as knowing who was calling on the telephone before answering it, or thinking about someone and then receiving a letter from that person on the same day the thought occurred, most of us need practice in being able to summon intuitive insights whenever we wish.

To get an idea of the depth of knowledge that can be attained, I recommend that you read at least one of the several books on intuition listed in the bibliography. If you have access to a teacher, the process may be learned even more quickly, for it seems that participating either in a group or with someone who is already "tuned in" makes it easier to learn the skill.

# 32

# Consciously Courting the "Yes!"

I use the term "yes" here to mean the creative insight, the "aha" moment when it all comes together. Creative problem solvers use a variety of methods to coax the "yes," and when it comes, it is laden with intuition. We have already defined creativity as making connections from disparate concepts or thoughts to produce something that is new and useful. However, when an idea is both unique and has appeal, when the response to it is, "Why didn't I think of that!" then intuition as well as creativity is often present, because it is your intuition that knows that the idea is not only unique, but also has merit.

## CREATIVE IMAGING

Creative imaging is a technique that many consultants use (several of their methods were explained in Part Five) that can be useful when a group is given the task of creating new products because last year's line isn't doing well this year. The first step in this three-step imaging technique is to envision the specific need for change. For example, you see that the present products are not maintaining market share, so that becomes the need. But you aren't sure what new product the market will respond to with enthusiasm, so you envision the product by first seeing in your mind's eye the "display" of empty shelves. The next step is to look at those empty shelves and, without regard to technical or financial constraints, allow your imagination to put different shapes, colors, and sizes of something on those shelves. Then, pool the "visions" of the group to see whether there are any similarities in what everyone has "seen" and note them. If several people envision one or more similar "new" products, they may become the winning product of the future.

Finally, in the third step, envision an action plan. One way to do this is to refine the image of the new product, visualize what it would look like one year from today, and "see" whether it sells. The group should then play with these "pictures" by building on one anothers' ideas to discover whether it will result in a viable action plan. Follow this with the necessary research to validate its feasibility and profitability, and chances are the visualization will become a successful new product.

## BODY-BASED INSIGHT

While the most common intuitive techniques rely on the visual sense, that is, being able to "see" pictures, some may find this difficult and prefer to use other senses to get information. Tactile knowing is a method that Sonia Choquette suggests, where you touch a variety of objects and imagine what they are and how they might relate to the problem you wish to solve—all done while wearing a blindfold.

Several intuitives report that they get their insights from being sensitive to changes felt in their bodies. They believe that the body is a receptor to an intuitive intelligence that is often unavailable to the conscious mind, which could explain, for example, why we sometimes get a queasy feeling in our stomachs, or a tightening in our throats when we sense danger. Here follows a real life example of how this body-based insight saved a company from hiring the wrong person (the names have been changed).

Bruce, the president of a communications company, had a black belt in the martial art of *aikido* and was trained to read signals from his environment as well as from his own body. He wanted to hire someone for a senior position in his company and had interviewed a strong applicant who had excellent references. He was about to offer him the position when, during their second meeting, he experienced a sudden "body rush," a feeling in his body that didn't seem right. He decided to wait until he could check out this candidate's history further.

In the course of the investigation Bruce learned that this applicant for the position of comptroller had very serious legal improprieties in his former position. Hiring him was out of the question. If Bruce had not listened and become aware of the feelings in his body, he would not have taken a closer look at the candidate's background. For those who can tune into how their body feels, whether by getting further training in *aikido*, bodywork, biofeedback, or other methods, it will be very useful for developing the intuitive understanding that resides in the physical body.

To test whether this technique is for you, begin by calming your mind while becoming aware of how your body is feeling. Take several deep breaths and let them out slowly. Then notice: Is your body calm or is it jumpy? Are any muscles aching? Is your stomach feeling full, empty, or comfortable? Once you have ascertained your present state, walk into a room where there is another person; sit there quietly and see if you can sense any changes in your body's feelings. If you become aware of any, note whether you are more or less comfortable, more or less achy, and so on. If you find yourself more uncomfortable than you were before, then there is something negative that your body may be picking up about the other person. If you feel less achy or more comfortable, there could be something good, something healing about this person.

Other body-based insights may come from listening to music or sounds of nature, which can activate your imagination to bring pictures into the mind's eye, similar to a dream, even though you are in a wakeful state. Once your body sensations allow you to see these pictures, you can use them as metaphors to solve the problem at hand. The pictures may be as important and as useful as those received in a dream state. For example, while listening to music you may get an image in your mind's eye of a quiet lake, with autumn leaves falling into the water and the trees surrounding it beginning to look quite bare.

If the problem you have been trying to resolve is what new product should we develop, and the company manufactures cutlery, the image may be telling you to think about special knives for cutting fish (the lake image) with colored handles on the cutlery (suggested by the autumn leaves) and a simple, spare design to the cutlery itself (like the bare trees). Or the image of the changing seasons may suggest a change in the demand for the product, with the bare trees of winter predicting less demand, or a "cold" attitude (water) that will affect sales. Any and all of these interpretations may be correct. How do you know which one to choose? Your intuition will tell you.

## THE ANTENNA APPROACH

This is called the "antenna approach" because you can train your mind to become a receptor, like an antenna, and pick up signals about others out of thin air—which is probably quite thick with information just waiting to be broadcast into your consciousness. The same process occurs with some intuitives; they seem to have something like a radar receptor in their heads that picks up apparently unknowable information, often with unsettling accuracy.

To learn this skill requires time to experiment with your imagination and to give yourself permission to be hopelessly off the mark. The following exercise will encourage you to explore your ability to become more intuitive by becoming more aware of information that you may think of as impossible to know. If you can relax your need to be right, and regard this as only a guessing game where you give yourself permission to be right or dead wrong, you will learn things that you never dreamed possible.

In one recent antenna-type experience, I was paired with a woman whom I had never met. We were told to imagine everything we "knew" about each other, to essentially make things up: imagine what kind of a house the other lives in, what colors are in her house, what kinds of things she likes, and so forth. While this may seem like an impossible task, it was surprising to me how many "hits" my partner and I had. Of course, we also had misses. However, when we analyzed the "misses," it turned out that those were based on culturally biased "knowledge" of what women who looked like us would be thinking or doing. In other words, when we took the clues of apparent age and how we were dressed and made judgments based on outward appearance, chances were 50/50 we would get it right. But when the information perceived from an intuitive knowingness poured in, not knowing from where, it seemed to be right on target. Perhaps a more accurate way of doing this would be to have one's eyes closed or wear a mask. Then there would be no signals from the way someone looked or dressed, and it would force us to use the intuitive rather than the deductive part of the mind. Innovation Associates often uses this technique as an ice-breaker in their seminars.

One challenge that many beginners experience with this exercise is not knowing whether the information they are receiving is from somewhere out there, or is coming from the projection of their own unconscious or conscious thoughts onto another person. The only way to know which is the case is to ask for feedback. With practice, you'll be able to reduce the number of projections and increase the number of intuitive "hits."

## BEING IN THE MOMENT

Sometimes we get insights during that time of day, usually sometime between lunch and dinner, when our brains are almost missing in action and we find ourselves losing concentration. It may come as a sudden touch of fatigue or mental fuzziness, and while a shot of caffeine helps, it never seems to help enough. Some theorists believe that this is the time of day when the four main regulatory systems that link mind and body are beginning to realign, to adjust themselves from daytime alertness to the more mellow mood of the evening. According to Laurie Nadel, these four physiological systems are:

- the autonomic nervous system that regulates a good many of the body's important functions;
- the endocrine system that regulates production of the pituitary, thalamus, hypothalamus, and thyroid hormone, among others;
- the immune system; and
- the system of information substance chemicals, such as neuropeptides in the brain (Nadel, 1990).

When these systems begin to realign, usually around 3 to 5 P.M., you may feel drowsy and lose attention, a signal that these changes are taking place. It is at this time when you are more apt to get a rare, sudden insight into a persistent problem. Rather than forcing yourself to push through the fatigue, this is a good time to take an intuition break. If you are working on a project and would like help from your intuition, this is the time to ask for it. Our rational defenses are weaker at this time, which makes it easier to access the unconscious mind.

It is interesting that the English have set this time aside for four o'clock tea, a time to stimulate the brain during this naturally lethargic time of day with a shot of caffeine and sugary scones. Latin countries often take a siesta sometime between 2 and 4 P.M., knowing that tiredness will occur anyway, so why not give in to it? Perhaps if we take a clue from the Latin cultures and sleep during this period, we may dream of solutions to problems. Many executives admit to taking catnaps during this time of day and report that they get their batteries recharged from it and are able to make better decisions.

# 33

# *Using Intuitive Imagery in Organizations*

We know from studying the images and symbols discovered on prehistoric cave walls and ancient Egyptian hieroglyphics, that the first means of communication were through pictures. Thus, we have a long evolutionary history of relating to visual cues or pictures. When asked to "see" an image of a particular scene with eyes either open or closed, most of us have no difficulty. For example, there's no problem in bringing the image of three white kittens in a basket to our minds. However, if we are asked to picture something that would conjure up feelings of revulsion, such as snakes, then we may have a negative emotional charge associated with the image. When imaging techniques are used by professionals, they usually do not involve pictures that would stir any negative emotional reaction.

## PICTURING THE FUTURE

In John Pehrson and Sue Mehrtens' book *Intuitive Imagery: A Resource at Work*, they share some interesting experiences using several types of imagery techniques to make crucial business decisions. In one, they have their clients focus on cards that ask questions about the business issues to be resolved. For example, the client may be trying to determine how to generate more sales, what new products to develop, or how to improve an operating system. While those participating in the group know that these are the specific issues for which solutions are needed, they do not know which problem has been written on the reverse side of each card; the specific content of each card is unknown to the cardholders. The session begins with a relaxation period, after which they are asked to visualize their thoughts as they look at the blank side of a card.

When Pehrson and Mehrtens work with groups of four or more people, there actually is a similarity in the images that each person offers, and it often predicts the final outcome. In one case, the group predicted that the company would have a new leader even though they had no idea of the question on the reverse side of the card, which happened to be, "Do we need new leadership?" Eighteen months later, the company was sold and, indeed, there was a new leader with a new CEO in charge.

Another client was a large urban holistic learning center that wanted to know what their core strengths and priorities should be in order to reposition the focus of the business, if necessary. They listed the following areas to be the key strengths of the learning center:

1. The unique role of the center in its community
2. The staff
3. The building
4. The center's future vision
5. The bookstore
6. The catalogue

7. The programming and teachers

8. The scholarship and volunteer program

9. The founder

The facilitator then asked the group to imagine playing the celebrity tic-tac-toe game, visualizing the boxes numbered 1 through 9. Each number represented one of the above listed strengths, although the group did not know which strength was represented by each number. They were asked to reveal which number or numbers lit up first in their mind's eye as they visualized the squares. Their responses were as follows:

Imager 1: Numbers 3, 5, and 7 light up

Imager 2: Numbers 7, 5, and 3 light up

Imager 3: Numbers 5, 7, and 9 light up

Imager 4: Numbers 5 and 8 light up

Imager 5: Numbers 3 and 4 light up

As you can see, four out of five picked either number 3 or 5; two people saw boxes 3, 5, and 7 light up; another saw 3; and the other 5. The interpretation is that there is a consensus among the imagers that the bookstore is the center's key strength when four out of five chose number 5, the bookstore. Three of the five people also agreed, when they "saw" numbers 7 and 3, that the programming and the teachers, along with the building, are also core strengths. Yet none of these people knew what each number signified when they imagined the squares. When the client looked at the results it agreed to focus the advertising around those core strengths, and it significantly improved their business.

In *The Intuition Workbook,* Marcia Emery tells of an intuitive approach to a marketing problem that required exercise, relaxation, and imagery. The story begins with her protagonist, Bob, who has developed a new product. Bob's boss questions his marketing plan and would like to have specific information on the sales forecast. Bob decides to tap into his intuition to give him the answers as to whether this product plan will be successful. The technique he uses to elicit this information begins with his getting up early the next day for a morning jog. When he returns, he settles down in a quiet space and uses some deep breathing and visualization techniques to get himself deeply relaxed. He then chooses the image of driving in a car as the means to find answers for several questions. The first thing he needed to know was, will the demand for my product rise or fall in the next year?

To get the answer, Bob imagines that he is in the car taking a trip. (Imagining being in a car can be very powerful, because for many of us, the car has become an extension of ourselves.) The car approaches a fork in the road, with one path leading up the mountain and the other going down toward a valley. Bob clearly sees his car beginning to climb the mountain, which he interprets as a growth in demand, that is, a demand curve. (It could also have been interpreted as an "uphill battle.")

The next question he needed to answer was, how much demand would there be for this product? As his car traveled above the tree line the only thing Bob noticed were large rocks and scrub, which suggested a very high altitude. He interpreted this image to mean that there would be a very high demand for the product. (I felt that this could also mean a barren market, but he is doing the interpreting, not me.)

Finally, Bob wanted to know when the demand for this product would peak. He imagined four quarters of a pie, representing the four quarters of his fiscal year. As he focused his attention on each successive quarter, the third "pie slice" becomes highlighted.

Emery's interpretation:

The imagery shows a bright overall picture. Then, Bob uses word associations to deepen his understanding: mountain suggests there will be hard work, which suggests more stress and strain to achieve goals—large rocks—steep mountain—decline on the other side is steep. Bob also remembers that his car is the only car on the road, so he can expect little competition in the near term.

Bob figures that demand for his product will grow quickly and peak in the third quarter of this year. Predicting that there will be a huge growth, he will need to convince his boss now to respond to the expected demand. Also, knowing that the market will be volatile, he thinks it may be a good idea to begin talking with his boss to prepare him for the radical shift ahead. As you can see, Bob's intuition told him much more than he could have otherwise known (Emery, 1994).

Could all of this imagery, and Bob's interpretation, be wishful thinking, that is, projecting what one would like to see, whether consciously aware of it or not, in order to make it seem positive? Perhaps. And it would be foolish for any business person to gamble on these images to make important decisions that involve thousands if not millions of dollars. However, the images can be a guide, whether they are negative or positive. In either case, more research would be needed before any final decision is reached.

Intuitive consultant Nancy Rosanoff suggests using similar imaging techniques when you want to determine the best timing for a new product release. To do this, have each team member imagine the product being introduced in three months, then six months, one year, and two years. Imagine an opening event that would take place, and imagine customers using the product at the different times. Compare images, feelings, and insights to see which provides the most unanimous feedback. When several people get the same or similar messages, it reinforces the validity of the intuitive sight.

Another technique she suggests is to write a question about a particular need and place it in a sealed envelope in the center of the table without stating what is written inside the envelope. Each team member is asked to imagine something about the piece of paper; after they have received some images, they share them with the group. When their reflections have been recorded, the envelope is opened and the question is read. When the group recognizes how their images are related to the question, many new insights may then occur.

To use a hypothetical example. Suppose the question inside the envelope asks, "Shall we develop and market our concept for ravioli-flavored ice cream?" Someone may say that he "sees" a refrigerator; another may say she "sees" a garden; and still another may say the image he received was of fruit. What does a refrigerator, a garden, and fruit have to do with marketing ravioli-flavored ice cream? A few possible interpretations: if they culti-vate their garden of product ideas, something "green," like money, may grow; if they put the idea on "ice" (refrigerator) for a while, it will give everyone time to let the possibilities emerge that may not be visible yet; or if they use red fruit instead of red ravioli, this ice cream idea may become fruitful. If ravioli, which is a pasta shell enclosing another food is translated into ice cream making, it may suggest using a shell type of packaging to encase a filling. The ravioli idea then becomes a chocolate casing around nuts or fruit within a raspberry flavored ice cream base. Ben and Jerry's, are you listening? This could be a winner!

When you have a decision that requires a "yes" or "no" answer, Rosanoff has the following suggestion:

> Sit down and make yourself comfortable. Take a few moments to breathe deeply. Let your breath allow you to relax. Let go of all the distractions of your day. Take a few more deep relaxing breaths. Allow your hands to rest on your lap, with your palms facing up.
>
> Now, think about the decision you need to make. Imagine that in one hand you are holding the word "Yes" and in the other hand you are holding the word "No." See the letters and feel their weight, sense their textures. Take a few moments to focus on the word "Yes." How does it feel? What does it do? How do you feel? Take as long as you would like to explore all of the sensa-tions, visions, and feelings that go with the word "Yes." Now take a few moments on the word "No." How does it feel? What

does it do? How do you feel? Take as long as you would like to explore all the sensations, visions, and feelings that go with the word "No." When you are finished, take a few more moments to breathe, and think about what your intuition has been communicating to you about your decision (Rosanoff,1988).

Frances Vaughan, author of *Awakening Your Intuition,* suggests that to stir your intuition, use your imagination in a structured visualization. Visualizing the image of a house can be one of the more easily obtained routes to one's unconscious mind and can offer much useful information because we often identify with our homes. In Vaughan's example:

Imagine a house that you are about to enter. See what it looks like on the outside. Notice the entrance. Enter your house and explore the rooms. See what the furniture is like and notice whether the windows and doors are open or closed. Go up to the attic and down to the basement. Are there any people in your house? What changes would you like to make?

She relates the story of a young woman who said that her imagined house:

"looked like a small one-story cottage covered with vines . . . the area around the house is all overgrown. I notice some climbing roses. The house feels pleasant and cheerful but . . . everything is a mess, and the furniture is old and crummy." The young woman's interpretation of this house was that it reflected the state of her mind. She felt that her head was cluttered with ideas, yet she was reluctant to start the overwhelming job of house-cleaning, which she interpreted as having to go into therapy or analysis.

It's useful to remember when experiencing this technique that similar images could represent something quite different depending on who is doing the visualization. Another person can see a very similar home and the interpretation could vary enormously. For example, "seeing everything covered with vines" to another person might mean that he feels choked and restricted by his life and perhaps forced to remain in a relationship or a job that he resents. The interpretation should be done by the person who does the visualization and not the outside observer, although the outsider may offer additional thought-provoking clarifications.

To use an imagery approach at work, close your eyes and become silent for a few minutes before any meeting, whether it is a team meeting, an interview, or a one-on-one with your boss. Then, in the actual meeting, focus on calming your mind to allow yourself to be aware of the other person's energy. If you are interviewing someone and would like to predict whether this person would be right for the company, imagine the candidate at the job six months from now. Be aware of how you feel and whether it conjures any images in your mind. Then imagine the person one year from now, see how your body feels, and again, watch for images. If you are in tune with slight differences in feeling, or get either negative or positive images, it will give you an insight into how this person will work out.

To know what new product idea is worth developing, another technique is to place the names of three or more new product ideas in separate envelopes. Seal the envelopes and shuffle them so that you have no idea what information lies inside each envelope. Then pick up one envelope at a time and hold it; try to sense whether one sends you more energy than another and notice your reaction. The envelope that sends you the strongest surge of positive energy is the product to choose. When you do this with a group, pool your results to see if the same envelope held the strongest energy for most people in the group.

In the event that you don't get any feeling in your body with this exercise, hold one envelope at a time and picture a bar graph on it. If the line on the graph goes up, this product would be a winner; if it goes down, a loser; and if it stays more or less on course, then this product may not be outstanding but will hold its own.

## HOW TO WIN AT THE RACES

While betting at the race track is not specifically related to business issues, except as a common metaphor for winning or losing, the Kentucky Derby offered me an opportunity to test John Pehrson and Nancy Rosanoff's suggestions for using cards or sealed envelopes in achieving intuitive insights. On the Friday before race day, I decided to experiment with their method to predict which horses would win the Derby. There were ten horses running in the race. I put the name of each horse on a separate card, turned the cards over, shuffled them, and numbered them on the back side from one to ten. The names of the horses were on the underside of the card. Then we (there were two of us) took about five minutes to get into a meditative state. We then held each card for a few minutes, looking at the blank side of the card, until we received a mental image of the horse and its position at the finish line. After writing down where we saw each horse finishing, we compared notes. To our mutual surprise, we had chosen the same two horses to finish within the first three places, although the 3rd horses we chose were different.

According to the racing experts, the two horses that we chose were also the favorites. The next day, about two hours before the race, we concentrated on the cards again. This time, using the same method, we chose the same three horses with the order of finish for the first and second place winners reversed. The result: I had chosen the exact order of the finish for the three horses. My partner picked the same three horses, with the first two in reverse order. Considering that the race was a photo finish, it could just as easily have been his line up that predicted the winners.

Laura Day, in her book *Practical Intuition*, has another method for winning at the races. She tells the story of going to the race track with $20 to bet. Just before the first race she sees in her mind's eye a girl running in a field. Meanwhile, her companion at the track began reciting the racing record of each horse and telling her of the "logical" reasons why one horse was more likely to win than another. Day looked down the list of horses running in this race and saw the name "Clover Girl." She bet $10 on this horse and it won. When asked by her friend why she would risk half of her betting money on that horse which had an undistinguished record, she said that she just knew it would win.

Day says that intuition is more likely to express itself through metaphors and symbols than is the reasoning mind, and is detached from its perceptions. The image that she received of a girl running in a field was a metaphor for "Clover Girl," yet she had no emotional attachment to this name or the horse. Day believes that,

> Searching intuitively is being open to perception without expectation. There is no feeling attached to it. A sure sign of your shifting from intuiting to reasoning, then, is when your internal dialogue begins eliciting emotions such as fear or anger in response to a question. Another sign that your rational mind is being hooked is when your internal dialogue begins to use words like "should" (Day, 1997).

At the race track, the nonintuitive knows that he "should" bet on a specific horse based on the horse's previous record. He may also experience fear if he is betting a lot of money that he cannot afford to lose.

This raises an interesting question. We know that Laura Day is a psychic and we assume the pictures she gets come from a place that perhaps the rest of us cannot access as easily. For those of us who are not psychics, how can we know if our images are predictions or mere reflections of projected reality? The answer is simple. Try it and see. Keep a score card reflecting hits and misses and test it for yourself.

# Card Tricks

There are many card games available today that will help elicit your intuition in creative problem solving for new product or service ideas, or in obtaining deeper insights for improving operating systems.

## BOFFO

Marilyn Shoeman Dow has invented one such card game. It is called BOFFO, or Brain On Fast Forward, and is guaranteed to stimulate creativity and creative problem solving. The game has two sets of cards, launchers and boosters, which when combined form interesting and often compelling word combination idea triggers. The first set of triggers, called "launchers," are cards with five words on them, such as Doll, Diaper, Banana, Glove, and Crutch. The second set of triggers, or "boosters," are cards that contain another five words, such as Freeze, Hug, Magnify, Minify, and Light. Two to eight people can play the game. The first person to go chooses a launcher card with five words on it, as listed above, and decides to choose the noun "Doll," for example. Then the second person takes a booster card and, from the five words on that card, selects the verb "Freeze." Using these two words, "Doll" and "Freeze," they may discover a new product idea such as Barbi popsicles. Or, with a launcher of "Diapers" and a booster of "Hug," the result could be to make diapers "huggable" by putting pictures of teddy bears on them. In a group setting there is no end to the intuitive clever ideas that BOFFO can generate.

## THE CREATIVE WHACK PACK

Roger Von Oech, author of *A Whack on the Side of the Head*, developed a card game to stimulate creative thinking, *The Creative Whack Pack*. While whacking upside the head may be reminiscent of some violent movies you have seen, the game, if used as directed, is actually quite benign physically—guaranteed not to draw blood, but rather creative ideas. While the intended use of these cards is to generate new ideas or solutions to problems, there are some companies that send cards from the Whack Pack to their salespeople for inspiration and encouragement. For example, one card may say, "Give Yourself a Pat on the Back," with the suggestion that the recipient should look for things he has done right lately, which helps to boost self-confidence. Most of us, whether salespeople or not, could use that advice at least once a day.

Another card may say, "Ask a Fool," which encourages you to question an idea or thought and turn it around, as the court jesters did for Renaissance kings to help them break out of the "group think" environment of their "yes-men" advisors. It was the fool's job to parody any proposal. As Van Oech explains: "He might extol the trivial, trifle the exalted, or reverse the common perception. To use the card, ask yourself what a fool would say about your assumption?" Again, this exercise is meant to spark intuitive ideas by asking you to take the reverse position of a commonly held view.

One example of this would be if TV networks ask, What if we did not have as many commercials in between segments of our programs, would we retain more of an audience? Would they still buy our products? Conventional wisdom says if you want to sell a product you need an ad. But if they mentioned the name of the product or service without a lengthy ad to interrupt the programming, perhaps more people would be predisposed to buy the product because fewer ads permitted greater enjoyment of the show. Could ad-less programming move the merchandise? Is this idea intuitive? If it is successful, then it would be intuitive as well as creative. As Van Oech says, "slaying sacred cows makes great steaks!"

Another technique Van Oech offers is to imagine you are the problem to be solved. As an example, imagine you are an oven. What would it feel like to be an oven? How would you bake breads or roasts? Would you do it any differently? This is actually the method that was used to invent the first intermittent windshield wiper. On his wedding night, Robert Kearns had been hit in the eye by the cork of a champagne bottle, which nearly blinded him. In his convalescence, he learned a lot about how the eyes work and how they clean themselves when we blink. He began to envisage the windshield as an eye that had to be cleaned periodically, and it sparked the idea to create a windshield wiper that "blinked"—that is, moved intermittently by being controlled by an electronic device. Late in 1963, he took the idea to Ford, which gave him an award for it and began using the idea without compensating him. Through many years of legal actions, after rejecting a settlement offer of $150,000 in 1980, he finally won his case ten years later and received a final settlement of $10.2 million.

The *Whack on the Side of the Head* and the accompanying *Whack Pack* include a wealth of thought-provoking ideas to drive anyone's creativity. Also, it is wonderfully irreverent toward accepted business practices; its perverse humor a delight!

# 35

# Still More Techniques to Stimulate Intuition

## USING METAPHORS

Metaphors are probably the single most effective technique for gaining insight to any problem, because when we ask the question, "How is this like that?" it forces connections to ideas that were previously unknown. This technique was developed into an art form by Synectics (described in Chapter 8), and today, many ideation consultants rely on the power of the metaphor to stimulate creative problem solving.

Edward de Bono, creator of the Six Hats™ technique, defined experts as those people in the deepest ruts worn by repeatedly experiencing the same issues over and over again. Once such "habits" form it requires an incredible amount of energy to struggle out of them. According to Bob Samples, author of *The Metaphoric Mind*, children without the "ruts of expertise" seem to be able to use metaphors quite naturally, "they do not have the habits created by experience, they invent solutions rather than rehearsing old ones."

To recapture the child's fluency with metaphors, several methods are offered. One example recommended by Frances Vaughan is most applicable to a situation where there is a person that you want to know better in your business or personal relationships. With your eyes open or closed, bring this person into your awareness as you become centered and quiet. Then, close your eyes and become aware of your breathing. Notice how you feel in your body and the thoughts going through your mind. Now, picture the person as an animal and think about all of the characteristics of that animal.

For example, suppose you see John Smith as a bull. Bulls are fierce, strong, powerful, and can be dangerous if you get too close. Which of these characteristics might apply to Smith? If he were to become a business partner, he could be a strong fighter to get our product into the market and powerful in acquiring new customers. On the other hand, bulls are also known for being temperamental. Would Smith be difficult to get along with? Now compare what you know of Smith to these characteristics and see which seem to fit him best. Is it possible that he is fierce, strong, and temperamental as well? If so, then you will need to judge whether this combination of both positive and negative characteristics would work well in your organization, or how you could construct Smith's role to minimize the effect of his temperamental nature.

## JOURNAL KEEPING

Dr. William Taggart, Professor of Management at Florida International University, teaches a course at the business school, "Discovering and Nurturing Your Intuitive Self." He asks his students to keep a journal of their intuitive experiences and record everything they think is intuitive, whether is turns out to be a hit or a miss. He asks, was the experience predictive of something and on target, or was it based on emotions, fear, or wishful thinking? Taggart says that knowing about the miss is as instructive as a hit, because it helps us to differentiate intuitive information from something else. "One key to understanding misses," he says, "may be that they represent situations when you were clearly aware that you were not in the intuitive mode. This may be sensed by your feeling 'out of the flow.'" In these circumstances, you may have an intuitive insight about not being intuitive! Yet your deeper self may be aware that you've missed an opportunity. A strong sense of not being in accord with what is happening may be a clear signal that you are experiencing "nonintuition."

The journal Taggart suggests keeping should contain several discrete entries, such as:

- Describe the intuitive experience
- The context of the situation
- When it occurred, date and time
- When it was recognized, date and time
- What happened just before the experience, in the moment, and right after?

Taggart also asks the students to describe the obstacles to the intuitive experience, the fears, and the desire felt, that is, was the intuitive experience expressing some desire. To dig deeper, he requests that they describe the mental clutter and the message the intuition was sending. He also recommends that the student try to get to the source of the message, that is, was it conscious or subconscious, internal or external, rational or intuitive? Once each experience is analyzed to this degree, it becomes easier to determine whether one did in fact have an intuitive experience, or whether it was based on something else. With practice, one should be able to discern the intuitive from the nonintuitive data.

One of Taggart's students offered the following experience in her journal. She had lost her driver's license and looked everywhere she could think of to find it. She was quite panicked about not having it, feared driving without it, and dreaded going to the motor vehicle registry to get another one. The night after she lost it she had a dream in which she saw herself in the car taking a cell phone from her purse and, in the process, the license fell under the driver's seat. The next morning she went to her car, and there was the license, exactly as she had dreamt it, under the driver's seat. Although this was an intuitive experience that came through a dream, it could have easily come during a meditation or guided imagery. The important point for the student was that she definitely had an intuitive experience, and it was right on target.

The physicist Fritjof Capra noted that "During periods of relaxation after concentrated intellectual activity, the intuitive mind seems to take over and can produce the sudden clarifying insights which give so much joy and delight." Finding a lost driver's license is a delight indeed!

## DREAM INTERPRETATION

For many people, dreams are a source of their most accurate and powerful intuitions. Some dreams come unbidden and bestow upon us unasked for yet deeply appreciated insights. Other dreams may require a bit of coaching to get them to reveal their secrets; the previous chapter offered some methods for incubating your dreams. However, one problem that many people share is that they often get very clear information from their dreams but are at a loss to interpret them.

Despite what the best-selling dream interpretation books would have you believe, a word of caution about their hints. Dream interpretation books cannot give you an accurate interpretation of your dream. There is no one "correct" interpretation of these symbols. The same symbol can mean different things to different people, depending on each person's unique experiences and background. That being said, the following are a few examples of some commonly experienced dreams and some suggestions of what to think about in terms of interpreting a symbol. But their most accurate meaning is the one that you find most relevant.

If you are thinking about a particular problem and dream that you are hiking along a path and it suddenly turns into a steep upgrade that is difficult to climb, this may indicate that to find the right solution—even though you are heading up the right path—will take a lot of work, because the path is difficult. If, on the other hand, you are contemplating buying a new business and you dream that you are in a car that crashes, it is not difficult to imagine that this is not a good sign that you should buy this business.

Sometimes, instead of seeing images, you may hear a voice speaking to you. In dreams, we often hear someone speaking to us as well as receiving images. Their words may be cryptic in meaning and not easily understood, but the meaning could be important for you to discover, and it may be worth your while to figure out the message and how it applies to you.

**36**

# *Playing Games with Your Intuition*

The following are a few ideas that you can practice every day without any elaborate preparation. They will help you to develop your intuitive ability when you need it to make more important decisions.

1.  If you are waiting at a bank of elevators, guess which elevator will arrive first. You will be surprised at how frequently you get it right. Although this will seem like guessing, keep a diary of how many times you predicted it and how many times you got it right. If you are correct more often than not, there's a good chance that something more than guesswork is going on here.

2.  If you have a question that can be answered with a "yes" or "no," try the pendulum exercise. To do it, get a small weight, such as a fishing lure weight, and put it on a string. Then hold the string with the pendulum steady in your hand. Ask a question and watch to see whether it moves forward and back, indicating "yes," or from side to side,

indicating "no." If it goes around in a circle, it may be confused by the question. One note of warning: Do not ask a question that you don't want the answer to if it's negative.

3. Keep a journal and record hunches and intuitive flashes. Note how many hits and misses you get. This will sensitize you to how your intuitive mind communicates its information to you, and you will learn what it feels like when you get a hit or a miss. Also, note how and when they come. Are they in dreams, while driving, walking, on the job, etc.

4. Dreams can be an excellent source for intuitive insights. Most often they tell us how we are feeling about specific events in our life that we may not wish to deal with on a conscious level. They can tell us how to market a product, whom to trust, and, as you have seen, how to retrieve lost items and predict the future.

Finding lost items seems to be a common occurrence in dreams. Recently, I met a man who told me a most remarkable dream. His wife had lost her diamond ring and although they searched for it everywhere, including their car, they could not find it. Several months later she died, and her husband was told in a dream in which she appeared that he could find the ring between the seats of his car. The next morning he went to the car prepared to take the seats apart. When he opened the door he found the ring just sitting there on the passenger seat.

As for predicting the future, I had a dream not long ago that did just that. In this dream I went to a restaurant, ordered a meal, and when the bill came, opened my wallet to discover that all my credit cards were missing. Although I had the exact amount of money to pay my bill in the dream, the idea that my credit cards had vanished was disturbing. The next morning I checked my wallet and the credit cards were still there. I was puzzled about the meaning of this dream until I opened a letter that was on top of a stack of mail that had been sitting there from the day before. It was from a bank, and the letter informed me that a check I deposited had bounced. Since I had already written a number of checks that would be drawn on the bounced check, I suddenly realized that my "credit" was gone. The lost cards in the dream were a symbol for credit, and the dream was warning me that I had indeed lost my credit.

5.  One of the simplest, and frankly most wonderful techniques to release your intuitive abilities is to purposely open your heart to feel love. Many writers on this subject suggest that those who receive the most accurate and frequent intuitive insights are people who can cultivate a deep compassion and empathy for people. It requires giving up feelings of anger and frustration and replacing them with empathic understanding and compassion. The bonus is that in the act of releasing angry thoughts, the body becomes healthier. When we have angry feelings and hold onto them, it seems to attack the physical self, which may include internal organs, nerves, bones, and the immune system. The phenomenon has been observed in the many books written on the mind/body connection.

6.  Being open to new experiences often reveals new insights. Michael Crichton, author of *Coma* and *Jurassic Park*, sought to have nearly every kind of adventure humanly possible, which he describes in vivid detail in his book, *Travels*. He writes about many physically challenging, some nearly death defying adventures, such as climbing to the top of the Himalayas or investigating hulks of shipwrecks buried hundreds of feet below sea level. Yet, of all the experiences he recounts, and many are fraught with the real life danger that we read of in his thrillers, none is more riveting than his travels into his inner world—or as some would call it, his higher world. These explorations related extraordinary experiences, such as feeling energy from others, seeing auras, having a conversation with a cactus, and being able

to bend spoons. When he went on this quest into his inner world, he began with a skeptical, yet investigative mind set, ready to call everything a hoax. Instead, he was profoundly moved by his own powers to tap into a mysterious, yet, real dimension of his own psychic ability. Crichton is well recognized for having a wonderfully imaginative, creative mind. Perhaps being open to having a multitude of unconventional experiences contributes to Crichton's genius; searching out similar adventures may stimulate our own creativity as well.

For those of us who may not have the opportunity or desire to search for such dramatic new experiences such as climbing the world's highest mountain, or plunging into frigid waters far below breathing space, we can still seek out the new experience in less extravagant, more homegrown ways. For example, go to a movie that you would never think of seeing and find something of interest in it. Try restaurants serving different ethnic foods, or visit different parts of the city than the areas you know. Take a day trip to a place you have never seen before, or at least not in recent years. Visit a zoo, a museum, a children's museum, an artist's studio. Learn how to throw a clay pot, draw a picture, sculpt a figure, change a flat tire, repair small appliances, become a mime, enroll in a variety of classes, such as improvisational acting, accounting, CPR, poetry, science, literature and language, or learn to play a musical instrument. These types of experiences can provide two benefits: first, you will have to adjust your thinking patterns to absorb something different, and second, it will give you time away from the problem at hand to allow your unconscious mind to work on it while your conscious mind is taking in the new experience. And, they will provide you with a new bank of connection-making factoids that you can draw on whenever a new problem arises.

# 37

# *Orchestrating Innovation*

If we define creativity as making connections between unlikely entities, as for example a burr and a closure for garments, as in Velcro, then the question is, what fosters this kind of connection-making in some minds and not in others? We have examined the left brain/right brain differences and located intuitiveness and creativity as a right brain function, most likely an inherited characteristic. Yet, we know that still does not completely define the creative act; we know that the left brain's logic must be involved, otherwise the right brain would spin out bizarre fantasies bordering on mania. So, how does the left and right brain communicate with one another to bring forth the creative innovation?

One possibility could be through the corpus callosum, those connecting links between right and left brains which pass messages between the two halves of the brain and are thicker among women than men; this is offered as one reason women are generally thought to be more intuitive than men (Moir and Jessel, 1991). One way we could increase our intuitive skills, then, is to thicken the strands of our corpus callosums.

A method to increase their density was offered by Don Campbell, author of *The Mozart Effect*, who suggested that this could be done by becoming a musician or listening to music more often. In recent studies on the brain, it was discovered that the corpus callosum of musicians is thicker and more fully developed than in other people, reinforcing the idea that music enlarges existing neural pathways and stimulates learning and creativity.

And, there is more evidence that music can stimulate creativity. From studies of Dee Coulter, Ed.D., Director of Cognitive Studies at Naropa Institute in Boulder, Colorado, she found that "the music of Miles Davis, John Coltrane, and avant-garde composer John Cage can lift the listener into theta consciousness—the highly creative brain wave state associated with artistic and spiritual insight" (Campbell, 1997).

I found this observation to be particularly interesting from a recent personal experience. Not long ago I was driving along a highway thinking about a problem, with no solutions coming readily to mind. In an attempt to divert my thoughts, I switched on the radio and soon found myself listening to a recording of an avant-garde piece, one of my very least favorite types of music. Usually, I do not relate to this music and would not willingly listen to it if something more interesting were on. However, I really wasn't listening to it; I was deep in thought and the music was simply there. Suddenly, I noticed the encroachment of ideas, first one, then another, until I had a multitude, whereas before the music was turned on I had none at all. Could there be a relationship between this music and the new influx of ideas? Coulter's work seems to suggest that this may very well be the case.

Then I experienced something even more profound during a Silva™ method course, which is designed to teach their participants, among other things, how to diagnose illnesses of total strangers. The instructor played a raw, somewhat unpleasant tone that we were told mimicked brain waves at the alpha frequency. The sounds were not particularly pleasant, but I found myself quickly evolving into an altered state of consciousness, and during this time became far more insightful than I had ever remembered being in my life! While in this state, I was able to diagnose illnesses of total strangers. The only information given to me was their names, ages, and where they lived. Of a 55-year-old man, I "saw" that he suffered from diabetes. Of a 42-year-old woman, I realized that she had had a hysterectomy. An 85-year-old woman appeared to have a dowager's hump and poor circulation. All of these "sightings" were correct, along with a fair number of "hits" on the description of their physical appearance and personality. From this experience, I can offer another possible explanation for heightened intuitive, or psychic, insight. It may be that those people who have extraordinary intuitive abilities have a lower brain wave frequency that comes naturally; they may be able to get their brains into the alpha or theta range at will and, thus, be able to pick up information about which the non-psychic person would be clueless.

Another form of music that has also released many insights in the form of memories for me was chanting: making sounds and tones that evoked long-distant memories. Some of the sounds resembled a mother's voice calling a child for supper.

That these sounds are universal was pointed out by Leonard Bernstein who noted that the familiar singsong school yard taunt, "nah nah nah, nah nah, nah," we have all grown up with is actually heard among children all over the world! Further, mothers, too, the world over, call in their children with the same two notes, "Charl . . . ee," "Pab . . . lo," "Gretch . . . en," "Moham . . . med," with the first syllable at a higher pitch than the second syllable. When we chant these simple notes, it brings memories of our own childhood, just as the scent of freshly baked madeleines (a French cookie) evoked memories for Marcel Proust that he recorded so eloquently in *Le Temps Perdue*.

Gunther Schuller, a world-renowned composer and musician, commented once that when he sees a painting, he hears music; some people report that when they hear music, they see pictures. This phenomenon is known as synesthesia, when our senses seem to cross wires as it were. In the movie, *Fantasia*, Disney created a synesthesic experience for us; he played classical music while we watched outrageous cartoon images. To this day, I can never listen to "The Sorcerer's Apprentice" without seeing in my mind's eye the dancing brooms. Apparently, once the image is implanted with music, it won't go away.

Using images with music was the type of synesthesia that Bulgarian psychologist Georg Lozanov used when he combined music and learning to accelerate the learning process. He discovered that slow Baroque music could bring students into a state of alert relaxation; the best music for learning being the violin and other string instruments that were rich in harmonic overtones, pulsing at 64 beats per minute. According to his research, his students learned in a fraction of the usual time it took to complete complex tasks, such as designing dresses or machine tools. In a single day, students reportedly learned half the working vocabulary, or up to a thousand words or phrases in a foreign language, with an average of 97 percent retention. He also discovered that brainwaves receive concrete information in both highly stimulated beta states as well as in extremely relaxed, near-dreamlike states. Accelerated learning courses today use these synesthesic techniques to enhance memory retention. For example, if you wish to remember a list of words, they suggest that you associate each word with a ridiculously bizarre picture in your mind. Then, when you "see" the picture, the word will be remembered. Lozanov's conclusion: when information is coded in both the conscious and unconscious minds, access to memory is far greater.

Perhaps this is the key to intuitive discovery: when we have access to memory of both the conscious and the unconscious minds, we can make connections far more easily than without this ability. And, if we would like to increase access to these memories, theta cycle sounds and music may be the best rhythm to cure the what-will-I-innovate-today blues.

The only question at this point is, which is the right music or sound for you? Perhaps the studies of Dorothy Retallack can give us a clue. Ms. Retallack, a graduate student at Temple Beull

College in Denver, decided to experiment with plants and music. She built five greenhouses, each one to grow corn, squash, marigolds, zinnias, and petunias. The greenhouses, all of the same size, received the same light, water, and soil. For several months she played different types of music to plants in four of the chambers. (As a control, the fifth had no sounds piped in.) One group of plants got Bach, the second Indian classical music, the third loud rock, and the last country-western. She found that the Bach and Indian music stirred the growth of the plants dramatically. The flowers were more abundant, and the vines even grew in the direction of the speakers! In the loud rock greenhouse, things were much worse. There were fewer flowers and the plants didn't seem to want to grow at all.

However, to Retallack's surprise, in the country-western greenhouse, the plants developed almost identically to those in the house where there was no music at all. Dan Carlson, another plant researcher, discovered that when his plants listened to sitar music, they couldn't get enough of it. They grew and grew, compared to those without music.

So, if plants are affected by music and we know human shoppers are affected by music (they buy more when certain types of music are played in stores), then why not use music as the catalyst to creativity?

Campbell does just that and tells of how he enhanced corporate creativity when he was invited to present a talk on music, stress reduction, and creativity to the board of a major computer company. His method:

> I began with a short exercise, playing music from Bach's Brandenburg Concertos. I asked the trustees to jot down the most vital points for their financial discussion. After six or seven minutes, I asked them to turn the page and set aside momentarily what they had written . . .
>
> I passed out two cheap, flexible paper plates to each person and asked everyone to move their chairs back a few inches from the boardroom table.

Then I played an Irish folk dance with a simple, spirited, and predictable melody, and asked them to follow along and imitate me. I brought the paper plates together as if I were playing the cymbals, then bounced them off my knees, chest, and head. After a few grumpy looks in my direction, all fifteen men managed to participate. Within three minutes they were smiling and, after the six minutes of this paper plate dance, their entire bodies had loosened up. They were laughing and relaxed. I put on the Brandenburg Concertos once again and asked them to write solutions to the problems that they had noted earlier. They wrote vigorously and pensively. After ten minutes, I excused myself and let them have their meeting.

The next day, I was called and told the board meeting was the most fruitful, creative session they had ever had. The board found itself able to concentrate more clearly after my visit.

While this story strongly suggests movement and music as factors that allowed more creativity to flow, it also suggests that removing some of the blocks to creativity is also useful. In corporate boardrooms, the blocks to creativity are often, but not limited to: stress, competitiveness, fear of making mistakes, being judged poorly and/or unfairly, etc. The physical activity as well as the music helped to put everyone in a more relaxed state, which removed some of the stress involved, thereby allowing for a more creative working atmosphere.

Apparently that computer company is not the only organization to recognize the value of music. Forty-three of the world's fifty largest industrial companies provide music to employees. DuPont introduced a listening program in one department that cut its training time in half, reduced its training staff by a third, and doubled the number of people trained. Apparently, DuPont not only listens to dreams; it listens to music as well, and has been enormously successful in the process.

# The Secret Idea
# Generator at IDEO, Inc.

To activate your intuition, all of the aforementioned may be extraordinarily helpful. However, let's look at the brainstorming method used at IDEO, Inc. Located on both the East and the West coasts, this company creates and designs new products for a wide variety of corporate clients. Its best known design is the computer mouse.

Tom Kelley, Vice President of Marketing, describes IDEO's brainstorming sessions as involving a group of six to twelve people who get together for one to one and a half hours. They state the problem, give a background synopsis of the issue, and then create categories for discussion, such as what technology would we need, what would the end user want, who are the competitors for this market, and what are the existing products along this line. They then take each category and throw out ideas, building upon each others' thoughts until they come up with perhaps 100 ideas. These are then distilled to about 20 of the best concepts that evolved from the brainstorming session. A written description and a sketch of each are sent back to the client for evaluation, at which point the client decides which idea he wishes to pursue. IDEO has grown from being a one-person shop twelve years ago to employing over 600 people today, and it has experienced phenomenal growth and success.

I asked Kelley to tell me the secret of their success. He disclosed that there is a little known element used in their brainstorming sessions that has, until now, been a carefully guarded secret. The mystery ingredient that actually underscores all of their creative innovations and new product designs begins with every employee involved in the project ingesting a massive dose of an uncontrolled substance. This appears to sharpen their minds and promote access to ideas never before dreamed of. What is this substance? *Chocolate chip cookies!* That's right, chocolate chip cookies. It is rumored that they munch hundreds of these dainty little morsels during every ideation session. In fact, their supply is never depleted, because with their help the job gets done.

Could chocolate chip cookies be the catalyst, the spark that allows the group's reactive chemistry to connect random thoughts into solid ideas? Actually, I believe they are onto something. (Please note: The following speculations were prompted while the tongue was firmly planted in cheek, but got hit by the sweet tooth in the process.)

Just think, chocolate was discovered by the Spanish conquistador Cortes in Mexico in the 1500s, who sent it to Spain where they kept it secret for 100 years. What had been invented up to that time? Telescopes, Spanish galleons, the printing press, the wheel. That's about it. Then, in the middle of the seventeenth century, a Frenchman discovered how to make finely ground cacao beans into cakes of chocolate. Is it mere coincidence that when chocolate became a staple in Switzerland, the Swiss developed more sophisticated clocks and watches, and as chocolate became a sustaining part of the Swiss culture, it culminated in a most creative moment a few years ago when an inventor, who was probably hung over in a chocolate stupor, produced the idea for the Swatch Watch which became a runaway success! This is no mere coincidence. European chocolates are said to be the best in the world, and having ingested sufficient quantities of this substance, European creativity was notably enhanced.

Further, when chocolate became popular in the United States, we got diesel train engines and automobiles. Until chocolate made it out of Mexico and Spain, invention was at a virtual standstill. It is obvious now that there could be a direct correlation between the introduction of chocolate to Europe and the United States and the sudden jump in creative technology never before experienced anywhere on earth! Is it any wonder, then, that the United States, the world leader in technology, is also the world's largest consumer of chocolate, as in 1.3 billion pounds annually? That breaks down to about 5.1 pounds of chocolate per person consumed in one year. However, you can readily see that far more than that is consumed at IDEO.

And, there's more. It was only after chocolate chip cookies were invented in 1915 at the Toll House Cookie factory in Whitman, Massachusetts that the airplane became perfected as a means of mass transit, not to mention the plethora of inventions that followed, such as televisions, microwave ovens, and computers. From this we can deduce that possibly the most creative people in the world are chocoholics. Women are known to crave chocolate and also to rely on their intuition more than men. Could there be a correlation between craving chocolate and intuitive ability? Now, this is only a hypothesis, but it would be an interesting research study for a chocolate-obsessed Ph.D. candidate. Then, if this were proven to have some validity, when it was time to hire a creative person there would be no need to ask for evidence of creative expression or impose all of those highfalutin' personality tests, there would simply be one question as a qualifier: Do you like chocolate? If the answer is "yes," the next question would be, how much do you like chocolate? And if that answer is something close to, "I never met a piece of chocolate that didn't seem friendly," chances are you may be looking at a creative genius. An alternative interviewing technique would be to have a large bowl of chocolates or chocolate chip cookies on your desk and invite the candidate to take as many as he or she likes; if you can see the bottom of the bowl within, say 15 minutes, you've got your hire.

With or without the chocolate connection, tune into your own intuition to experience more clever, more profound and more profitable ideas. Then, trust it.

# Conclusion

As you have read, there are many pathways to reach the unconscious mind, such as through visualization, music, metaphors, dreams, pendulums, and card games, among others. Some of these will work well for you, others less so, depending on whether your individual thinking pattern is more inclined to receive cues from visual or kinesthetic techniques. If you can be open to experiencing something new that may seem far-fetched and incredible, it may become one of the most effective stimulants to charge your intuition to produce successful innovations.

In the next, and last, part of the book, we will look at how to know when you are receiving an intuitive insight and why it is so important to cultivate your intuition. Tapping into your intuition can have a profound effect on your well-being, including your health, relationships, and work life. Is there anything else that is more important?

# PART TEN

## New Beginnings

The leader who would create a vision sufficiently compelling to motivate associates to superior performances must draw on the intuitive mind.

...J. NAISBITT AND P. ABURDENE, *Re-Inventing the Corporation*

Intuition flourishes when it is valued.

...FRANCES VAUGHAN

Intuition leads to innovation. It is the muse, the spark, the beginning, the end. If you want more innovative thoughts and ideas or products and services, you must learn how to court your intuition and listen to its voice when it speaks.

Joseph Campbell warned us several years ago, "Technology is not going to save us. Our computers, our tools, our machines are not enough. We have to rely on our intuition, our true being."

When he wrote those words, Campbell was most likely unaware of a company called Invention Machine Corporation (IMC) that was founded in 1989 by Valery Tsourikov. Its business is creating software that helps engineers invent new products.

Their software is a database that uses artificial intelligence to become a brainstorming partner for an engineer; the engineer may take solutions suggested by the software and apply them to a particular problem. For example, suppose an engineer wants to invent a self-cleaning floor. IMC's software will offer her ideas and concepts from previously invented products that bear a similarity to this project, to give her additional information in areas that lie outside of her expertise. It demonstrates how similar problems were solved by experts in other fields. So, when asked for a method to invent an electronic ice cream scoop, the computer's database would deliver 200 related ideas in one minute. This may ultimately take the place of creative connection-making that many ideation seminars offer, because now the engineer has been given 200 possible connections, some of which she may never have made for herself.

But the next problem is, how would the engineer know which of the 200 ideas will be useful? Will it result in a trial-and-error game for all 200 possibilities until the right match is made? Or, will she use her intuition to zero in on the precise ideas she needs to develop the invention? As you can see, even with the very latest and most sophisticated technological advances, intuition continues to remain indispensable.

That's one reason Campbell felt that we needed our intuition to survive. Another is that it can protect us from the world this technology has created. In many respects, it is a world as hard as the computer's metal casing. Human values, such as being authentic and ethical, are often devalued in favor of being skilled at manipulation and deceit. We see it in the court system, where a jury is often selected for its prejudices and its emotions are manipulated by lawyers. We see it in sales strategy, where the client is played like a piano, hitting the soft keys of enticement or the strident notes of threat, whatever it takes to make the sale. Remember that old-fashioned value of paying your bills on time? That now may be passé.

The bank that holds BJ's Wholesale Club's credit cards has recently revoked the credit of thousands of customers who have always paid their bills on time. They are considered undesirable credit customers. The bank, much to BJ's dismay, wants customers who cannot pay their bills on time so that more money can be earned on their purchases by charging interest. Our technology, it would seem, has been a partner in changing these values because it has provided the technology to permit the demand of interest payments, and if one does not want to pay interest, no credit is offered. In this starkly competitive world, can BJ's afford to lose these thousands of customers because they like to pay their bills on time? Technology values the deadbeat, or those who want it all but can't afford it, and encourages them to get into unconscionable debt. Our values, it would seem, must keep at least one step ahead of the technology, or we will be lost.

How can intuition be of value? It can warn us of the predator who would convince us to buy an inferior system; it can help us discern the valuable from the junk offerings of the marketplace; it can offer insight when we have an innovative idea; and predict future trends in the marketplace; in short, it can bring us the most valuable knowledge when the timing is critical.

And there is one more reason to develop intuition: it will be the status symbol of the future. Futurist Watts Wacker believes that the social trend will be what he terms "downward nobility." Satisfaction and domestic contentment will be the status symbols of the future rather than money, and status will hinge on what is scarce, like these intangibles, and not manufactured goods, which anyone with money can buy. One more intangible that he predicts will be a very high status commodity: spiritual experiences. People who are in touch with their spirituality are a small yet very special clique. When you tap into your intuition, you will begin to experience that spiritual connection. This book is the first step toward that future as well as a map for the present.

How will you be able to recognize an intuitive insight? The following are a few guidelines:

A.  Through the Mind
    - a hunch
    - a symbolic message, as in an image, a sudden memory, or lyrics to a song
    - a relevant dream
    - internal seeing or hearing
    - a significant insight popping suddenly into one's mind
    - a new realization of how disparate ideas are connected
    - a gradual awareness of how certain knowledge explains a situation or indicates how to proceed
    - an awareness that events are flowing in a certain direction
    - a glimpse of the big picture

B.  Through Body and Feeling Changes
    - a muscle contraction or a sudden upset stomach
    - an energy increase or decrease relative to an action to be taken
    - an unexpected change in one's feelings about a situation

C.  Experiences One Didn't Initiate
    - a synchronistic experience
    - an unhappy experience (like a job loss that may lead to a better job)
    - the disappearance of all options but one in a situation, indicating that this is the path you should take
    - the realization that when one door closes another opens

Jagdish Parikh, author of *Intuition, The New Frontier of Management*, has described other ways to know when intuition is present:

- Sometimes we feel a bodily or physical sensation, or we experience a kind of warmth, comfort, or vibration of positive energy.

- Sometimes we hear an inner voice.
- There could be a different kind of quality or clarity in the mind, or we experience a feeling of certainty, which is also more intense.
- A feeling of excitement is experienced when intuition informs us either to do or not do something.
- Some people say that they experience a different kind of consciousness, as though it were a luminosity or glow.

Harvard Professor Daniel Isenberg suggested the following ways senior managers could improve their thought processes:

- Bolster intuition with rational thinking. Recognize that good intuition requires hard work, study, periods of concentrated thought, and rehearsal.
- Offset tendencies to be rational by stressing the importance of values and preferences, of using imagination, and of acting with an incomplete picture of the situation.
- Develop skills at mapping an unfamiliar territory by, for example, generalizing from facts and testing generalities by collecting more data.
- Pay attention to the simple rules of thumb—heuristics—that you may have developed over the years. These can help you bypass many levels of painstaking analysis.
- Don't be afraid to act in the absence of complete understanding, but then cherish the feelings of surprise that you will necessarily experience.
- Spend time understanding what the problem or issue is.
- Look for the connections among the many diverse problems and issues facing you to see their underlying relationships with each other. By working on one problem you can make progress on others.
- Finally, recognize that your abilities to think are critical assets that you need to manage and develop in the same way that you manage other business assets (Isenberg, 1984).

These descriptions and advice may or may not apply to your own experience, because each individual experiences it differently. For most people who trust their intuition, when they get an intuitive insight, they know it. It may take practice, analysis, and trust to become proficient at knowing when intuition is being delivered to you.

But when the message is received, it will generally be the right one for you.

Writer Rudolf Steiner explains that the spiritual world—from which intuitive information comes, presumably—is very different than our physical reality. In fact, he says that one of the ways you can be sure that the information is intuitive is that it seems a bit strange or comes in images that are rather odd. While the following experience does not quite fall into this category of being odd, for me it was unusual.

# 39

# *Trust Your Intuition*

My experience was not a major, earthshaking event. It was only a small, gentle lesson in learning how to pay attention to my intuition. For several months I had been attending a class once a week and always chose the same route to get there. I usually found a convenient place to park on the side of the street that I habitually entered. One day, as I was leaving to go to class, I had a sudden thought to take a different route that would bring me to the opposite side of the street to look for a parking spot. It seemed unusual to me that the thought came the moment I backed out of the driveway. It wasn't couched in a "should I do this or that" decision-making pattern; rather, it was a clear message to take another route.

Ignoring that message, I began an internal dialogue. I said to myself, "No, I always find a place to park on the side of the street that I usually enter, so chances are, based on previous experience, I will find one there today." I decided to follow my customary route, and when I arrived there were no places to park on that side of the street, but several were available on the opposite side, as my intuition had told me. I had made the decision based on the pattern of my prior experience, which in this case turned out to be irrelevant. Had I listened to my intuition, even though it was contrary to my experience, I would have found a parking spot far more readily.

It would seem, then, that we get these thoughts for a reason, and if we can learn to trust them and not try to impose what seems like logic based on experience, they will make our lives a little easier. The skeptic might ask, but how many times have you had thoughts such as these and it turned out to be wrong? The crucial point here is the phrase, "thoughts such as these." Most of us, when we plan to go anywhere, first decide on what we think is the best route to take based on prior experience or a map. However, this thought was different. It did not come as a result of trying to decide which route to take; I was quite sure of the route that I wished to take. Therefore, this thought literally came out of nowhere. And perhaps that is the key to understanding the difference between an intuitive insight and a logical approach. If one begins to think about several possible alternatives and chooses one that seems to be the best guess, that decision is based on using a conventional logical approach. If, on the other hand, a message saying "Go this way" flashes in your head, then I believe that is intuition.

## CHRISTOPHER REEVE AND THE DOGWOOD TREE

On April 1, 1997 the Northeast was hit with a surprise winter finale, a blizzard that downed trees and power lines and made our lives more solitary than usual, with snow drifts and electrical wires blocking the efforts of the snowplows. The storm hit when the trees were just thinking about renewing their blossoms for another year, and we worried about all of those badly severed limbs and whether they would destroy the beauty of our spring, or would they stubbornly blossom anyway.

About a month later, as I walked by a neighbor's home, I saw a beautiful white dogwood tree in full flower with one of its largest branches resting on the grass. About 90 percent of the limb had been severed from the tree trunk by the earlier storm, yet its white blossoms were full and dazzling in the bright sunlight and seemed to beckon to the passersby to come and visit for a moment. The branch was bent so low that it rested on the grass and was easily accessible, unlike the stately dogwoods near my home whose branches reached for the sky and seemed to say, "You may look but don't touch." Was this a miracle of nature? How could a limb, cut off by over 90 percent from the trunk and seeming to hang on by a mere splinter of wood, continue to blossom with lush white flowers? The branches had never seemed so full and so beautiful.

And then I thought of Christopher Reeve, the actor who is now a quadriplegic. He, too, is functioning with perhaps even less than 10 percent of his body's ability. He cannot move arms or legs or even speak or breathe without a respirator. Yet, when you look at his face, it seems to be shining with a special inner glow. Where does this glow come from? I don't know, perhaps Mr. Reeve can tell us. What I do know is that with less than 10 percent of his physical ability to function, he has not only touched everyone's heart, but he is also engaged in productive work, such as directing a movie and being a spokesperson for several charitable organizations. Like the dogwood tree, with only 10 percent of its visible connection to a life source, Reeve, too, seems to radiate an almost unearthly beauty.

What does this have to do with developing intuition? According to Myers Briggs, the great majority of us prefer the sensor way of perceiving life, which means that perhaps 90 percent of the time we perceive the world only through our five senses. If that is so, then that leaves only 10 percent of the time for us to be open to our intuition, the sixth sense. If we can become aware of that intuition only 10 percent of the time, then it is possible we could achieve as much success in our world as Christopher Reeve or the dogwood tree. If we can cultivate this ability using only 10 percent of our time to practice and refine this skill, it could make a meaningful difference in our lives. We have seen how 80 percent of the most successful executives rely on intuition; how consultants tap into it for new product development, sales, and marketing direction; and, how the wisest firms call on intuitive and psychic consultants to get as much information as possible before making important decisions.

Knowledge is power. Intuition is knowledge that is gained in a nonlinear way. One person who has attained enormous power by being aware of this subtle ability is David Geffen, a billionaire partner in DreamWorks who is described as "perhaps the most powerful man in Hollywood ... He is not a strategic or a systemic thinker. Like the old-time moguls, Geffen makes decisions as much with the gut as with the brain" (Seabrook, 1998).

The question is not whether intuition is useful; we have seen that it is. The critical benefit our intuition offers is that it gives us the ability to work smarter, not harder—to be the most efficient and creative we can be. If the advancements of technology today are helping us to do more in less time and with more efficiency, then why not make the same advances with our minds? Why shouldn't we, too, as humans, use our minds to mirror the advances and capabilities that technology is achieving?

Land and Jarman put it another way, stemming from their observations:

> Many men and women prefer the more down to earth tools of rationality and common sense that seem to move them ahead in the working world. The fact is that color, fantasy, poetry, romance, imagination, intuition, music, emotion, irrationality, tenderness, and relaxation are the most powerful aspects of the effective and productive creative life (Land and Jarman, 1992).

All of this is to say that if you want to be creative, allow emotion, irrationality, imagination, and intuition to penetrate into your experience of life.

We have gone from dreams to corporate problem solving, to intuitive and psychic consultants, to intuitive diversity, and to do-it-yourself intuition. The practice of intuition is an art, not a science, so do not expect a replication of the experiment each time you try it. Nevertheless, try intuitive knowing; it is better than depending on luck, maybe more accurate than market research results, and can be the most important guide to your future. An idea begins with intuition.

> They say that ideas are a dime a dozen. They are not. Ideas are diamonds, and they are stocked and stored in the great structure that we call our mind-body system. Beneath the surface crust or ordinary consciousness, we are all filled with ideas and associations linking with other ideas—the very stuff of evolution moving in us to emerge as innovation (Houston, 1997).

Let this book, then, be a guide to inhabiting, extolling, deepening, and reveling in our burgeoning ability to know more, create more, become more.

Certainly, in the interest of improving the bottom line for your business, to not attempt generating creative, intuitive ideas would be foolhardy. "Innovate or evaporate" has been the threat and the challenge. Intuition will help you meet that challenge by stimulating innovation. It makes it happen. Tap into your intuition now and watch ideas burst forth like sparklers on the Fourth of July.

# APPENDIX

# Consultant Resource Directory

American Management
   Association
1601 Broadway
New York, NY 10009-7420
800-262-9699

Robert Beachy, Principle
The Axiom Group, Inc.
1401 W 76th St., Suite 420
Minneapolis, MN 55423
612-861-9533
fax 612-861-9511

*The Whack on the Side of the Head*
   and *Whack Pack*
Barnes and Nobles Bookstores or
U.S. Games in Stamford, CT or
Creative Think
Box 7354
Menlo Park, CA 94026

BOFFO
Marilyn Shoeman Dow
ThinkLink
1411 4th Ave.
Seattle, WA 98101
206-622-2212

Sonia Choquette
P.O. Box 408996
Chicago, IL 60640
773-989-1151
http://www.inner-wisdom.com

Mary Ann Cluggish
Wellesley, MA 02181
617-237-2316
mcluggish@aol.com

Barbara Courtney
Redwood Shores, CA 94065
415-508-9621
fax 415-508-1808

*I Speak Your Language*
Drake Beam and Associates
100 Park Ave.
New York, NY 10017
212-692-7700
fax 212-953-0194

Marcia Emery
1502 Tenth Street
Berkeley, CA 94710
510-526-5510
PowerHunch@aol.com

Richard Feder
President
The Marketing Group, Inc.
74 Rogers Road
Stamford, CT 06902
203-359-8888
fax 203-359-9778
feder@tmg.com

Violet Frayne
American Greetings
One American Road
Cleveland, OH 44144
216-252-7300 ext. 4330
fax 216-252-4391

Bob Gill
Product Development
    Partners, Inc.
114 Waltham St.
    Suite 12
Lexington, MA 02173
781-860-0654

Cheryl Gilman
Career Coaching & Consulting
Belmont, MA 02178
617-489-4243
fax 617-489-1132

Nancy Gust
Stage One
11 Lennon Road
Arlington, MA 02174
781-636-4932

Robert L. Hanig
Associate Director
Innovation Associates, Inc.
100 5th Ave.
Waltham, MA 02154
617-398-8555
fax 617-398-8523
hanig.robert@adlittle.com

Herrmann International Group
2075 Buffalo Creek Road
Lake Lure, NC 28746
704-625-9153
fax 704-625-2198

Bob Johnston, Principle
IdeaScope
Union Wharf,
    Suite 214
Boston, MA 02109
617-492-7666
bob_johnston@ideascope.com

The Tale of O
Rosabeth Moss Kanter
Barry Stein
Goodmeasure
100 Memorial Drive
Cambridge, MA 02142
617-621-3838

The Keys Instrument
Dr. Teresa M. Amabile
Graduate School of Business
    Administration
Harvard University
Soldiers Field Rd.
Boston, MA 02163
617-495-6871
fax 617-496-5305
tamabile@hbs.edu

Bryan Mattimore
The Mattimore Group
Three Landmark Square
Stamford, CT 06901
203-359-1801
fax 203-359-8127

Deborah McConchie
Bottom Line Marketing
    Consulting
Newton, MA 02160
617-969-0915
fax 617-965-5587
dmcconchie@aol.com

Christopher W. Miller, Ph.D.
Founding Partner
Innovation Focus
841 Flory Mill Rd.
Lancaster, PA 17601
717-519-1900
fax 717-560-3778
innovation@what-if-u.com

Laurie Nadel, Ph.D.
56 7th Ave.
Suite 7G
New York, NY 10011
212-647-1134
fax 516-889-5580
LNADE@aol.com

John Pehrson
Creative Change Technologies
Placitas, NM 87043
505-876-3068
jbpehrson@aol.com

Predictive Index
Praendex Inc.
40 Washington St.
Wellesley, MA 02181-1888
617-235-0959
800-832-8884 (toll free)
ilenem@praendex.com
Ilene McCune, Consultant

Lynn Robinson, M.Ed.
Intuitive Readings and
    Training
53 Langley Road, Suite 260
Newton Centre, MA 02159
888-543-3356 (toll-free)
617-964-0075
lynn@lynn robinson.com
http://www.lynn robinson.com

Winter Robinson
Tor Down Publishing Co.
430 Simpson Rd.
Saco, ME 04072
207-929-6960
fax 207-929-6901
well:tordown@mix-net.net.

Nancy Rosanoff
Nancy Rosanoff & Associates,
    Inc.
109 Sunnyside Avenue
Pleasantville, NY 10570
914-769-7226
fax 914-769-4473
rosanoff@tiac.net
http://
    www.intuitionatwork.com

Barbara L. Schultz
Consultant to Organizations
22 Forbes Ave.
San Rafael, CA 94901-1741
415-456-6441
fax 415-456-1044
BLSI-Intuit@aol.com

Lynn Schweikart
LKS Creative Counsel
252 Marlborough St.
Boston, MA 02116
617-247-2087
fax 617-536-4426
LKSCHWEIK@aol.com

Mark Sebell, President
Creative Realities
17 Arlington St.
Boston, MA 02116
617-246-1313

Bill Taggart
Professor of Management
Florida International University
9030 SW 125th Ave., #108
Miami, FL 33186-7161
305-595-6177
fax 305-398-3278

Gigi Van Deckter, President
The Van Deckter Co., Inc.
2109 Broadway, Suite 13-109
New York, NY 10023
212-724-6272
fax 212-724-1299
gigigram@aol.com

Shira White, CEO
S. P. White, Inc.
HC 1 Box 311C
Leeds, NY 12451
518-622-9825

# Bibliography

Agor, Weston. 1989. "Intuition and Strategic Planning," *The Futurist Magazine*. Nov-Dec: 20-24.

American Management Association. 1997. *Intuitive Leadership: Turning Gut Feelings into Competitive Advantage*. New York: American Management Association.

Arredondo, Patricia. 1996. *Successful Diversity Management Initiatives*. Thousand Oaks, CA: Sage Publications.

Associated Press. 1997. "Pair Held in Slaying of Pizza Deliverers." *The Boston Globe*, 22 April: 4.

Auerbach, Jon. 1997. "Charity Case." *Wall Street Journal*, 11 September.

———. 1997. "Jewish Loan Societies Rethink the Tradition of Helping All Comers." *Wall Street Journal*, 11 September: A1.

Bentov, Itzhak. 1977. *Stalking the Wild Pendulum*. New York: Dutton.

BenTov, Sharona. 1995. "Theodorakis' Ballad." *Virginia Quarterly Review*, 71 (3): 499-500.

Blakeslee, Sandra. 1997. "In Work on Intuition, Gut Feelings are Tracked to Source: The Brain." *New York Times*, 4 March.

Bosnak, Robert. 1996. *Tracks in the Wilderness of Dreaming*. New York: Delacorte Press.

Brodie, Richard. 1996. *Virus of the Mind*. Seattle: Integral Press.

Buzan, Tony. 1994. *The Mind Map Book*. New York: Dutton.

Cameron, Julia. 1992. *The Artist's Way*. Los Angeles: J.P. Tarcher/ Perigee.

Choquette, Sonia. 1997. *Your Heart's Desire*. New York: Three Rivers Press.

Coleman, Debi. 1997. "What It Means to Lead." *Fast Company Magazine*, Feb-Mar, 99.

Cooper, Paulette, and Paul Noble. 1996. *The 100 Top Psychics in America*. New York: Pocket Books.

Covey, Stephen. 1996. *The Seven Habits of Highly Effective People*. New York: Simon & Schuster.

Crichton, Michael. 1988. *Travels*. New York: Knopf.

Crisp, Tony. 1990. *The Dream Dictionary*. New York: Dell.

Csikszentmihalyi, Mihaly. 1996. *Creativity, Flow, and the Psychology of Discovery and Invention*. New York: HarperCollins.

Day, Laura. 1996. Practical Intuition. New York: Villard.

Dean, Douglas, and John Mihalsky, et al. 1974. *Executive ESP*. New York: Prentice Hall.

de Beauport, Elaine. 1996. *The Three Faces of Mind: Developing Your Mental, Emotional, and Behavioral Intelligences*. Wheaton, IL: Theosophical Publishing House.

DeBecker, Gavin. 1997. *The Gift of Fear: Survival Signals that Protect Us from Violence*. New York: Little, Brown.

DeBono, Edward. 1992. *Serious Creativity*. New York: Harper Business.

Delaney, Gayle. 1988. *Living Your Dreams*. New York: Harper & Row.

————. 1991. *Breakthrough Dreaming*. New York: Bantam Books.

Diamond, David. 1997. "What Comes after What Comes Next." *Fast Company Magazine*, Dec-Jan: 72-80.

Drake Beam and Associates. 1972. *I Speak Your Language Manual*. New York: Drake Beam and Associates.

Emery, Marcia. 1994. *The Intuition Workbook*. New York: Prentice Hall.

————. 1995. "Intuition: How to Use Your Gut Instinct for Greater Personal Power." Chicago: Nightingale-Conant. Audio cassette.

Faraday, Ann. 1972. *Dream Power*. New York: Berkeley Books.

Flatow, Ira. 1992. *They All Laughed*. New York: HarperCollins.

Gallos, Joan V., and V. Jean Ramsey. 1997. *Teaching Diversity*. San Francisco: Jossey-Bass.

Gardner, Howard. 1983. *Frames of Mind: The Theory of Multiple Intelligences*. New York: Basic Books.

————. 1993. *Creating Minds: An Anatomy of Creativity*. New York: Basic Books.

————. 1995. *Leading Minds: An Anatomy of Leadership*. New York: Basic Books.

Garfield, Patricia. 1974. *Creative Dreaming*. New York: Ballantine.

Gendlin, Eugene. 1986. *Let Your Body Interpret Your Dreams*. New York: Chiron.

Gilberd, Pamela. 1996. *The Eleven Commandments of Wildly Successful Women*. New York: Macmillan, Spectrum.

Gilligan, Carol. 1982. *In a Different Voice*. Cambridge, MA: Harvard University Press.

Gilman, Cheryl. 1997. *Doing the Work You Love*. Chicago: NTC/ Contemporary Books.

Goleman, Daniel. 1995. *Emotional Intelligence*. New York: Bantam Books.

Guiley, Rosemary Ellen. 1995. *The Encyclopedia of Dreams*. New York: Berkeley Books.

Hall, Doug. 1995. *Jump Start Your Brain*. New York: Warner Books, Time Warner.

Hamel, Gary, and C.K. Prahalad. 1996. *Competing for the Future*. Cambridge, MA: Harvard Business School Press.

Herrmann, Ned. 1988. *The Creative Brain*. Lake Lure, NC: Brain Books.

Higgins, James M. 1995. *Innovate or Evaporate*. Winter Park, FL: New Management Publishing.

———. 1994. *101 Creative Problem Solving Techniques*. Winter Park, FL: New Management Publishing.

Houston, Jean. 1997. *A Passion for the Possible*. New York: Harpers Publishers.

Isenberg, Daniel. 1984. "How Senior Managers Think." *Harvard Business Review,* Nov-Dec: 80-90.

Jackson, Gerald. 1987. *Executive ESP*. New York: Pocket Books.

Jampolsky, Gerald, and Diane Cirincione. 1992. *Wake Up Calls*. Carson, CA: Hay House.

Jaworsky, Joseph. 1996. *Synchronicity*. San Francisco: Berrett-Koehler.

Kamenitz, Rodger. 1997. *Stalking Elijah: Adventures with Today's Jewish Mystical Mysteries*. San Francisco: HarperSF.

Kantor, Rosabeth Moss and Barry Stein. 1979. *The Tale of O*. Cambridge, MA: Goodmeasure. Film.

Kaplan, David. 1997. "Silicon Samurai: The Oracle." *Newsweek*, 4 Aug.

Keirsey, David and Marilyn Bates. 1978. *Please Understand Me*. Del Mar, CA: Prometheus Nemesis Books.

Kock-Sheras, Phyllis R. 1995. *The Dream Sourcebook*. Los Angeles: Contemporary Books.

Kohn, Alfie. 1986. *No Contest: The Case against Competition*. Boston: Houghton Mifflin.

———. 1993. *Punished by Rewards*. Boston: Houghton Mifflin.

Land, George, and Beth Jarman. 1992. *Breakpoint and Beyond*. New York: Harper Business.

Landrum, Gene. 1994. *Profiles of Female Genius*. Buffalo, NY: Prometheus Books.

Langer, Ellen J. 1997. *The Power of Mindful Learning*. New York: Addison Wesley.

Langreth, Robert. 1997. "Hey Guys, for Your Next Party Try Borrowing Women's Genes." *Wall Street Journal*, 12 June: B1.

Lown, Bernard. 1996. *The Lost Art of Healing*. Boston: Houghton Mifflin.

Lynch, Frederick R. 1997. *The Diversity Machine: The Drive to Change the "White Male Workplace."* New York: The Free Press.

Mattimore, Bryan. 1993. *99% Inspiration*. New York: Amacom.

Maynard, Herman Bryant, Jr., and Susan Mehrtens. 1997. *The Fourth Wave*. San Francisco: Berrett-Koehler.

Michalko, Michael. 1991. *Thinkertoys*. Berkeley, CA: Ten Speed Press.

Moir, Anne, and David Jessel. 1991. *Brain Sex*. New York: Carol Publishing Group.

Moss, Robert. 1996. *Conscious Dreaming*. New York: Crown Trade Paperback.

Mowen, John C. 1993. *Judgment Calls*. New York: Simon & Shuster.

Munn, Michael. 1996. "Intuitive Meditation at Work: Solving Science and Business Problems." In *Intuition at Work*, eds. Roger Frantz and Alex N. Pattakos. San Francisco: New Leaders Press.

Myss, Caroline. 1996. *Anatomy of the Spirit*. New York: Harmony Books.

Nadel, Laurie, Judy Haims, and Robert Stempson. 1990. *Sixth Sense*. New York: Prentice Hall.

Naparstek, Belleruth. 1997. *Your Sixth Sense*. San Francisco: Harper.

Ogilvy, David. 1983. *Ogilvy on Advertising*. New York: Crown.

Osborn, Alex. 1979. *Applied Imagination*. New York: Scribner's.

Parikh, Jagdish. 1994. *Intuition, The New Frontier of Management*. Malden, MA: Blackwell Publishers.

Pehrson, John, and Susan Mehrtens. 1997. *Intuitive Imagery: A Resource at Work*. Newton, MA: Butterworth-Heinemann.

Peters, Tom. 1994. *The Pursuit of Wow*. New York: Vintage Books.

————. 1997. *Circle of Innovation*. New York: Random.

Popcorn, Faith. 1996. *Clicking*. New York: HarperCollins.

Prince, George. 1970. *The Practice of Creativity, A Description of Synectics*. New York: Collier Books.

Ray, Michael. 1993. *The New Paradigm in Business*. New York: J.P. Tarcher/Perigee.

Ray, Michael, and Rochelle Myers. 1986. *Creativity in Business*. New York: Doubleday.

Reed, Henry. 1989. *Edgar Cayce on Mysteries of the Mind*. New York: Warner Books.

Rogers, Carl. 1961. *On Becoming a Person.* Boston: Houghton Mifflin.

Rosanoff, Nancy. 1988. *Intuition Workout*. Santa Rosa, CA: Aslan Publishing.

Salk, Jonas. 1983. *Anatomy of Reality*. New York: Columbia Union Press.

Samples, Bob. 1976. *The Metaphoric Mind*. Reading, MA: Addison-Wesley.

Schnabel, Jim. 1997. *Remote Viewers*. New York: Dell.

Seabrook, John. 1998. "The Many Lives of David Geffen." *The New Yorker Magazine*, 23 February: 108-119.

Shawcross, William. 1997. "Turning Dollars into Change." *Time*, 1 Sept., 50.

Silva, Jose, and Philip Miele. 1972. *The Silva Mind Control Method*. New York: Simon & Schuster.

Sims, David. 1996. "You Can Almost Hear the Gears Turn Inside His Head." *Smithsonian*, January, 46.

Sonnet, Andre. 1961. *The Twilight Zone of Dreams*. Radnor, PA: The Chilton Company.

Stack, Jack. 1997. "Measuring Morale." *INC Magazine*, January, 29.

Steinem, Gloria. 1992. *Revolution from Within*. Boston: Little, Brown.

Taylor, Kristin Clark. 1985. "Thinking Rationally Can Kill Good Ideas." *USA Today*, 29 Oct.

Taylor, Jim, and Watts Wacker with Howard Means. 1997. *The 500 Year Delta*. New York: HarperBusiness.

Taylor, William. 1997. "What Comes After Your Success." *Fast Company Magazine*, Dec-Jan, 82.

Van de Castle, Robert. 1994. *Our Dreaming Mind*. New York: Ballantine.

Vaughn, Frances. 1979. *Awakening Intuition*. New York: Anchor Books.

Von Oech, Roger. 1983. *A Whack on the Side of the Head: How to Unlock Your Mind for Innovation*. New York: Warner Books.

————. 1986. *A Kick in the Seat of the Pants: Using Your Explorer, Artist, Judge, and Warrior to be More Creative*. New York: Harper & Row.

————. 1992. *A Whack on the Side of the Head*. Menlo Park, CA: Creative Think.

Zebrowitz, Leslie. 1997. *Reading Faces*. Boulder, CO: Westview/ Harpers.

Zukav, Gary. 1989. *The Seat of the Soul*. New York: Simon & Shuster.

# Butterworth-Heinemann Business Books . . . for Transforming Business

*5th Generation Management: Co-creating through Virtual Enterprising, Dynamic Teaming, and Knowledge Networking, Revised Edition,*
Charles M. Savage, 0-7506-9701-6

*After Atlantis: Working, Managing, and Leading in Turbulent Times,*
Ned Hamson, 0-7506-9884-5

*The Alchemy of Fear: How to Break the Corporate Trance and Create Your Company's Successful Future,*
Kay Gilley, 0-7506-9909-4

*Beyond Business as Usual: Practical Lessons in Accessing New Dimensions,*
Michael W. Munn, 0-7506-9926-4

*Beyond Strategic Vision: Effective Corporate Action with Hoshin Planning,*
Michael Cowley and Ellen Domb, 0-7506-9843-8

*Beyond Time Management: Business with Purpose,*
Robert A. Wright, 0-7506-9799-7

*The Breakdown of Hierarchy: Communicating in the Evolving Workplace,*
Eugene Marlow and Patricia O'Connor Wilson, 0-7056-9746-6

*Business and the Feminine Principle: The Untapped Resource,*
Carol R. Frenier, 0-7506-9829-2

*Choosing the Future: The Power of Strategic Thinking,*
Stuart Wells, 0-7506-9876-4

*Conscious Capitalism: Principles for Prosperity,*
David A. Schwerin, 0-7506-7021-5

*Cultivating Common Ground: Releasing the Power of Relationships at Work,*
Daniel S. Hanson, 0-7506-9832-2

*Flight of the Phoenix: Soaring to Success in the 21st Century,*
John Whiteside and Sandra Egli, 0-7506-9798-9

*Getting a Grip on Tomorrow: Your Guide to Survival and Success in the Changed World of Work,*
Mike Johnson, 0-7506-9758-X

*Knowledge in Organizations,*
  Laurence Prusak, 0-7506-9718-0

*The Strategic Management of Intellectual Capital,*
  David A. Klein, 0-7506-9850-0

*The Rhythm of Business: The Key to Building and Running Successful Companies,*
  Jeffrey C. Shuman, 0-7506-9991-4

*Setting the PACE® in Product Development: A Guide to Product And Cycle-time Excellence,*
  Michael E. McGrath, 0-7506-9789-X

*Time to Take Control: The Impact of Change on Corporate Computer Systems,*
  Tony Johnson, 0-7506-9863-2

*The Transformation of Management,*
  Mike Davidson, 0-7506-9814-4

*What Is the Emperor Wearing? Truth-Telling in Business Relationships,*
  Laurie Weiss, 0-7506-9872-1

*Who We Could Be at Work, Revised Edition,*
  Margaret A. Lulic, 0-7506-9739-3

*Working From Your Core: Personal and Corporate Wisdom in a World of Change,*
  Sharon Seivert, 0-7506-9931-0

To purchase any Butterworth-Heinemann title, please visit your local bookstore or call 1-800-366-2665.

# About the Author

Sandra Weintraub began Management Resources over twenty years ago as a training and management development consulting firm, specializing in developing executive and supervisory skills and, more recently, ideation seminars to create new products and services.

She has provided management training for many Fortune 500, educational, and governmental organizations, and she has served as an adjunct professor in management skills at Brandeis University. An inventor of novelty and household products that received worldwide publicity, she has also been an invited speaker to many organizations, such as the Product Developers and Management Association, The American Creativity Association, and an *Industry Week Magazine* conference, among several others. She was also a requested speaker at DuPont's Oz Network, a forum where leading thinkers on creativity are invited to address their members.

Her publications include several articles on Management Training in professional journals. Following her studies on dreams with Dr. Arthur Bernard of The Dream Center in Van Nuys, CA, she also published several articles on how dreams have been an integral part of the creative process for hundreds of years.

The author can be reached at:

Management Resources
P.O. Box 340
Newtonville, MA 02160
617/332-2990